The Progressive Dilemma

The Progressive Dilemma

DAVID MARQUAND

HEINEMANN : LONDON

William Heinemann Ltd
Michelin House, 81 Fulham Road, London SW3 6RB
LONDON   MELBOURNE   AUCKLAND

First published 1991
Copyright © David Marquand 1991

A CIP catalogue record for this book
is available from the British Library
ISBN 0 434 45094 4

Phototypeset by Input Typesetting Ltd, London
Printed and bound in Great Britain
by Clays Ltd, St Ives Plc

Contents

Foreword

At the start of the last decade of the century, the contours of British electoral politics have more in common with those of thirty years ago than with those of the recent past. The 'mould' which the SDP famously set out to break in the early 1980s has survived all assaults on it. For the moment the two-party system which took shape in the 1920s, when Labour replaced the Liberals as the main anti-Conservative force in British politics, looks more secure than it has done for nearly twenty years. Once again, the battle that matters is the battle upon which Ramsay MacDonald sought to focus the attention of the electorate in the early 1920s – the battle, as he put it, between 'Tory Government and Labour Opposition'.

The return to two-party politics has been greeted with rejoicing in the labour movement. Understandably so: in recent years, at any rate, Labour's fortunes have been symbiotically linked with those of the existing two-party system. Had the system collapsed, Labour would have been the most obvious victim; it is because Labour recovered from the troubles of the early 1980s that the system recovered as well. Yet there is a paradox here, which few Labour politicians are anxious to confront. The two-party system which has now returned to health has been a much better friend to the British right than to the British left. To be sure, the Labour Party suffered more in the 1980s, when the system seemed on the point of collapse, than in earlier periods in opposition. But the difference was one of degree, not of kind. The Conservatives were as hard to dislodge in the 1930s, and almost as hard in the 1950s. In the 1930s and 1950s, almost as much as in the 1980s, electoral failure was both cause and consequence of destructive factional disputes within the labour movement. The seventy-odd years since Labour became the main anti-Conservative party in the state have seen only two decisive Labour victories. The governments produced by those victories have held office for a total of only nine years. Apart from a brief period in the early 1980s, Labour has always been strong enough to prevent anyone else from offering a serious challenge to the Conservatives. For most of the time, it has been too weak to make its own challenges effective.

That combination of strength and weakness provides the central theme of this book. Interwoven with it are a number of related themes: the complex mixture of assertiveness and defensiveness, of sectional fragmentation and group loyalty, which have shaped the labour culture and contributed to the paradoxical conservatism of the labour movement; the constraints which Labourism has placed on the actions, and even on the thinking, of individual Labour politicians and intellectuals; above all, the tensions and ambiguities in the relationship between the Labour Party and the progressive intelligentsia on which it depends for ideas and which alone can validate its claim to be a potential party of government rather than the vehicle for a social interest. These continuities shine through the obvious contrasts between different periods of Labour history. They also define and explain the 'progressive dilemma' of my title. For they hold the key to the party's failure to construct an enduring Labour-led equivalent of the heterogeneous, ramshackle, but extra-ordinarily successful progressive coalition which the Liberals led before the First World War.

In the first part of the book I discuss these themes directly, and in a historical context. More particularly, I try to explore some of the similarities and dissimilarities between the pre-1914 Liberal coalition and the narrower Labour coalition which partially (but only partially) succeeded it, to disentangle the conservative practice from the radical rhetoric of the latter, to probe the relationship between New Liberalism and Fabian democratic socialism, and to speculate about the reasons why no significant Communist Party grew up on British soil. In the second part the discussion takes a different form. The same broad themes are present in the back-ground, but instead of discussing them directly I have tried to focus on the way in which they have manifested themselves – for good or ill – in the careers of selected politicians and intellectuals. Ernest Bevin and Stafford Cripps represent the golden age of Labourism, when, for a glorious moment, the Labour ethos and the national mood ran so close that a Labour Government seemed to embody a progressive conscience, extending well beyond the confines of its own constituency. Their lesser contemporaries, Herbert Morrison and Hugh Dalton, are included in my portrait gallery as reminders of the limitations which helped to ensure that the moment did not last. The essays on Hugh Gaitskell and Aneurin Bevan deal with the two outstanding representatives of the silver age. In different ways and for different reasons, both found themselves kicking against the pricks of Labourism; despite the earnest courage of the former and the wayward genius of the latter, neither managed to transcend it. Their failure to do so led straight to the deepening crisis of the 1960s, 1970s and 1980s, when the old tensions of Labourism and the newer tensions of revisionist social democracy fed on each other to such effect that the party's ability to govern was called into question. I have tried to illustrate that unhappy interaction through the contrasting figures of Richard Crossman, Douglas Jay, Michael Stewart, Harold Wilson and Tony Crosland, with David Owen as a kind of counterpoint.

In the last three chapters I look at the contemporary scene. I begin by examining the paradoxical resurgence of Labourism under Neil Kinnock, and the accompanying collapse of the Alliance. I then try to explore the potentialities for a revised revisionism, social democratic in its ethic but liberal in its politics, based on the twin notions of citizenship and community. Finally, I argue the case for a new kind of bottom-up progressive coalition, transcending the familiar categories of left, centre and right and cutting across the party lines which still divide the intellectual descendants of the old, pre-1914 progressive coalition from each other. Whether such a coalition can in fact be constructed I do not know. I am more than ever convinced that it is a necessary – though not sufficient – condition for a change of regime.

David Marquand, May 1990

Acknowledgements

Some of the chapters were written specially for the occasion. Others began as essays, written for a variety of different periodicals; most of the latter have been revised to provide continuity, to expand the argument or to take account of new material which has appeared since they were first published. I am grateful to the editors of *Encounter*, the *New Statesman*, *The Listener*, the *London Review of Books*, *The Times Literary Supplement*, *Marxism Today* and *Government and Opposition* for permission to republish material which first appeared in their pages. The curious may like to know that earlier versions of Chapters 2 and 4 first appeared in *The Listener* on 27 March 1969 and 23 November 1978 respectively; of Chapter 5, part of Chapter 6 and part of Chapter 10 in *Encounter*, of April 1969, April 1984 and June 1963 respectively; of Chapters 7, 13 and 15 and part of Chapter 10 in the *London Review of Books* on 21 March 1985, 22 January 1981, 1 July 1982 and 7 May 1987 respectively; and of Chapters 9 and 12 and part of Chapter 6 in the *New Statesman* on 12 March 1965, 28 September 1973 and 21 April 1967 respectively. Part of Chapter 8 first appeared in *The Age of Austerity*, ed. Philip French and Michael Sissons (London, Hodder & Stoughton, 1964), and part of Chapter 15 in *Thatcherism, Personality and Politics*, ed. Kenneth Minogue and Michael Biddis (London, Macmillan Press, 1987).

I should also like to thank Mrs Pat Bellotti and Mrs Kath Capper for help in word-processing, and my long-suffering editor, Tom Weldon, for forbearance, insight and support.

D.M.

I

The Paradox of British Democracy

Liberalism never has been nor ever can be anything but a diversified crowd. . . . It is a gathering together of all the smaller
interests which find themselves at a disadvantage against the
big established classes, the leasehold tenant as against the land-
owner, the retail tradesman as against the merchant and money-
lender, the Nonconformist as against the Churchman, the small
employer as against the demoralising hospitable publican, the
man without introductions and broad connections against the
man who has these things. . . . It has no more essential reason
for loving the Collectivist state than the Conservatives; the small
dealer is doomed to absorption in that just as much as the large
owner; but it resorts to the state against its antagonists as in
the middle ages common men pitted themselves against the
barons by siding with the king. The Liberal Party is the party
against 'class privilege' because it represents no class advantages, but it is also the party that is on the whole most set
against Collective control because it represents no established
responsibility. It is constructive only so far as its antagonism to
the great owner is more powerful than its jealousy of the state.
It is organised only because organisation is forced upon it by
the organisation of its adversaries. It lapses in and out of alliance
with Labour as it sways between hostility to wealth and hostility
to public expenditure.

H. G. Wells, *The New Machiavelli*, 1911[1]

Wells was unmistakably a man of his own time. Yet his scorn for
the Liberal Party of that time provides an ideal starting point from
which to explore a dilemma which still haunts the British left. By
1911, he had broken with Sidney and Beatrice Webb, lampooned in
The New Machiavelli as the half-sinister, half-ludicrous Oscar and
Altiora Bailey, but he still shared the quintessentially Fabian assumption that the intellectually and organisationally tidy should and

would prevail over the variegated, the spontaneous and the unruly. The weight of numbers might, for a time, enable a 'diversified crowd' to overwhelm its rivals, as the Liberals overwhelmed theirs in 1906. But such success could only be temporary. In government as in war, heterogeneity, diversity and variety were handicaps. Lasting success went to the expert, the disciplined, the well drilled: in a word, to the new 'Samurai' to whose rule Wells had looked forward in *A Modern Utopia* a few years before.[2] Further assumptions followed. One was that the omnicompetent 'collectivist state', managed by tidy-minded experts, was bound to be the wave of the future. Another was that it was a wave which the undisciplined and disorganised Liberal Party could not ride. A third was that the fragmented and divergent social interests which supported the Liberal Party were in some sense marginal or obsolescent; and that Liberalism was therefore doomed to be ground out between the upper and nether millstones of organised capital and organised labour, the big and disciplined interests which would shape the twentieth century, and around the struggle between which its politics would revolve.

These assumptions must have seemed vindicated by the Liberals' misadventures thereafter. In the general election of 1906, five years before *The New Machiavelli* was published, the Liberal Party had obtained 400 seats, a majority of 130 over all other parties combined. Most of the thirty Labour Members had been returned with Liberal support. In 1916, Asquith's replacement as Prime Minister by Lloyd George precipitated a split in the Liberal Party which lasted for seven years. Eventually it was patched up, but the patching came too late to maintain the Liberals as a major party. By 1926, they were indisputably in third place in the House of Commons, with only forty seats and a share of the popular vote, in the preceding general election, of only 17.6 per cent. In 1936, they had twenty seats, having won 6.4 per cent of the popular vote. Nearly thirty years were to pass before their share of the vote reached double figures again.

The main essentials of what was to become the orthodox explanation for this long decline are to be found at their most persuasive in George Dangerfield's exuberant post-mortem on *The Strange Death of Liberal England*, first published in 1935 and reissued several times since.[3] With captivating wit and panache, Dangerfield tried to show that the soul of Liberal England had perished long before the body. Liberalism was a nineteenth-century creed, the creed of an age 'where neither Wealth nor Work would ever combine; where a comfortable and independent bourgeoisie would make profits not too large to be indecent; where social ills would be medicined but never cured'. It could not cope with the bleaker realities of a century whose hallmark was combination; and it was forced to take refuge in wriggles and evasions. The Liberal ministers of the pre-war period, ghosts of a heroic but vanished past, were swept this way and that by every wind that blew, seeking harmony where none existed and compromise where none was possible. If the First World War had not arrived in time to save them, they would have faced a civil war in Ireland, and perhaps a general strike on this side of St George's Channel as well. They were powerless to satisfy the demands of organised labour, because they were inhibited from attacking capital. They could not reconcile the claims of the southern Irish home rulers (on whom, after 1910, they depended for their parliamentary majority) with those of the Ulster Protestants, because the two sets of claims were inherently irreconcilable. Above all, their ideology – the vague and sentimental Liberal faith in an illusory Progress – could no longer satisfy the needs of a harder, tougher century, without illusions. The death of Liberal England was, in reality, not strange at all. It was the inevitable result of the inability of the Liberal Party to represent the working class, and of the inability of Liberalism to inspire answers to the psychological and economic problems of the modern world.

Dangerfield did not draw explicit conclusions for his own time. The implicit conclusion, however, emerged unmistakably from the narrative. The future would lie with a party that did represent the working class, and with a creed that could solve contemporary problems. For most people on the left, the identities of the party and creed in question were not in doubt. On the eve of the First World War, Ramsay MacDonald had warned that, if the Liberals did not make concessions to Labour, politics would be dominated by 'a great Labour Party and a strong reactionary party, with a small Liberal Party standing between, cut off from every source of inspiration and opportunity of growth'.[4] Left-wing intellectuals of the 1930s were often as impatient with the vacillations and hesitations of the Labour Party as H. G. Wells had been with the incoherence and indiscipline of the Liberal Party before 1914, but few doubted that MacDonald's prophecy had come true; that the choices which the Liberal Party had tried for so long to evade were now inescapable; that battle between capital and labour had been joined in the political as well as in the industrial sphere; or that, in consequence, the Labour Party was now the only alternative to reaction.

In one sense, of course, MacDonald's prophecy *had* come true. Even in the 1930s, the Liberal Party was by no means 'cut off from every source of inspiration'. Keynes and Beveridge, the two leading intellectual architects of the settlement which was to define the political agenda for nearly a generation after 1945, were both Liberals, not socialists. In spite of the intellectual vitality of Liberal summer schools, however, the Liberal Party had ceased to be a serious contender for power. Labour had, without question, replaced it as the leading anti-Conservative party in Britain, and has continued in that position ever since.

But there was a paradox about Labour's achievement – a paradox which has been central to British electoral politics ever since the achievement was accomplished. As everyone knows, the Labour Party of the 1980s fared extraordinarily badly in general elections. Many explanations have been canvassed: the formation of the SDP; the attractions of 'Thatcherism'; the spread of 'consumerism'; the effects of the new technologies; the party's swing to the left. In all the excitement, however Labour's record in previous decades, before the SDP, Mrs Thatcher, consumerism, the new technologies or the swing to the left were heard of, has been comparatively neglected. Yet that record holds the key to the party's more recent misadventures. It would have come as a bitter disappointment to the ardent spirits who rejoiced in MacDonald's warning that a 'great Labour Party' would, if pushed, take over the Liberals' role as the alternative to the party of reaction.

Underlying MacDonald's tone of menace was the tacit assumption that, if it had to play the Liberals' old role, Labour would play it at least as successfully as the Liberals had done: that when the hard choice between capital and labour was put to it, the electorate would be bound to opt for labour. In the event, the seismic shift in political allegiance which drove the Liberals to the margins of electoral politics and made Labour the main anti-Conservative party in the state has benefited the Conservatives as much as, in some respects more than, the Labour Party. The two-party system which prevailed from 1868 to 1918 – the system of Conservatives versus Liberals – produced a total of twenty-seven years of Conservative or Conservative-dominated government, against twenty-three of Liberal. The Conservative-versus-Labour system which succeeded it has produced a strikingly different pattern. Conservative or predominantly Conservative governments have been in office for fifty of the seventy-odd years since the Labour Party first became the official Opposition in the House of Commons, and Labour governments for only twenty. Even if the ten years from 1979 to 1989 are left out of the reckoning, the score is still forty to twenty in the Conservatives' favour. Most of the Labour governments concerned, moreover, have either been in a minority in the House of Commons, or have commanded majorities too small to allow them to legislate as they wished. Only twice – under Attlee in 1945 and under Harold Wilson in 1966 – has the Labour Party won a parliamentary majority in double figures. The governments at the head of those majorities held office for a total of only nine years. Liberal England may have died, but Labour England has failed to be born.

Yet a sociological investigator from Mars, knowing nothing of the last seventy years of British history, but aware of the main elements of Britain's social and political structure, would probably expect the Labour Party to have held office more often than not. In its early years, it is true, only part of the working class had the vote, so some of its potential constituency was still, in Gladstone's famous phrase, beyond 'the pale of the Constitution'. In 1918, however, the belated arrival of manhood suffrage removed that handicap. On the other hand, its assets were formidable – particularly in comparison with those of other European socialist and working-class parties. The United Kingdom is the oldest industrial society in Europe, and the British working class, on some definitions at any rate, the most mature. There is no peasantry and, in most of mainland Britain, no serious religious cleavage. In the nineteenth century there were, of course, important differences between working-class Anglicans and working-class nonconformists, but in the twentieth century these differences ceased to bite. Even in the nineteenth century, they went nothing like as deep as the gulf between believers and unbelievers which has dogged the working-class movement in some continental countries. In a different sphere, the British Labour Party was the only working-class party in a combatant country which contrived not to split over the question of participation in the First World War; partly because of this, it has never had to contend with a powerful Communist Party, rooted in national traditions and national experiences, on its flank.

The paradox does not end there. The debates which punctuated the slow broadening of the franchise in the course of the nineteenth century had been haunted by the fears of the propertied and the hopes of the propertyless, or at any rate of their champions. Grant universal suffrage, Macaulay had declared in the House of Commons debate on the People's Charter in 1842, and 'it matters not at all what else you withhold. . . . My firm conviction is that, in our country, universal suffrage is incompatible, not with this or that form of government, but with all forms of government, and with everything for which forms of government exist; that it is incompatible with property.'[5] Give working men votes, Robert Lowe had echoed in the debate on the 1867 Reform Bill, 'and the machinery is ready to launch those votes upon the institutions and property of this country'.[6] For his part, Karl Marx had declared that, in Britain, universal suffrage would have as its 'inevitable result . . . the political supremacy of the working class'.[7] After 1918, these predictions could be put to the test. Working men all had votes; and the self-proclaimed party of the working class stood ready to receive them. As we have seen, the outcome was two generations of Conservative hegemony, broken by only two majority Labour governments. As the young Peter Shore asked in 1952,

> Once the mass of the people had the vote, Socialists were convinced that Conservatism and all it stood for would be swept away. Their victory seemed certain, for Conservatism which was based on privilege and wealth was inevitably a minority creed, whereas Socialism, with its appeal to social justice and economic self-interest, would recruit the big battalions of the poor and unprivileged. . . . Yet it is clear that events have falsified these predictions . . . the question which must now be asked is why the fruits of universal suffrage have taken so long to ripen. How is it that so large a proportion of the electorate, many of whom are neither wealthy nor privileged, have been recruited for a cause which is not their own?[8]

Shore's question has called forth a flourishing academic industry. Disraeli's famous 'angels in marble' – the Conservative working-class voters without whom the modern Conservative Party would never have won a general election – have been exhaustively investigated. A battery of sociologists and political scientists has tried, with the aid of increasingly sophisticated statistical techniques, to define their social characteristics and uncover their political preferences. Much has been discovered, much of it of value. As so often, however, number-crunching social science reaches only part of the problem. It has told us who the Conservative working-class voters are, or at any rate who they were when the relevant studies were carried out. It cannot tell us why they are – why they resisted Labour's blandishments; why Labour offered the kind of blandishments it did; what blandishments, if any, they would have accepted; under what circumstances, if any, they would have accepted the blandishments Labour actually offered.

Because it cannot tell us these things, the unwary reader may jump to the conclusion that Conservative working-class voters were bound to think and vote as they did, and that nothing could have persuaded them to think and vote differently. For the very precision of its findings creates a misleading impression of determinacy. The contours of existing political attitudes are traced with such care and sophistication that it is easy to forget that these are not the only possible attitudes: that the mix of values and experiences they register might have taken a different form. Yet political attitudes are not set in stone. They are affected by a range of factors, not least by the words and deed of politicians. As an illuminating recent study of British voting behaviour puts it, politicians 'shape' the voters' values, or try to.[9] They have to tailor their appeal to existing preferences, but if they have any sense they also try to restructure existing preferences to suit the purposes for which they are appealing. One reason why Conservative working-class voters exist is that a succession of Conservative politicians tried, quite consciously, to bring them into existence. One reason why the death of Liberal England was not followed by the birth of a comparable Labour England is that Labour politicians have been less good at 'shaping' values than have their rivals. So if we want to understand the paradox through which the Conservatives have profited more than Labour from the belated coming of a democratic suffrage, it is not enough to examine the voters whose allegiance Labour failed to win. It is also necessary to examine the structure and beliefs of the party which failed to win it. And, if we are to understand these, we must look again at the complex and baffling process through which it toppled the Liberals from their perch.

At this point in the argument, re-enter H. G. Wells and *The New Machiavelli*. His picture of the Liberal Party was, of course, a hostile caricature, not a rounded portrait. Like all good caricatures, however, it contained a large enough element of truth to make it recognisable. The Liberal Party of 1911 *was* a motley, even ramshackle,

11

coalition, which included in its bearlike embrace teetotallers, small businessmen, nonconformists, leasehold tenants, successful professionals and radical intellectuals, as well as the occasional whig aristocrat and business magnate. After 1910, moreover, the Liberal Government depended on the parliamentary support of an even wider and more heterogeneous coalition, which also included the usually reliable but occasionally fractious Labour Party (itself a loose-knit federation of socialist sects and largely non-socialist trade unions) and the single-issue Home Rule Party. The ideological span of that wider coalition extended from ILP on the left to Gladstonian relics like Lord Crewe, the Lord Privy Seal and Secretary of State for India, on the right. On a deeper level, both the Liberal Government, in the realm of action, and Liberalism, in the realm of doctrine, *did* seek to reconcile the claims of labour and capital. Liberal ministers were indeed trying to improve the condition of the working class, while remaining within the framework of a privately owned market economy. Though they did not put it in these words, the essence of their whole project was to find a middle way between the *laisser-faire* capitalism of sixty years before and the 'collectivist state' of Wells and the Fabians.

Heterogeneous, loose-knit and unwilling to choose between capital and labour though the Liberal coalition was, however, it does not follow that the Liberal Government was a spent force, still less that Liberal England was dying. As Wells noticed in the paragraph immediately after the one quoted at the head of this chapter, the Liberal Party of 1911 was remarkably similar, in composition, attitude and ethos, to the American Democratic Party of the same period. Yet, while the British Liberals went under, the American Democrats survived and prospered. The decade that saw the Liberal Party split three ways between the Simonite National Liberals, the Samuelite free traders and an isolated Lloyd George rump saw Roosevelt in the White House and the New Deal in spate. The 'Roosevelt coalition' which carried the New Deal through, and was in turn cemented by it, dominated American electoral politics for nearly forty years, and still retains some of its old power. There are, of course, innumerable reasons: the contrast between the effect of the First World War on Britain and its effect on the United States; the even more dramatic contrast between American prosperity and British economic stagnation in the 1920s; the relative weakness of the American trade unions; the fact that American socialism was essentially an immigrant creed, with few roots in native American soil; the ethos of the frontier and the sense of social mobility associated with it compared with the class-stratification and class-consciousness of Britain. Wherever the true explanation may lie, however, it plainly cannot lie in the extra heterogeneity of the Liberal Party or in its anxiety to follow a middle way between capitalism and socialism. The Roosevelt coalition of Southern whites, Northern blacks, labour unions, farmers, liberal intellectuals and small men resentful of big business and Wall Street was at least as heterogeneous as, and in many ways reminiscent of, the pre-1914 Liberal coalition in this country. *Mutatis mutandis*, its generous, flexible and imprecise ideology – insofar as that rather slippery term is appropriate – was equally reminiscent of the social liberalism around which the Liberal coalition took shape. And to these it owed much of its success.

In spite of the obvious differences between the two societies and periods, the same was true of Britain's pre-1914 Liberal coalition. It was, of course, a difficult coalition to manage: Wells and Dangerfield were right about that. But managing difficult coalitions is what politicians are paid for. So long as the managers were sufficiently resilient and adroit to keep the coalition together, the social heterogeneity and intellectual diversity which caused their difficulties were assets, not handicaps, enabling them to fight the political equivalent of a war of movement instead of being bogged down in long-dug trenches. And what stands out most sharply from the vantage point of nearly eighty years later is precisely their skill, *élan*, ability to seize the initiative and capacity for renewal. After a feeble start in the Government's first two years of office, they tamed the Lords; greatly extended the scope of the regulatory state, which had grown up by fits and starts since the Factory and Public Health Acts of the mid-nineteenth century; and laid the groundwork for the welfare state of the mid- and late twentieth. More portentously still, the budgets of Asquith and Lloyd George produced a substantial shift in the incidence of taxation, deliberately designed to favour the poor at the expense of the rich, and tried to establish the principle that society has a special claim on socially created wealth. Especially when taken together with the Land Campaign which Lloyd George launched in 1913, the net effect was a challenge to the rights of property more radical than any seen in previous British history, and in some ways more radical than any mounted by any subsequent peacetime government, apart from Attlee's. Whether or not the Liberal coalition would also have solved the Irish Question, and kept a partially self-governing Ireland within the United Kingdom, can never be known. To put it at its lowest, the solution its leaders were pushing through Parliament on the eve of the war was at least as promising as anything proposed since. If, as Michael Bentley suggests, the Liberal Government led a 'charmed life',[10] part of the explanation lies in its own mastery of the black arts.

This does not mean that it could have continued indefinitely on the path it was following in 1914. But by 1914 it was no longer following the path on which it had set out in 1906. Like its Conservative opponents and its Labour allies, it was caught in a complex crisis of the political economy, which had called the old, nineteenth-century relationship between the state and civil society into question, and with it the character of the political order, the territorial constitution and the authority of government. Like all politicians in such situations, the Liberals sometimes stumbled, but for most of the time they showed a remarkable ability to address new questions in new ways. We cannot know if their capacity for renewal would have been equal to the tests it would have faced if war had been avoided. We do know that it was equal to the tests imposed upon it before August 1914.

Underlying the notion that the Liberal Government was a spent force are the assumptions that Liberalism was a spent force: that the framework of values and beliefs within which Liberal ministers took their decisions was obsolescent, decaying and unable to stand up to the strains of the twentieth century: that, since the claims of capital and labour are in fact irreconcilable, the social-liberal middle way was a blind alley. These assumptions are more difficult to evaluate. Plainly, it is impossible to prove that Liberalism was not a spent force: 'spentness', like beauty, is in the eye of the beholder. Moreover, Liberalism, like the Liberal Party, was not all of a piece. Sometimes it seems that there were as many Liberalisms as Liberals. To complicate matters still further, the relationship between Liberalism as a system of belief and Liberalism as a set of policies is as complex and as difficult to define as that sort of relationship usually is. The notion that that tough and leathery old pro, Herbert Henry Asquith, was consciously seeking to put an explicit Liberal ideology into practice does not carry much conviction. In all the confusion, however, two things seem clear. The first is that some of the Government's attitudes – notably, its adherence to the free-trade principles which most of Britain's competitors had abandoned and the priority

14

it gave to archaisms like Welsh Disestablishment and non-denominational education – were redolent more of the past than of the future. The second is that that is exactly what one would expect of a party in transition, trying to cope with the unforeseen problems of a society which was also in transition.

The important question is not whether the Liberals of 1906–14 were in some respects the prisoners of their own ideological pasts. They were bound to be. It is whether the doctrines which they had inherited from the past were sufficiently elastic to be adapted to the needs of the present and future, and whether the Liberals themselves were sufficiently flexible to try to adapt them. Some were not. But some were; and the most striking thing about these is how sharply their eclectic 'New Liberalism' differed from the Liberalism of the nineteenth century. To be sure, the values which lay at its heart were closely related to the values of earlier Liberals. It is not difficult to detect echoes of John Stuart Mill in the 'moral reformism' of such New Liberals as L. T. Hobhouse, J. A. Hobson and C. F. Masterman.[11] That is hardly surprising: the New Liberals were, after all, Liberals. But the means through which they wished to realise their values, the questions they were trying to address and the preoccupations which led them to believe that those questions needed addressing looked forward to the new century, not backward to the old. They redefined the core liberal principles of liberty and personal fulfilment to justify an active state, capable of securing 'positive' freedom as well as 'negative'. In the language of a still later period, political citizenship was to be supplemented by social citizenship: constitutional democracy by social democracy. That may have been a vain ambition, but it was hardly an obsolescent one.

Hobson and Hobhouse spoke only for themselves, of course. New Liberalism was not the official doctrine of the Liberal Party or even the unofficial doctrine of the Liberal Government. But that does not detract from its importance. The New Liberals offered the Liberal coalition a rationale for further changes, a vocation for a possible future. Their approach to the immediate issues of the day was very close to the equally eclectic socialism of the Independent Labour Party and the Fabian Society – one reason why the handful of Labour MPs who thought of themselves as socialists found it so easy to remain within the coalition, and why so many former New Liberals saw the Labour Party as a suitable vehicle after the First World War. Unlike their socialist allies, however, the New Liberals believed that they could realise their ambitions within the confines of a capitalist economy. They wished to limit the rights and extend the obligations of property, not to expropriate the property owner. They were groping for a way to humanise and moralise the market – to distinguish between worthy and unworthy forms of property; to cut across the divide between propertied and propertyless; to establish a divide between exploitative and non-exploitative property instead – and, in doing so, to incorporate labour into a reformed capitalism. For such a politics, the Liberal coalition was ideally suited.

This was their real offence in socialist eyes. If socialism was right in holding that the claims of capital and labour could not be reconciled, then their whole enterprise was doomed. But if they were right, then socialism was unnecessary. Yet there was an irony there, which no one could have spotted at the time. If New Liberalism was doomed, it was doomed in surprising company. Since 1945 a succession of Western governments has tried to reconcile capital and labour much as the New Liberals tried; and by a strange quirk of ideological transference, many of the governments concerned have belonged to the socialist tradition. In theory, as well as in practice, the post-Marxist, revisionist 'social democracy' of Scandinavia and Central Europe has had much more in common with the New Liberalism of 1906–14 than with the Marxism of the same period. This is less true of Britain, since the British Labour Party has never been explicitly revisionist. But even in Britain the 'operational code' of the Attlee and Wilson governments was shot through with assumptions from the same ideological stable as New Liberalism, while the explicit revisionism of Anthony Crosland and Hugh Gaitskell looked forward to a reformed capitalism much closer to the New Liberal vision of the future than to Keir Hardie's or even to Sidney Webb's. In the struggle for intellectual ascendancy between socialism and New Liberalism, socialism won the first battles. Posthumously, and without acknowledgement, the New Liberals won the war.

This leads on to a wider point. All industrial societies have to solve the problem of how the 'labour interest', immanent in the very structure of modern industry, is to express itself in politics. One solution, tacitly implied in the theories of the new right and vigorously exemplified in the practice of Stalinist Russia, is to make sure that it can do nothing of the sort. Another, the solution of the American New Deal, is to incorporate it into a broad-based, cross-class political coalition, of which it becomes a crucial, but not dominating, part. Scandinavia and post-war Central Europe have found the solution in social democratic parties, closely associated with, but organisationally separate from, centralised trade unions originally created under social democratic inspiration. For most of this century, the British solution has been Labourism. The labour interest, in other words, has been sustained by, and embodied in, a Labour Party. That party has deliberately chosen to identify itself as the instrument of the labour interest rather than as the vehicle for any ideology. It has usually been led by middle-class professionals; and for most of its history it has been committed, in principle, to a rather inchoate socialism. But, in a sense not true of its social democratic counterparts on the mainland of Europe, it has been a trade union party, created, financed and, in the last analysis, controlled by a highly decentralised trade union movement, which was already in existence before it came into being. Above all, its ethos – the symbols, rituals, shared memories and unwritten understandings which have shaped the life of the party and given it its unmistakable style – has been saturated with the ethos of trade unionism.

Because Labourism has been the British solution, because it has helped to shape the structure of British politics and the assumptions of British politicians and voters, British commentators are apt to assume that no other solution was possible. This is to beg one of the central questions in twentieth-century British history. In world terms, Labourism is the exception – and a fairly rare exception at that – not the rule. More important still from our point of view, the real meaning of almost all the items on the New Liberals' agenda lies in their search for a different solution. If they had found it, it would, of course, have been *sui generis*, shaped by national traditions and the interplay of national forces. But, although there can be no certainty, there is not much doubt that it would have been closer in some ways to the American and in others to the Scandinavian than to the solution actually adopted.

As everyone knows, the search failed. But it does not follow that it was bound to fail. What ensured its failure, and destroyed the Liberal coalition, was the fatal conjuncture of three developments: the 1916 split in the Liberal Party; Labour's departure from the wartime coalition and decision to fight the 1918 election in opposition to it; and the huge wartime increase in the size and self-confidence of the labour movement which made it possible for the Labour Party to become an independent contender for power. There

17

is no doubt that premonitory signs of the last two were in evidence before the war. One was the sudden chill in the Government's relationship with its Labour allies which lay behind MacDonald's Lear-like warning of the terrors which would follow the emergence of a 'great Labour Party'. Another was the industrial unrest of the period. What all this implies, however, is not that the coalition was doomed, but that the tacit terms and conditions around which it had taken shape would have had to be redefined in Labour's favour to keep Labour on board. In the stratified class society which Britain had become by the early twentieth century,[12] a class politics of some sort was almost certainly inevitable. The question is whether it could have taken a different form from the one it took after 1918.

There is some evidence that something of the sort was beginning to emerge on the ground. According to P. F. Clarke, the Liberals had, in practice, become the party of the working class in industrial Lancashire.[13] On a different level, Lloyd George seems to have been edging his way towards a redefinition of the terms and conditions of the pre-1914 coalition, on the basis of which a different kind of class politics might have become possible. For all MacDonald's huffing and puffing, there is not much doubt that the Labour leadership would have been much happier coming to terms with the Government than fighting it. In the end, of course, the coalition was not redefined; Labour did not stay on board; and class politics settled into a Labourist pattern. But it is unlikely that the responsibility lies with an inexorable fate. The evidence suggests that Liberal England died, not because its death was set in the stars, but because the Liberals did not move quite fast enough along the path they had tentatively begun to follow.

Against that background, Labour's tribulations after 1918 fall into place. After an interregnum, the pre-war Liberal coalition was gradually replaced by a Labour coalition of a rather similar kind. Just as Lloyd George had tried to redefine the Liberal coalition so as to keep Labour on board, so Ramsay MacDonald did his best to redefine the Labour Party so as to win over former Liberals. Just as the Liberal leadership had courted the labour interest without which it could not win the battle for votes, so the Labour leadership courted the radical intelligentsia without which it could not win the battle of ideas. And just as the Liberal Party had slowly been turning itself into the political vehicle of the working-class voters who later went to Labour, so the Labour Party gradually became the vehicle of the progressive professionals who had once been one of the mainstays of the Liberals. The process took some time, of course. In the 1920s, the Labour Party was still overwhelmingly working class at the bottom, and predominantly working class, at least in origin, at the top. None of the 'Big Five' in MacDonald's Cabinets had been to university, and all of them had known poverty in their youth. In the next fifteen years, however, the radical intelligentsia embraced the Labour Party as warmly as it had once embraced the Liberals. Three of Attlee's 'Big Five' were public-school university graduates, one of them a Wykehamist and one an Etonian. The bright young professionals who swept on to the Labour benches in 1945 – the Hugh Gaitskells, Harold Wilsons, Michael Foots, John Freemans, Barbara Castles, Patrick Gordon Walkers and Christopher Mayhews – were products and symbols of a social alliance, which looked at first sight like a new version of that of 1906.

But only at first sight. There were at least three critical differences between the Labour coalition which achieved its apotheosis in 1945 and the Liberal coalition which the First World War cut off before its prime. In the first place, the Labour coalition was much narrower. To be sure, it too was a 'diverse crowd' or, as Harold Wilson liked to put it, a broad church. Visionary socialists jostled uneasily with closet revisionists; Christian pacifists with social patriots; Marxist ideologues with down-to-earth trade unionists; 'intellectuals' with 'workers'. As for the unions, they were divided between white collar and manual; skilled and unskilled; craft, industrial and general. But these diversities only qualified a fundamental homogeneity. Only part of the extraordinary Liberal caravanserai which had so astonished H. G. Wells came over to Labour when the Liberal Party went into its decline; indeed, there is some evidence that more Liberal voters switched to the Conservatives after 1918 then to Labour.[14] At the heart of the Labour coalition, giving it its bedrock vote and its fortress seats, was the unionised working class in the old industrial areas, employed in the old staples of the Industrial Revolution and marked by its scars. There, and for these, Labour was 'our' party: the embodiment of a history and a culture as well as, perhaps more than, the vehicle of an interest. The tribal loyalties which grew out of that history and culture gave the Labour coalition a reservoir of almost automatic support, available in bad times as well as good, and a corresponding durability and toughness, which its Liberal predecessor had lacked. Unfortunately, the loyalty of its fortresses did not compensate for the doubts and fears of the much more extensive sociological countryside around them, where the history and culture were different, and where the scars of the Industrial Revolution were either forgotten or non-existent.

Even in its great victory of 1945, when its majority was almost as large as the Liberals' in 1906, and when most of what had once been Liberal territory fell to it, Labour's support was more narrowly concentrated than the Liberals' had been.[15] At other times, its social and geographical span was narrower still. In his famous *English Journey* in the early 1930s, J. B. Priestley discovered a classless third England – an England of 'Woolworth's, motor coaches, wireless, hiking, factory girls looking like actresses, greyhound racing and dirt tracks'[16] – distinct both from the industrial England of slag heaps and slums and from the rural England of oak beams and village greens. George Orwell said much the same thing in *The Lion and the Unicorn*, when he looked to the 'skilled workers, technical experts, airmen, scientists, architects and journalists, the people who feel at home in the radio and ferro-concrete age' to lead the social revolution which he thought would follow the Second World War.[17] As Orwell and Priestley both sensed, the intermediate third England ought to have been natural territory for a party hostile to class privilege and committed to equal opportunity. Its American equivalent was, for a long time, natural territory for the Roosevelt coalition. If Britain's class politics had taken a different route, it might have been natural territory for a reconstituted Liberal coalition. Labour captured a large part of it in 1945 and 1966, and held some of it in all elections. But it never became Labour territory. The technicians and so-called 'black-coated workers' whom Herbert Morrison wooed before 1945 – nephews and great-nephews of Mr Polly; parents of the C1s and the more qualified of the C2s of later pollsters – had Labour voters in their ranks, but they did not really belong to the Labour coalition. As technological and economic change swelled their numbers, and the gap of aspiration and attitude between the Labour fortresses and the wider society grew, there was much talk of the decomposition of the working class, and of the obstacles it placed in the way of a Labour victory. In reality, technological and economic change only added to an obstacle which had been present from the first.

The second difference between the post-1918 Labour coalition and the pre-1914 Liberal coalition is more nebulous, but equally revealing. It is that the Labour coalition never managed to renew itself in office in the way that the Liberal coalition had done. As everyone knows, the minority governments of the 1920s were distinctly unimpressive. In the case of the first, no disaster ensued. Less than five years after its defeat in 1924, Labour was back in office. The second Labour Government was another matter. Its *immobilisme* in 1930 and collapse in 1931 drove the party back into its fortresses, and handed the middle ground of politics to the right. In some ways, however, the records of the governments of 1945–51 and 1964–70 are more instructive. Like the Liberals in 1906, both began by embodying a popular mood wider and deeper than their parliamentary majorities. Though neither contained a political genius of the stature of Lloyd George, the personnel of both could stand comparison with the Liberals'. And although the Wilson Government's achievements were modest, Attlee's carried through a programme of constructive legislation on the scale of that of 1906–14. Yet, with all its achievements, even the Attlee Government ran out of steam well before its term was over, and left office intellectually and politically exhausted. The Wilson Government did not have much steam to start with, and spent its last two and a half years hagridden by the after-effects of the forced devaluation of 1967. No doubt, the accidents of personality and contingencies of politics were partly to blame, but that does not mean that nothing more can be said. Fate helps those who help themselves. Labour's problem was not lack of ability, or even bad luck. It was a kind of woodenness, a lack of political imagination, a hardness of the intellectual arteries, which prevented Labour ministers from creating new opportunities and turning the flanks of their opponents in the way that Roosevelt and Lloyd George so often did. It is hard to escape the conclusion that part of the explanation lies in the structure and mentality of the Labour coalition itself.

This leads on to the third and most important difference. The Labour coalition had its roots in the labour interest and the ethos of Labourism. It could not transcend these without betraying its vocation and dishonouring its origins. In a phrase which the German socialist, Egon Wertheimer, once applied to Ramsay MacDonald, it was the 'focus for the mute hopes of a whole class'; and it was to that that it owed the extraordinary, sometimes almost pathetic, loyalty of its core constituency. But in spite of the fears of middle-class observers – in spite, for that matter, of the stubborn courage displayed in periods of industrial unrest, and of the rituals of solidarity which commemorated it – these hopes were defensive, not offensive: consolations for defeat, not spurs to victory. The Labour ethos, perfectly symbolised by the mournful refrain of the 'Red Flag' – 'Though cowards flinch and traitors sneer / We'll keep the red flag flying here' – was an ethos of resistance, not of attack; of the objects of history, not of the subjects. The labour movement was a product of the world of 'us' against 'them', but it existed to protect 'us' against the injustices perpetrated by 'them', not to enable 'us' to join 'them', and still less to replace 'them' by 'us'. In theory, it was committed to huge changes – common ownership of the means of production; a socialist commonwealth – far more radical than anything ever contemplated by the Liberal coalition. In practice, as it showed again and again in government, its instincts were cautious, even conservative, to a fault. That did not mean that the commitments had no significance. As Gaitskell discovered when he tried to change them, they were sustained by fierce and unshiftable loyalties, shared not only by the left of the party, but by gnarled and supremely unideological trade union leaders on the right. On two occasions – after the defeats of 1931 and 1979 – they had a direct influence on party policy. But, for most of the time, their significance was emotional and symbolic, not operational. Their function was to show that the party was true to its roots, properly respectful of past sacrifices and the memory of the pioneers, not to proclaim a doctrine.

As well as being defensive rather than offensive, the Labour ethos was, in an odd way, exclusive rather than inclusive. Co-operation with other parties was at best suspect, and at worst a symptom of treachery. In 1930 and 1931 and again from 1976 to 1979, minority Labour governments had to co-operate with the Liberals in order to stay in office. But they did so half-heartedly, almost furtively, as though ashamed of what they were doing. Later in the 1930s, Stafford Cripps was actually expelled from the party for advocating a popular front against Neville Chamberlain. A more subtle exclusiveness can be detected in the party's approach to its own composition. Recruits from outside the labour interest were always welcome. The renegade aristocrats, Sir Oswald Mosley and Sir Charles Trevelyan; the upper-middle-class professionals, Hugh Dalton and Hugh Gaitskell; the *déclassé* intellectuals, Sidney Webb and Harold Laski – all these rose high in the party, and some of them found a place in its heart. But it welcomed such recruits conditionally, not absolutely. They were guests, not family; and there was always a certain tension, a lingering unease, in their relationship with the hosts, beautifully captured in an entry in Richard Crossman's diary, describing a conversation with Gaitskell:

22

Of Roy Jenkins, he said, 'He is very much in the social swim these days and I am sometimes anxious about him and young Tony [Crosland]. We, as middle-class Socialists, have got to have a profound humility. Though it's a funny way of putting it, we've got to know that we lead them because they can't do it without us, with our abilities, and yet we must feel humble to working people. Now that's all right for us in the upper-middle class, but Tony and Roy are not upper and I sometimes feel that they don't have a proper humility to ordinary working people.'[18]

A good way to epitomise the differences between the Labour coalition and its Liberal predecessor might be to imagine Asquith solemnly explaining to Haldane or Grey why they ought to be 'humble' to the chapel-goers and small shopkeepers in their constituency associations.

The same was true, in a still more subtle way, of the party's approach to the electorate. Of course, no one ever suggested in so many words that middle-class voters should be 'humble' to working-class ones, or Conservative voters to Labour ones. Yet the ethos, style and, for that matter, very name of the party all conveyed a tacit and often unintentional message to that effect. According to Clause Four of its constitution, the Labour Party existed to win justice for 'the workers by hand and brain'. It was bound by its very nature to stress class identities and appeal to class loyalties. Only if its potential constituents saw politics in class terms would it succeed: only if they were right to see politics in class terms would its success be justified. It was because it persuaded most working-class voters to do this that it became a major party. But its appeal to class loyalty and class identity was inevitably double-edged. The large minority of working-class voters which did not see politics in class terms became, by implication, disloyal; non-working-class voters became, at best, slightly inferior auxiliaries, a kind of political Wavy Navy, and at worst adversaries. This logic, it is true, rarely became overt. Only occasionally, as when Emmanuel Shinwell declared that no one but the organised working class mattered 'a tinker's cuss' or when the 1974 election manifesto looked forward to 'an irreversible shift of wealth and power to working people and their families', did the attitudes it implied come to the surface. Overt or not, however, it made itself felt in a thousand ways – in the sudden shift of mood when a group of Labour canvassers crossed from a council to a private estate; in the rhetoric of a factory-gate meeting during an election campaign; in the ethic of group solidarity which lay behind Arthur Henderson's aphorism, 'the plural of conscience is conspiracy'; in the style and atmosphere of the party's annual conference; in the very language of 'our people' which Labour politicians used almost without realising what they were doing. It was as apparent to the voters outside the core constituency as to those within. It did more than any other single factor to keep them out.

Hence the dilemma which has haunted non-Conservative Britain for nearly seventy years. It was a dilemma, in the first place, for the radical intelligentsia – for the suppliers of ideas, the framers of policy, the makers of ideological claims, without whom Labour could never be more than a glorified pressure group. By the late 1920s, at the latest, it was clear that the old Conservative-versus-Liberal two-party system had given way to a Conservative-versus-Labour system. Radical intellectuals' had to decide whether or not to enlist in the emerging Labour coalition. If they stood aloof from it, they might help to perpetuate Conservative rule and cut themselves off from political influence into the bargain. Yet, if they threw in their lot with it, they would be expected to internalise the interests of a class to which they did not belong, and to accommodate themselves to an ethos alien to the impulses which had made them radicals in the first place. For radical intellectuals were radicals because they were also dissenters, because they had chosen to reject the inherited values of their own class and milieu. The rank and file of the labour movement also rejected those values, of course, but in doing so it was affirming its inheritance, not dissenting from it. Intellectual recruits who imagined that because Labour welcomed them as allies it had some special sympathy for dissent as such were soon disabused. Its highest value was group loyalty; it approved of dissenters in the enemy ranks, but it displayed little tenderness to dissenters in its own. Josiah Wedgwood, the maverick radical who joined the Labour Party after the First World War, was not alone in provoking distrust among the trade unionists 'to whom his ideas, the outcome of a different kind of education and background, seemed dangerously liberal, in every political and moral sense'.[19] Of course, many radical intellectuals did throw in their lot with Labour. Some also did their best to make the necessary accommodation to the culture of Labourism. But others refused, objecting with Keynes that, while an appeal to justice and good sense might have converted them, 'the class war will find me on the side of the educated bour-

24

geoisie'.[20] There is no way of telling how many belonged to the second category. They were enough to ensure that it was only on rare and intermittent occasions that the Labour coalition managed to dominate the moral and intellectual debate in the way that the Roosevelt coalition dominated it in the United States.

A similar dilemma confronted potential anti-Conservative voters outside Labour's core constituency. Labour's class appeal has always been fundamental to it. But class is subjective, not objective. What counts is how identities are defined – to which dimension of a usually complex identity its possessor gives primacy and for what purposes. At the heart of Labour's class appeal lay the assumption that the class dimension must, by definition, have primacy over all other dimensions: that class divisions were somehow fundamental or superordinate and that other social divisions were trivial in comparison. Closely related to that assumption were the assumptions that working-class interests had a special legitimacy denied to other class interests, and that only the malevolent or foolish could deny such obvious truths. Labour rose as far as it did because these assumptions seemed to millions of working-class voters to make sense of their experiences. It failed to rise further because it did not make sense to others: because many people whom sociologists would have classified as working-class obstinately refused to give primacy to the class dimension of their lives, while others, whom sociologists would not have so classified, could not see why the working-class, as a class, had any moral claim on anyone else. To those in the first category, Labour's class appeal might well seem less a call to arms than a patronising, even insulting, denial of individuality. To potential sympathisers in the second, it might seem a slap in the face. It is too soon to tell if these dilemmas will survive the changes of policy and style which the Labour leadership forced through in the 1980s. What is clear is that, for nearly seventy years, they held the key to the weakness of non-Conservative Britain.

Asquith's Ghost

Perhaps only because it prevailed for so long, perhaps because it was associated with class divisions and justified in class terms, the Conservative-versus-Labour party system which dominated British politics from the late 1920s to the early 1970s has often been seen as the product of some inexorable sociological law. The truth is more complicated. No one could deny that sociological factors played an important part in its emergence. The Labour Party saw itself as a class party and appealed, quite explicitly, to class loyalties. Yet the demise of the Liberal Party as a serious contender for power and even the transformation of the Labour Party into a potential party of government owed less to class divisions than to differences of feeling and belief which cut across them: less to sociology than to politics. Liberalism perished because some Liberals abandoned it, while others made only fitful and half-hearted efforts to stick to it. Labour replaced it because many Liberals came to believe that it had become the best available custodian of the Liberal ideal.

The first, though not the last, big nail in the Liberals' coffin was Asquith's fall from power in December 1916. With that, class had nothing to do. For the first sixty-two years of his life his career had been a long succession of triumphs. Until pre-war loyalties were twisted out of shape by wartime passions, no one could reasonably have expected the triumphs to cease. As a boy at the City of London School, as an undergraduate at Balliol, as a barrister at Lincoln's Inn, the solidest, if not the most glittering, prizes of late-Victorian middle-class England seemed to fall into his grasp, almost without effort on his part. It was the same when he entered the House of Commons. From the first, as Roy Jenkins pointed out in his lucid and compassionate biography,[1] Asquith spoke as though he were already a front-bencher; from the first, his colleagues accepted him at his own valuation. At forty – only six years after his first election to Parliament – he was Home Secretary in Gladstone's last Cabinet. During the furious controversies which divided the Liberal Party in the 1890s, his stock steadily rose. By 1906 he was the only possible successor to Campbell-Bannerman as Liberal leader.

The pattern continued after he became Prime Minister in 1908. Asquith held the premiership for an unbroken period of eight years and almost eight months, a record unequalled since the early nineteenth century. His Government was perhaps the most successful reforming administration which this country has ever had, as well as the most distinguished. Under its aegis, the 'New Liberalism', which sought to adapt the individualistic radicalism of the nineteenth century to the social needs of the twentieth, momentarily became a political force. The reforms it enacted were substantial achievements in themselves. More important still, the logic behind them pointed the way to further advance. It is true that the Liberal Party was frequently divided over policies and over personalities, sometimes bitterly so. But its divisions were a product of its strength. The clash of powerful and ambitious leaders in the Cabinet was due, at least in part, to the amazing abundance of political talent which it contained; the disputes over policy reflected the breadth and generosity of Liberalism as a creed. In the summer of 1914, in fact, it would have made sense to look forward to an almost indefinite continuation of Liberal rule – or at least to the gradual emergence of an acknowledged centre-left coalition of Liberalism and Labour, which might have provided this country with a hegemonic progressive coalition analogous to the Roosevelt coalition which dominated American politics from the 1930s to the 1960s.

It would be wrong to suggest that the 1916 split was solely responsible for preventing the emergence of such a coalition in this country. But there is no doubt that when Lloyd George arrived at 10 Downing Street the moderate left in this country received a blow from which it took thirty years to recover. By a curious and terrible irony, Asquith's swift rise in the councils of his party, and his sage conduct of affairs during his first six years as Prime Minister, pale into insignificance compared to his fall. The man whose career was one long celebration of the ethic of bourgeois success is memorable chiefly as a failure.

Why did he fail? In August 1914, when he steered a virtually united Cabinet into what was to become the first total war in history, Asquith's authority was beyond challenge. By December 1916 it had become a hollow shell. To maintain it, he had first made a coalition with the Unionist Opposition, and then succumbed to the clamour for conscription. These concessions were of no avail. Opponents of compulsion were dismayed by his surrender to 'Prussianism'. Supporters condemned him for surrendering too slowly. Lloyd George, by now the leading champion of the 'fight to the finish', convinced himself that Asquith did not have the energy and drive to win the war. The newspaper magnates, Northcliffe and Max Aitken, were determined to destroy him. So were the diehard Unionists, Milner and Carson. Against that background, Lloyd George produced his famous proposal that a committee of three, chaired by himself, should direct the war effort. Asquith would stay on as Prime Minister, but as a figurehead in the background, detached from what was now the central area of public policy. Carson supported the idea with enthusiasm. After some hesitation, Bonar Law was persuaded to support it as well. Not surprisingly, Asquith rejected it. More surprisingly, he then accepted a modified version of it, only to reject it again the following day. The day after that he left office, never to return.

But, although the facts are clear, their meaning and implications are swathed in controversy. Like many of history's murderees, Asquith suffered a double indignity. Not only did he lose power; he lost reputation as well. Unlike Chamberlain in 1940, he was brought down by covert intrigue, not by open revolt. The intrigue was started by his chief lieutenant, who ended by supplanting him. Because of all this, the intriguers and their friends had to take exceptional pains to justify their actions, to themselves as well as to others. Only the most unselfish patriotism, called forth by an extraordinary national emergency, could excuse what, in ordinary times, would have been flagrant disloyalty. But Lloyd George and his associates could be patriots, overcoming an extraordinary emergency, only if Asquith were extraordinarily culpable. His guilt was the condition of their innocence. Only by blackening him could they remain unspotted themselves.

In practice, they blackened him in two ways. Lloyd George insisted that he had wished not to supplant Asquith, but only to infuse greater vigour into the direction of the war. The crisis came only because Asquith reneged on his agreement to set up the three-man war committee; Lloyd George himself became Prime Minister only because Asquith, having resigned, selfishly refused to serve under Bonar Law or Balfour. Secondly, and more damagingly, Lloyd George and his associates insisted that, in any event, the only way to save the country was to take control over the war effort out of

Asquith's feeble hands. Asquith, as they depicted him, was a figure of supine indolence and failing powers, an inveterate procrastinator and compromiser whose favourite motto was 'Wait and see' – competent enough in peacetime but, in Lloyd George's flamboyant metaphor, not a man to keep on the bridge in the 'raging typhoon' of war. They mutinied because it was the only way to avoid shipwreck.

The first charge was true in form. Lloyd George and his associates did not force Asquith out of 10 Downing Street; he left of his own accord. If he had been willing to accept the war committee as Lloyd George proposed it, he could have stayed. But this only pushes the real argument one stage further back. If Asquith had stayed on Lloyd George's terms he would have been not so much a lame duck as a crippled one. Everyone would have known that he had been forced to accept Lloyd George's terms; that, in a decisive trial of strength between the Prime Minister and his chief lieutenant, the Prime Minister had lost; that real power now rested with Lloyd George; and that in any future trials of strength Lloyd George would be the man to back. Conceivably, the arrangement might have lasted. More probably, it would have broken down in acrimony and recrimination, leaving Asquith's authority even more depleted than it had been to start with. This is not to say that Lloyd George did not want his plan to be accepted or to work, or that he was dishonest when he denied that he wished to become Prime Minister himself. Like most people, Lloyd George found it easy to persuade himself of what it was convenient for him to believe; at the start of the crisis, when most of the leading Conservatives were still uneasy about him, it was convenient for him to believe that he wanted only to direct the war effort and not to head the Government. All the same, Asquith was right in his initial instinct that a Prime Minister who surrenders the substance of power to a subordinate will be Prime Minister only in name. And it was on that primordial fact of political dynamics, not on personal likes or dislikes, that the Government foundered.

The second charge raises more complex issues. The suggestion that Asquith was too indolent to win the war makes nonsense of his earlier career. Indolent men do not win large practices at the Bar or enter the Cabinet at forty. Nor do they head vigorous reforming governments with still unsurpassed skill and authority. The truth is that Asquith was not indolent, but patient; and patience may be a virtue even in wartime. It is true that the phrase 'Wait and see' was, in some ways, typical of Asquith; but, as Roy Jenkins showed, it

29

was coined as a warning, not as an evasion, and the use made of it by Asquith's enemies during the war was a propaganda device, not a piece of scholarly analysis.

The wider charge that his qualities were suited to peacetime rather than wartime leadership is more difficult to assess. It is easy to see why his enemies thought so. By December 1916, the war had lasted for more than two years, and victory was as distant as ever. The agony of the Somme had gone for nothing, and the generals only offered more bloodletting. At such times, men look for scapegoats; Asquith, with his measured periods and ostentatious calm, was the ideal scapegoat for a febrile political nation, thirsting for the appearance of energy. But that does not make the charge true – or, of course, false. The truth is that no one has managed to devise an aptitude test for wartime leaders, or, for that matter, for peacetime ones. The only test is success; and that is retrospective. Moreover, success owes at least as much to the contingencies of battle, the chemistry of personal relationships and the weight of impersonal social and economic forces as to the character of the man at the top. Was Hitler a good wartime leader? In 1940 most of his countrymen thought so. By 1945, they had changed their minds. Was Lincoln? Was Churchill? Was Stalin? Judged by the test of eventual success, the answer must be 'yes'. But their methods differed greatly; they all made grievous mistakes; they all went through bad times as well as good; and if any of them had died in the bad times, he would probably have been judged a failure.

Lloyd George and Asquith differed in temperament and taste; inevitably, their styles of leadership differed as well. Asquith's style was consultative or, as Lloyd George complained, 'judicial'; Lloyd George's was authoritarian. Asquith collected the voices and reached his conclusions after pondering the opinions he had heard; Lloyd George led from the front, and sought to impose his will on those behind. Even in quiet times, there are many who long for the certainties of a great man's will – who yearn to place the burdens of decision on stronger shoulders than their own. In war, such yearnings are even more common. Those who experience them are bound to prefer the second style to the first. It is not self-evident that they are right. In his memoirs, Lloyd George listed the qualities of a good war minister and concluded that Asquith lacked them. But his conclusion was hardly surprising: the qualities he listed were those he thought he possessed himself, and in which he thought Asquith was deficient. Yet if the charge against Asquith is merely that he was not Lloyd

George – and, consciously or unconsciously, that is what many of his critics really meant – it does not get us very far.

The real issues lie deeper. In spite of the immense advantages which the British system of government confers on the Prime Minister in possession, Asquith resigned – against his will, and with his faculties intact. He was not sick, as Eden and Macmillan were when they retired from office, nor senile as Churchill almost was. He was not the prisoner of basically uncongenial political allies, as Ramsay MacDonald had become by 1935. He was not faced by a sizeable revolt in the division lobbies of the House of Commons, as Chamberlain was in 1940. Nevertheless, he fell. He fell, moreover, because at the moment of crisis the pivotal Unionist members of his own Cabinet were unwilling to support him. It is true that the way in which their unwillingness was manifested is a matter of controversy. In one version, Asquith resigned because he thought that Lloyd George would be unable to form a government. By forcing the issue, he hoped to demonstrate his rival's weakness and return to power stronger than before. Another holds that Asquith resigned because Bonar Law had given him a misleading impression of the attitude of the Unionists, as a result of which he believed that it was no longer possible for him to carry on. But this controversy is irrelevant to the basic question. The harsh fact is that the Unionist members of Asquith's Cabinet switched their allegiance to Lloyd George, and that they did so because they no longer believed that Asquith had the better claim to their support.

The most important of these Unionist ministers was, of course, Balfour. Once Balfour joined Lloyd George's camp, Asquith's game was up. Roy Jenkins had hard words for Balfour. Balfour, he wrote, 'had an unusually strong, though carefully concealed love of office, and a complete faith in his own ability to look fastidious in any company'. Perhaps he had. But that is not an adequate explanation of his conduct. For, as Jenkins himself pointed out, Balfour's switch of allegiance was 'the most decisive single event of the crisis'. If he had stood by Asquith, Asquith might have stayed in power. But, if Balfour's switch was decisive, it follows that Lloyd George's victory did not become inevitable until after it had taken place – and it was not until after Lloyd George's victory had become inevitable that love of office alone could impel existing office-holders to support him. The truth, surely, is that Balfour and his Unionist colleagues were moved only partly by love of office and partly by patriotism. They had no special loyalty to Asquith: he was, after all, the leader of the opposing party. But by the same token they had no special fondness for Lloyd George. What they wanted was a prime minister who could carry on the war. If Asquith could do so, well and good; if he could not, they would desert him for someone who could. Once it had become clear to them that Asquith's ship was no longer seaworthy, they ratted. It is hard to see how they could have been expected to do anything else.

It is true that Asquith's ship became unseaworthy, not so much because of navigational errors on the part of the captain, as because of insubordination on the part of the first mate. The traditional Asquithian view, according to which Asquith was the innocent victim of his chief lieutenant's vaulting ambition, the Duncan to Lloyd George's Macbeth, has much to commend it. His authority was ebbing well before December 1916, but the responsibility for fomenting the crisis which finally destroyed it belongs unquestionably to Lloyd George. It is true too that, among the confused mixture of motives which drove Lloyd George, a ruthless will to power and a restless hunger for activity bulked much larger than any attachment to principle. He was a chameleon of the political emotions, instinctively changing his colour to suit the changing colours of his habitat – a radical 'pacificist' before the war, one of the earliest Liberal converts to conscription in 1915, and the arch-exponent of the 'knock-out blow' in 1916. But that does not mean that his quarrel with Asquith can be understood in exclusively personal terms, or that principle played no part in it. There was truth in the charge that Asquith compromised and procrastinated: the long months of argument and manoeuvre which preceded his Cabinet's decision to substitute conscription for voluntary recruiting are proof of that. What his critics often forgot, however, was that he procrastinated in order to keep his unhappy and divided party together. The reason why it was unhappy and divided was that total war – or, to put it more precisely, the kind of total war which it found itself waging – ran against its grain. The reason why Lloyd George was so contemptuous of Asquith's procrastination was that it did not run against his. And the reason why the split had such an edge of bitterness was that Asquith and his supporters could not help noticing the differences between Lloyd George's grain and their own.

A. J. P. Taylor's suggestion that the Asquithians were too 'fastidious' for wartime politics[2] contains an element of truth, but it just misses the real point. For most of his career, Asquith had been a tough, canny, rather coarsely textured party politician, with a strong

32

appetite for power. He did not suddenly lose these attributes in August 1914. It was not fastidiousness that hampered him thereafter, but ambivalence – his own, and still more his party's. Some have discerned the roots of this ambivalence in the Liberal Party's historic attachment to *laisser-faire* principles, and in the inevitable conflict between those principles and the demands of wartime. To win the war, government had to mobilise all the nation's resources; market forces had to give way to state control; a hitherto liberal economy had to become, at least in part, a command economy. Liberals, so this argument holds, were naturally more attached to economic liberalism than were their Conservative contemporaries. For them, the break with *laisser-faire* was particularly painful, and some of them were unable to make it. At first sight it is a plausible argument, but it does not square with the record of either party before the war. The social reforms of 1906 to 1914 contravened the precepts of economic liberalism as thoroughly as did the interventions of 1914 to 1918; in the economic sphere, at any rate, the wartime state was merely the New Liberal state writ large. Nor, for that matter, does the record of the pre-war Conservative Party suggest that state intervention was intrinsically more congenial to it than to the Liberal Party. In both parties, attitudes to intervention varied with the kind of intervention proposed, and with the interests that stood to benefit from it. In both, men favoured intervention if they thought the cause was right.

The agony of wartime Liberalism went much deeper than economics. It sprang from the innermost recesses of what Michael Howard has called 'the liberal conscience'.[3] At first, most Liberals justified the war on the grounds that Britain was fighting to defend the liberal values of democracy, self-determination and the rights of small nations against Prussian militarism. The mounting casualty lists, the wild, almost racialist, anti-Germanism of the popular press, the mobs that broke up anti-war meetings, the erosion of civil liberties and the hounding of dissenters gave that justification a hollow ring. 'Prussianism', it seemed, was not confined to Prussia: liberal war aims did not guarantee a liberal war. Ugly questions followed. Were liberal values any safer in Britain than in Prussia? How long would they remain so? Might it not be that the atmosphere and imperatives of war – or, at any rate, of the mass war which alone offered any hope of total victory – were inherently illiberal? If so, was there not a danger that liberalism would lose, no matter which side won? These questions did not seem to disturb Lloyd

George. As he made clear in his war memoirs, he had nothing but contempt for the 'sectaries' in his own party, who seemed more anxious to keep their liberalism intact than to win the war. Other Liberals suspected uneasily that victory on Lloyd George's terms would be a kind of defeat. It is hard, in retrospect, to quarrel with their suspicions.

That, of course, is why Lloyd George won and Asquith lost. The Unionist ministers who switched their allegiance to him realised that he was ruthless, power-hungry and unburdened by scruples. They also realised that mass war is a ruthless business. Once confronted by a clear choice between Asquith and Lloyd George, they were bound to turn to Lloyd George – not because they trusted him or admired his moral character, but because they sensed obscurely that his ruthlessness provided a greater hope of victory. When Asquith complained of the 'blackguardly press' which had persecuted him, as he did after his fall, he showed how fatally he had misjudged the temper of the times. For the 'blackguardly press' had sensed the mood of the political nation better than he had. It realised, as he did not, that in war blackguards can easily become heroes. He might have kept the shadow of power if he had been willing to concede the substance. The one thing he could not do was to keep the substance once Lloyd George had made up his mind to seize it.

His fall has an element of personal tragedy about it, but it deserves less sympathy than it has sometimes won. He was dragged from power by the dogs of war, maddened by the scent of blood. The dogs had been let loose, not only or even mainly by Lloyd George, but by the Liberal Government of which Asquith was the head. Asquith and his followers would have liked to restrain them in some way, but they made no effort to return them to their kennels. The alternative to the hysteria and illiberalism of mass war was not a calm and liberal limited war: no such war was on offer. The alternative was peace. We cannot know on what terms peace would have been available. To be sure, we do know that Germany's war aims were remorselessly expansionist. But the notion that a negotiated peace was, by definition, unattainable – that the advocates of the 'fight to the finish' were, by definition, right in thinking that total victory over Germany was the only alternative to total defeat at her hands, and that it was a waste of time to see if compromise was possible – is much too deterministic to be taken for granted. What is certain is that Asquith and the Asquithians gave no comfort – either before or after his fall – to the tiny and beleaguered handful which argued the case for compromise in the face of ostracism and even persecution. The truth is that the Asquithians were as willing as the Lloyd Georgites to wound. Their trouble was that they were afraid to strike.

Their havering inflicted as much long-term damage on their party as did Lloyd George's contempt for their scruples. Because of it, Ramsay MacDonald and the anti-war minority of the Labour Party were able to run off with the liberal conscience; and it was because the liberal conscience seemed safer in its new home than in its old that Labour replaced the Liberals in the role of political executor to the progressive intelligentsia. That, in turn, helped to transform it from a glorified pressure group, concerned only with the 'low politics' of interest and section, into a true political party, with roots in the historic culture of a recognised part of the political nation and a vocation for the 'high politics' which preoccupy that nation. Labour could not have begun to replace the Liberals as the main anti-Conservative party in the state without its class base. But it needed more than its class base to complete the process. It had to look like a potential party of government; it had to offer a governing philosophy capable of stirring imaginations and mobilising emotions; above all, it had to justify its claim to be the heir of all that was best in Liberalism.

Without the progressive intelligentsia it could have done none of these things; and the progressive intelligentsia was attracted to it by its wartime record at least as much as by its economic doctrines. If Asquith had put himself at the head of the campaign for a negotiated peace, risking the odium which that would have brought him, the Ponsonbys, Trevelyans, Wedgwoods and J. A. Hobsons who deserted to the Labour Party might have stuck to their old allegiance. He, rather than MacDonald, might have been the 'man of the people' when wartime passions cooled; under his aegis, the Liberal Party might have continued to dominate the moral high ground. As things were, the tradition of mandarin progressivism which Asquith's Government had embodied more fully than any other before or since flowed, in the main, into Labour channels.

The consequences went further than might appear at first sight. As John Campbell has shown in his mordant and thought-provoking study of Lloyd George's attempts to break the tightening grip of the Conservative-versus-Labour party system in the late 1920s,[4] the forces which gave the victory to that system owed their strength to a deep-seated, all-pervading resistance to change. This was most obviously true of the forces which produced the Carlton Club revolt against him in 1922 – the forces for which Baldwin's notorious warning, that 'a dynamic force is a very terrible thing', was a welcome, as well as an appropriate rallying cry. But conservatism with a small 'c' was not confined to Conservatives with a big 'C'. Despite its theoretical commitment to a new social order, the Labour Party was equally conservative – and not only for the familiar reason that its parliamentary leaders were extremely conservative people. Much more important was the fact that the interests which the Labour Party had come into existence to further were rooted economically, psychologically and ideologically in the past. Then, as now, Conservative speakers hard up for a peroration would dilate on Labour's leanings towards Bolshevism. Then, as now, the real charge against the Labour Party was not that it was planning to overturn the status quo, but that it was wedded to it: that a party which saw itself as the political instrument of a working class whose attitudes and aspirations had been shaped in the nineteenth century, and whose bread and butter depended on the survival of the industrial pattern of the nineteenth century, was bound to find it extraordinarily difficult to meet the challenges of the twentieth.

The Conservative and Labour parties were locked in battle, or at any rate talked as though they were locked in battle, over the question of who should own and control an economic machine which was already obsolescent and uncompetitive. Though both paid lip-service to the need for change, neither gave serious thought to the question that really mattered – the question of how to overhaul the machine, so that it would become competitive in the new conditions of the 1920s and 1930s. Britain in the 1920s needed a radical programme of economic modernisation, designed to shift resources out of the old staple industries, in which the comparative advantage had passed to others, and into new technologies where she might have led the field if only she had tried. What she got was a long and debilitating argument over whether 'socialism' should replace 'capitalism', conducted with a theological rigidity which made it even more difficult than it would have been in any case to call a halt to the class war which was one of the chief causes of her decline.

Would Lloyd George have done any better? This is clearly a crucial question, and Campbell can fairly be accused of approaching it in too one-sided a fashion. He was captivated by Lloyd George's sparkling wit and bubbling intellectual exuberance; he assumed too readily that because Lloyd George, the Opposition leader, could pour withering scorn on the Labour and Conservative dullards on the Treasury bench, a Lloyd George government would have been able to solve the problems which baffled the two big parties. He forgot that even Lloyd George, in spite of his marvellous ability to see through the cant of Whitehall and the Bank of England, was the prisoner of some pretty silly cant of his own, notably on the crucially important fiscal question. Lloyd George, he assured us, really did believe in free trade. But Lloyd George also believed in the Liberal policy of loan-financed national development. And, as Keynes recognised, in conditions of worldwide depression, free trade and loan-financed national development were incompatible.

Yet, when all the qualifications have been made, it is hard to dispute that, on the central issue of the time, Lloyd George's strengths were more remarkable than his weaknesses. For he really did try to answer the questions that mattered. He saw, more clearly than any other political leader, that Britain could survive in a changing world only if she changed herself; he also saw what Campbell called the 'false dichotomy' between capitalism and socialism gave no guidance to the sort of changes that were needed. And this, of course, was his undoing. For his answers cut across the 'false dichotomy'. They were neither 'capitalist' nor 'socialist'; they were designed to use the power of the state to make capitalism work properly. As such, they were much more modern in conception than anything else on offer at the time. But in the climate generated by the struggle between 'capitalism' and 'socialism' they did not look modern. They looked irrelevant, opportunistic and, in an odd way, out of date. So, by a terrible paradox, the most creative and adventurous politician of the day appeared to most of his countrymen as a querulous and self-seeking voice from the past. Despite the 'Yellow Book' and *We Can Conquer Unemployment* – the two most impressive political documents produced in inter-war Britain – the Liberals won only seventeen more seats in 1929 than they had won at their nadir in 1924.

The question is, why? Part of the answer, of course, lies in the weight and power of the vested interests rooted in the past. Part lies in the attitudes and assumptions inherited from the first Industrial Revolution. By a cruel paradox, part lies in the weakness of the Liberal Party which Lloyd George was trying to correct. By the time he became their leader, the Liberals were clearly the third party in the state. They could not possibly form a government, and Lloyd

George knew it. Their best hope was to hold the balance in the House of Commons. But, as David Steel discovered fifty years later, there is not much point in holding the balance if you tie yourself so firmly to the bigger of the two big parties that you become virtually indistinguishable from it. Lloyd George was well aware of that danger, and bent over backwards to avoid it – intriguing with Churchill in February 1929 about a new 'anti-socialist' coalition based on free trade and electoral reform and, in the early months of the 1929 Government, urging on the Conservative diehards to revolt against Baldwin's policy of support for the Irwin Declaration on dominion status for India. Such manoeuvres were indispensable if the Liberals were to avoid giving the impression that they had been taken prisoner by the Labour Party. But there is no doubt that they added to the already deep-seated suspicion of Lloyd George, in the Labour Party and elsewhere.

Part, however, lies in the legacy of war and the post-war coalition. Because of this, all three parties were full of devoted enemies of Lloyd George. Indeed, one of Campbell's main themes was the 'obsession' shared by Baldwin and MacDonald with making sure that Lloyd George never did clamber back to office. Another was the rancorous hostility with which the Asquithian Liberals pursued him, even after he had succeeded Asquith as Liberal leader. Campbell himself was inclined to dismiss all this as a symptom of the jealousy which small men feel for great ones, or as a reflection of the unease which Lloyd George's contempt for party shibboleths was bound to inspire in the solid party wheelhorses who make up the vast majority of any House of Commons. It was both of these, of course, but it was something else as well. The fact is that liberal-minded people in all parties had been shocked by Lloyd George's conduct as Prime Minister – not just because he was a Welshman, an 'outsider', and disdained party shibboleths, but because he appeared to have no principles and no loyalties, party or otherwise – and that, partly because they were shocked by his conduct after reaching 10 Downing Street, they became retrospectively uneasy about the route he had taken to get there.

The impression was, in some ways, unfair. As Campbell and, more recently, Kenneth Morgan have both argued, there were discernible threads of attitude and instinct, linking Lloyd George, the coalition Prime Minister, to Lloyd George, the People's Chancellor. But, unfair or not, it went very deep, not only among envious Asquithian grandees and small-minded party politicians, but also among numbers of ordinary voters with no axes to grind. Lloyd George might have been able to eradicate it in office; Churchill, after all, managed to eradicate a rather similar impression when he returned to the Admiralty in 1939. But he would not have found it easy. He had found it comparatively easy to vanquish the living Asquith. Asquith's ghost was a harder nut to crack.

3

Revolution Averted

In the first week of January 1919, 10,000 British soldiers mutinied at Folkestone, and refused to obey their orders to return to France. Along the coast at Dover another 4,000 demonstrated in support of them. Fifteen hundred Service Corps men at Osterley Park seized lorries, drove to London and demonstrated in Whitehall; other soldiers demonstrated outside 10 Downing Street. Before the end of January another 20,000 men had refused to obey orders at Calais, and the sailors on HMS *Kilbride* had hoisted the red flag to the masthead, with the declaration: 'Half the Navy are on strike, and the other half soon will be.' In February 1919 armed troops demonstrated on Horse Guards Parade, and the War Office sent a confidential questionnaire to the commanding officers of all units to find out whether their men would remain loyal in the event of a revolution.[1]

It was a good question. By now, Glasgow had been paralysed by a general strike, involving over 100,000 men. The red flag had been flown from the municipal flagpole; the city had been ringed with troops and tanks; and the strike had culminated in a great riot in George Square, ending with a baton charge by mounted police. The miners' union had voted six to one in favour of a national strike for higher pay, shorter hours and the nationalisation of the pits; and there was a serious possibility that, if the strike took place, they would be supported by the railwaymen and transport workers as well. Even the police could not be relied on. In August 1918 the London police had gone on strike, leaving the capital without adequate forces to maintain law and order; and since then the police union had increased its membership from 10,000 to 50,000.

All this took place against a background of revolution and disorder in Central and Eastern Europe. After the collapse of the German Empire in November 1918, a republic had been proclaimed and a socialist government had taken office. But the extreme left of the German labour movement, represented by the revolutionary shop stewards and the so-called Spartacus league, rejected parliamentary democracy, and tried to force the German revolution along the path which the Bolsheviks had taken in Russia. In January 1919 they rose in revolt, and were brutally crushed. In March, the foundation congress of the Communist International was held in Moscow. 'Revolution is gaining strength in all countries,' Lenin declared in his greeting to the foreign delegates. 'The Soviet system has won not merely in backward Russia, but even in Germany, the most developed country in Europe, and also in England.' Many Englishmen would have agreed with him. 'Our real danger now,' wrote Field-Marshal Wilson in November 1918, 'is not the Boche, but Bolshevism.' Events since then appeared to bear him out. The wave of disorder which swept over the armed forces in the early months of 1919 gradually subsided as the men were demobilised, but the wave of industrial unrest which accompanied it lasted much longer. Between the beginning of 1919 and the end of 1921, an average of forty million days a year was lost in strikes – a figure twice as high as that recorded in the bitterest period of labour unrest before the war. Most of the strikes were caused by a straightforward economic conflict between employers and unemployed, but some of them were directly political in character, and almost all of them had political overtones. Working men and women were in revolt against an economic system which treated them as 'hands', without a voice in the decisions that shaped their lives. During the war, they had made great gains in power and self-confidence. They were not prepared to lose them now without a fight.

This wave of industrial unrest went hand in hand with a sharp turn to the left in the political wing of the labour movement. Between 1918 and 1920 the Independent Labour Party – which saw itself, with some justification, as the spearhead of the organised working class – increased its membership by 50 per cent. Since its foundation, the ILP had eschewed revolutionary Marxism and preached a characteristically British brand of Christian socialism, in which the labour theory of value took second place to the Sermon on the Mount. Yet in December 1919, the Scottish divisional council of the ILP voted in favour of affiliation to the Communist International, and at the full party conference the following April a motion to disaffiliate from the social democratic Second International was carried by a large majority.

Four months later, in August 1920, when it looked as though Lloyd George was planning to go to war against Russia in alliance with Poland, even the mandarins of the Parliamentary Labour Party and TUC threatened a general strike. If war broke out, declared the railwaymen's leader, Jimmy Thomas, a life-long opponent of unconstitutional methods, Labour would 'challenge the whole constitution of the country'. If Thomas's challenge had been made, it might well have been successful. 'On every side ex-servicemen are saying that they will never take part in any war again,' the Cabinet was told by its advisers. 'The workers are dead against a war with Russia.' Such comments were by no means unusual in this period. For at least two years after the First World War, it seemed perfectly conceivable that Britain might be on the verge of a revolutionary upheaval of a kind she had not experienced since the Chartists, and that the left wing of the British labour movement might evolve into a broadly based Communist Party of the kind which had come into existence in France and Germany.

In fact, of course, neither of these things happened. The wave of industrial unrest died down after the collapse of the post-war boom in 1921, and although the Communist Party of Great Britain was founded in 1920 it never offered a serious threat to the Labour Party or acquired a hold on the loyalty of the working-class electorate. But the fact that no revolutionary upheaval took place does not mean that the failure of the revolutionary left was inevitable. There was no divine law which decreed that London should escape the fate of Berlin or that the British labour movement should remain broadly united in the social democratic fold while the French labour movement split. If the ILP had joined the Communist International, as its French and German equivalents did, and as the Scottish divisional council wanted it to, a powerful Communist Party might have come into existence on British soil, able to speak in native accents and appeal to native traditions. In the turbulent climate of 1919 and 1920, such a Communist Party might have made considerable headway. The fact that this did not happen cannot be explained merely by easy generalisations about the British national character or political culture. History is made by men and women, not by sociological abstractions; and the failure of the revolutionary left in these years can be explained only by examining the behaviour of the people who made it up.

Walter Kendall's study of the revolutionary movement in Britain in the first two decades of this century provides an ideal starting point for such an examination. Before he wrote, the far left of the British labour movement in this period had been almost ignored by serious historians, and as a result a vital part of the story had not been told. Kendall examined the development of the Marxist sects on the fringe of the labour movement before 1914, of the shop-stewards' movement during the war, and of the complex eddies and cross-currents which came together in the British Communist Party in 1920. In doing so, he torpedoed one obvious explanation of the failure of revolutionary Marxism after 1918, and went some way to establishing a less obvious one.

The obvious explanation of the failure of revolutionary Marxism in 1919 and 1920 is that it was somehow un-British, and therefore doomed from the start. Yet the first socialist party in Britain was the Marxist Social Democratic Federation. If length of pedigree is the criterion, Morgan Phillips's famous aphorism that the British labour movement owes more to Methodism than to Marxism ought to be stood on its head. It is perfectly true that the Social Democratic Federation made very little headway, and that it was easily overtaken by its younger rival, the ILP. But this was not primarily because its ideology was Marxist. It was because it was inept, pig-headed, authoritarian in structure, and singularly badly led.

In any case, as we have seen, the social climate of 1919 and 1920 was by no means as hostile to revolutionary action as this explanation implies; and the true explanation for the failure of the revolutionary left to exploit their opportunities must therefore be found elsewhere. The explanation given by would-be revolutionaries at the time, and by those who sympathise with them in retrospect, is that the working class was betrayed by its established leaders. But this explanation is even less convincing than the first one. The established leaders of the working-class movement were not revo-lutionaries, and never had been. The reason they did not engage in revolutionary action was not that they were afraid to, and still less that they had somehow been bought off by the ruling class, but that they were convinced democrats who believed in parliamentary government.

It is perfectly true that the opposition of the established leadership to joining the Comintern provides one important reason for the failure of the revolutionary left. Thanks to his stand during the war, Ramsay MacDonald was easily the most popular figure in the ILP during these years. He was also the most effective and determined opponent of the Leninist left, and from mid-1919 to the end of 1920 he devoted most of his time and talent to a passionate campaign to save the ILP from the Leninist embrace.

But, although MacDonald played an important part in preventing the establishment of an effective Communist Party on British soil, he did not play the most important part. The most important part was played by the communists themselves – to some extent in Britain, and even more in Russia. The British Communist Party, unlike its French and German equivalents, was always an entirely artificial creation. It came into existence, not because of what was happening in Britain, but because the Russian leaders of the Comintern decided to bring it into existence. It was sustained, not merely by the moral example of the Russians, but in a direct and crucial way by Russian money and Russian men. The organisations which came together at its foundation conference were mostly tiny and uninfluential sects. The exception was the British Socialist Party, the heir of the old Social Democratic Federation. But even the BSP had affiliated to the Labour Party on a membership of only 10,000, which was less than a quarter of the membership of the ILP. Kendall estimated its true membership at around 4,000 and thought that the total membership of the new Communist Party when it was founded was almost certainly little more. This feeble conglomeration of Marxist sects was maintained, not by the pennies of the workers, but by generous financial subsidies from Moscow; and, since its leaders had no real constituency in the British working class, they soon became nothing more than paid *apparatchiki* of the Comintern. In the long run, the same thing happened to the French and German parties as well.

Even this might not have mattered if the Russian leadership and its British followers had had the remotest understanding of British conditions and the balance of forces in the British labour movement – or for that matter the remotest understanding of the Marxist sociology that they preached. One example stands out. As a result of its 1920 party conference the ILP sent a delegation to Russia to find out exactly what membership of the Communist International would entail and how closely a British party which joined it would be expected to conform to the Russian model. MacDonald ridiculed the idea of making this enquiry, on the grounds that Lenin had already made it clear that membership of the Comintern would involve an absolutely slavish conformity to the Russian model. Despite MacDonald's scorn, however, the ILP delegation duly departed – and, when it arrived in Russia, the Russian leaders proceeded to prove that everything MacDonald had said was right.

One of the things the ILP wanted to know was what the dictatorship of the proletariat really meant in British conditions, and what scope there was for parliamentary action there. The Russian answer was that 'in no country can the dictatorship of the proletariat be applied better or more directly than in Great Britain'. As for parliamentary action, it was merely a diversion. The workers should prepare, 'not for an easy parliamentary victory, but for victory by a heavy civil war'. Another of the ILP's questions was how communism differed from other forms of socialism. The answer to this question was even more illuminating. Communism, the Russians declared, was the only form of socialism. Whatever else went under the name of socialism was either 'wilful deception by lackeys of the bourgeoisie' or the self-deception of those who hesitated 'between life-and-death struggle and the role of assistants to the expiring bourgeoisie'. After this, it is hardly surprising that the ILP did not join the Comintern. The only surprising thing is that some of its members still wanted to.

Lenin's admirers might argue that this merely proves that Lenin was an honest man, who was not prepared to coax foreign parties into his International by deceiving them about its true nature. But this argument does not stand up, since on other occasions Lenin was perfectly prepared to deceive people, if he thought it would serve a revolutionary purpose. The real reason why the Russians' reply to the ILP was so uncompromising was not that they were honest men. It was that they were unbelievably arrogant. They thought they knew what Britain was like better than the British did themselves, and that because they had succeeded in seizing power in a backward peasant autocracy they were entitled to give orders to Western socialist parties with older and stronger traditions than their own. As a result, they threw away the chance of winning over the ILP, with its 45,000 members, its deep roots in the working-class movement and its proud history. In exchange they got the rump of the British Socialist Party and a handful of insignificant splinter groups. The conclusion is irresistible. Insofar as any single person deserves the credit for preventing a revolutionary outbreak in post-war Britain it is not Lloyd George or even Ramsay MacDonald. It is Lenin.

4

Varieties of Reform

'Why cannot the leaders of the Labour Party face the fact that they are not sectaries of an outworn creed, mumbling moss-grown demi-semi Fabian Marxism, but the heirs of eternal Liberalism?' So asked John Maynard Keynes, the most creative and original Liberal thinker of his day, in a *New Statesman* article in January 1939.

The question sounds through the history of the British left like a tolling bell. When Keynes asked it, Neville Chamberlain was Prime Minister, at the head of a nominally National, but in reality over-whelmingly Conservative Government, with a majority of more than 200 in the House of Commons. The Liberal Party had not formed a government for almost a generation; and could not realistically hope to form a government in the foreseeable future. It had few distinctive policies, hardly any organised support and no coherent doctrine to which it alone could convincingly lay claim. The only alternative to indefinite Conservative rule – and to Conservative rule of a kind which seemed peculiarly reactionary to most people on the left – was Labour rule.

But the Labour Party had held office only twice, for a total of only three years. The second Labour Government had perished ignominiously by its own hand, and since then the party had spent nearly eight years in impotent and unproductive opposition. Most of the available evidence suggested that it would be defeated again in the election which was due at the latest in 1940. For, although the Labour Party had replaced the Liberals as the main anti-Conservative party in Britain, it had captured only part of the old Liberal constitu-ency. Labour had recovered surprisingly quickly from the catas-trophe of 1931; but its vote in the 1935 election had been no higher than its vote in 1929, even though the Liberal vote was four million down. In striking contrast to the American Democratic Party, in other words, the Labour Party was still a minority party, rooted in a sectional interest, and perceived as such by the electorate. And that, of course, was one of the main reasons why it was in opposition and the Conservatives were in office.

Yet, as Keynes noticed, one of the main reasons why the Labour Party had failed to enter its inheritance as the 'heir of eternal Liberalism', and why it had failed to construct an Attlee coalition on the lines of the American Roosevelt coalition, was that it had not really tried. In the 1920s, Ramsay MacDonald had done his best to widen the Labour Party's intellectual and social base, and to present it to the country as the only legitimate descendant of the Edwardian Liberal Party rather than as the political instrument of the organised working class. But, after 1931, MacDonald and MacDonaldism were hopelessly discredited in Labour circles. In the 1930s, the Labour Party turned defiantly, almost ostentatiously, in on itself, its energies absorbed in savage theological disputes between a curiously rigid and mechanical Marxist left and an authoritarian trade union right. Liberal intellectuals like Keynes could hardly fail to prefer the Labour Party to the Conservative Party. But they had been given no reason to identify themselves with it emotionally, in the way that their American counterparts identified themselves with the party of Roosevelt and the New Deal, or that their predecessors had identified themselves with the party of Lloyd George and the people's budget.

Keynes's question is therefore one of the central questions facing the historian of the British left between the wars. For Labour's inability to establish itself as the electoral heir of the Edwardian Liberal Party was, in large part, the product of its indifference to the intellectual legacy of Edwardian liberalism. Intellectuals may not command many divisions, but they draw the maps by which the divisions march. Before 1914, the maps had been Liberal maps. One reason why they were not Labour maps in the 1930s is that the Labour Party did not try hard enough to mobilise the map-makers.

All this gives a double significance to Peter Clarke's *Liberals and Social Democrats*, a sensitive and absorbing composite portrait of four of the most impressive Liberal intellectuals in the generation before Keynes – L. T. Hobhouse, the social theorist; J. L. Hammond, the social historian; J. A. Hobson, the economist; and Graham Wallas, the pioneer of political science.[1] In the first place, it is an important contribution to the intellectual history of early twentieth-century Britain. It also throws important new light on the enduring tensions in the relationship between the Liberal intelligentsia and the labour movement, and hence on a crucial aspect of present-day British politics as well.

As Dr Clarke's title implies, all four of his heroes were Liberals with a big 'L' for varying periods, and liberals with a small 'l' throughout their adult lives. All four were also what we would now call social democrats, seeking more social and economic equality within an essentially capitalist framework, and opposing wholesale public ownership for its own sake. Though none ever sat in Parliament, all four were active in politics and journalism, and devoted as much intellectual and emotional energy to the day-to-day political battles of the time as to the life of the mind. All four helped to shape the style and objectives of the new 'social' liberalism which provided the agenda for the pre-1914 Liberal governments, and all four sympathised strongly with the nascent labour movement in those years.

Yet only J. A. Hobson joined the Labour Party when it became clear that the Liberal Party was no longer an effective political force. And what Dr Clarke shows above all, it seems to me, is that the barriers which kept the other three from following Hobson's example were the products of a coherent set of emotions and intellectual attitudes, which governed the behaviour of a large number of other liberal intellectuals as well – both then and since.

His central thesis is that the progressive mentality can take one of four possible forms, which reflect a fundamental division between optimistic and pessimistic views of human nature. There are, he points out, obvious grounds for associating a belief in original sin with social conservatism. But, he goes on,

> even for revolutionists, it makes a crucial difference whether an optimistic or pessimistic view of human nature is postulated. On an optimistic view, progress can be assumed. A moral change, a change of heart, a new consciousness, will be the agent and sanction of a transformation within society. But the revolutionist who takes a pessimistic view has no such confidence; instead, he is impressed by the ideological conditioning which has flawed the social consciousness of the very groups who ought to bring change about. Nevertheless, he knows that revolution is correct, and concludes that it must if necessary be made from above if spontaneous forces fail. Mechanical methods have to be substituted instead.[2]

Thus, the early Marx was a moral revolutionist and Lenin a mechanical one. And a similar distinction can be drawn between moral and mechanical reformists. Just as mechanical revolutionists believe that

48

revolution will have to come from above, so mechanical reformists, while, differing from their revolutionist counterparts in believing that change can be brought about peacefully, believe that recalcitrant human nature can be prodded into the right path only by coercion, and that the primary aim of those who seek social change must be to get their hands on the instruments of coercion. For the moral reformist, on the other hand, social change is above all the product of persuasion and leadership, and state-imposed progress is inherently suspect.

Clearly, these distinctions must not be pushed too far. The line between moral and mechanical revolutionists is not hard and fast. There was a streak of anarchistic, 'moral' revolutionism in Lenin, and more than a streak of coercive, 'mechanical' revolutionism in Marx. The same is true of the line between moral and mechanical reformists. Even the most optimistic moral reformist must presumably believe that state power is worth having, and that some of the obstacles to social progress can be removed only by the appropriate use of that power. Even the most cynical mechanical reformist must believe that there are limits to the extent to which change can legitimately be forced down society's throat. Otherwise the whole concept of reformism would be meaningless.

All the same, it seems to me that Dr Clarke's four categories reflect divisions of attitude and feeling which can be detected quite clearly in the real world. It also seems to me that they do a great deal both to answer the question which Keynes asked in the *New Statesman* fifty years ago, and to explain why he asked it.

For what emerges most clearly from Dr Clarke's study is that all four of his heroes, and, indeed, the pre-1914 liberal intelligentsia as a whole, were moral reformists to the fingertips. They were, of course reformists, not quietists. They thought it worthwhile to engage in a struggle for political power; and they thought that, because they believed that political power could be used to further the social and economic changes which they believed to be right. Indeed, their greatest achievement was to help redefine traditional, Gladstonian, socially quietist liberalism so as to permit – and indeed oblige – a consistent liberal to use the power of the state to achieve social reform. But they did not believe that the state could be the sole, or even the main, agent of social change; and they were instinctively hostile to any suggestion that reform should be pushed through by force or manipulation.

The second important conclusion to emerge from Dr Clarke's

book, however, is that this was not true of the labour movement –
or not, at any rate, of the intellectuals who fashioned the ideology
of the labour movement. As Keynes pointed out, labour's ideology
was drawn from two sources – Fabiansim and Marxism. But
although the early Marx was a moral revolutionist in Dr Clarke's
sense, it was the later Marx – and, indeed, the later Marx as
mediated by the arch-mechanist, Engels – who influenced the British
labour movement. And if the Marxist element in labour's ideology
was mechanical, the Fabian element, Dr Clarke suggested, was even
more so.

To be sure, one of his heroes, Graham Wallas, was a prominent
Fabian for many years, and, indeed, contributed to the famous first
volume of Fabian essays. But that strengthens his argument. For
Wallas became estranged from the Fabian Society precisely because
Fabianism, at any rate as interpreted by Bernard Shaw and the
Webbs, became more and more mechanical in Dr Clarke's sense of
the term, and diverged more and more sharply from moral reformism. And what was true of Wallas was even more obviously true
of Hobhouse, Hobson and Hammond. There were three great litmus
tests of political allegiance at the beginning of this century – the Boer
War, the 1902 Education Act and tariff reform. Moral reformers
instinctively supported the Boers, opposed paying for Church schools
out of the rates and supported free trade. On all three, orthodox
Webbian Fabians were either indifferent or on the other side.

There were, of course, other elements in the labour movement
besides Fabianism and Marxism. There were, most obviously, the
trade unions and the Independent Labour Party. But although the
unions were sometimes swept away by a wild and heady mood of
moral revolutionism, as in the strike waves before and after the First
World War, they were generally led by sober mechanical reformers,
with a world-view very close to that of the Webbs. The ILP, it must
be admitted, was a more complicated kettle of fish, and it is a pity
that Dr Clarke does not say more about his quartet's relations with
it. Some ILPers were reformers, particularly before the First World
War, and others were revolutionists, particularly after it. But virtually all fell squarely on the optimistic, 'moral' side of Dr Clarke's
moral–mechanical dividing line. They were therefore closer emotionally to the moral reformers in the Liberal Party than was any other
section of the labour movement; and it is not an accident that when
the Liberal moral reformers did come over to Labour, as many did
after 1918, they tended to do so by way of the ILP. Indeed, Hobson,

though not a member of the party, became a kind of ILP guru in the mid-1920s. But, although the ILP contributed a great deal to the mood and style of the labour movement, it did not contribute much to its ideology. In ideology, the mechanists prevailed, with only occasional shouts of protest from the moralists; and, although there have always been plenty of instinctive moral reformers in the labour movement, they have never had a coherent moral reformist creed to give their instincts an intellectual cutting edge.

Nor, of course, has anyone else. The New Liberalism which Dr Clarke's quartet helped so powerfully to develop before the First World War provided only partial and intermittent guidance to would-be moral reformers between the wars; and although many of the social reforms introduced by the wartime Churchill Government and the post-war Attlee Government can be traced back to seeds sown by Liberal moral reformers before 1914, the exercise has little point. What matters is that no one managed to articulate a coherent moral reformist creed to take the place of pre-1914 New Liberalism in the conditions of today. Perhaps the chief lesson of Dr Clarke's book is that that is now one of the most pressing intellectual tasks of our time.

5

The Politics of Deprivation

In September 1927, Beatrice Webb noted in her diary that she was about to begin a new investigation into the administration of out-door relief to the able-bodied. Her diary entry was remarkably pessimistic in tone. She asked herself gloomily whether her strength would hold out, and then continued, in a passage of almost brutal self-revelation:

> I am not confident that either Sidney or I have the mental vigour and resilience to tackle new problems – we can still collect and marshal already known categories and facts – perhaps as skilfully as ever. But can we discover the *new* issues and gauge the new proportions of the problems involved, e.g. chronic unemployment? And is there any practicable solution, should this unemployment prove not only to be chronic but also progressive? If such a disaster is actually imminent will any change in administration, policy and procedure avail to alter the result? Might it not be a question of muddling through, curbing and checking the present Poor Law administration, until a lowered birth-rate, emigration, and an even higher death-rate brought about a new equilibrium of population with national resources? These pessimistic doubts, are they themselves signs of senility? It seems ridiculous, with the immense strides in the technique of production and the opening out of the world's resources that there should be less work – fewer commodities and services to divide among an industrious and active-minded people! . . . But have we or any other contemporary investigators and thinkers the capacity to discover how to prevent unemployment and how best to treat the unemployed?[1]

In the general election two years later, the Labour Party became the largest single party in the House of Commons; for the second time the unfortunate Ramsay MacDonald faced the delicate task of heading a minority government dependent on tacit – but highly volatile – Liberal support. In 1924 he and his party held office in similar circumstances for ten months. Their record was a creditable one, particularly in foreign affairs. His second Government was less fortunate. A few months after his arrival in Downing Street, the American stock market collapsed and the great depression began. For the next two years he and his colleagues struggled unavailingly with falling exports and a steadily rising total of unemployment. When they came into office in June 1929, 1,164,000 insured workers were unemployed. By July 1930 the figure was over two million. By the following December it was two-and-a-half million, and by June 1931 it had reached 2,700,000. Beatrice Webb's forecast that unemployment might prove not only chronic but progressive had apparently come true: and the Government of which her husband was a leading member turned out to be as incapable of solving the problem in practice as she had been of solving it in theory.

It is true, of course, that no government anywhere in the world managed to halt the depression when it first broke. But that was small comfort. Labour had based its claim to power, in large part, on the proposition that the evils of recurrent trade depressions and bouts of mass unemployment could be eradicated only by a socialist party, committed to the total transformation of society: that as a socialist party, it possessed both a special sensitivity to the sufferings of the unemployed and a special competence in handling the problem of unemployment. Yet, so far from displaying any such sensitivity or competence, the 1929 Government presided over the biggest increase in unemployment since the turn of the century. To be sure, it was a minority government and, as such, lacked the power to carry out the social transformation to which its members were committed. Even minority governments can formulate policies, however, and on the issue which the Labour Party had itself identified as the most important of the day, the 1929 Government formulated none. It rejected the Liberal policy of loan-financed public works. It also rejected the Conservative policy of protection. That left it with no logical alternative to the orthodox Treasury doctrine that depressions would sooner or later cure themselves, provided that governments balanced their budgets and refrained from increasing the public debt. But although Philip Snowden, the Chancellor of the Exchequer, accepted that doctrine himself and made manful efforts to persuade his colleagues to put it into practice, his efforts did not succeed. Later mythology notwithstanding, Snowden's budgets were not balanced. Though the Government refused to borrow for public works, it did borrow – and borrowed, moreover, on an increasingly lavish scale – to cover the growing deficit in the unemployment fund. All the options, in short, were rejected, except the fatal option of waiting for something to turn up. As in somewhat similar circumstances in the 1970s, what turned up was a sterling crisis which only the bleakest Treasury orthodoxy could resolve.

Yet the Government's *immobilisme* was not due to indifference or complacency. Before the First World War, MacDonald had won his spurs as a parliamentarian by his advocacy of a 'Right to Work Bill' based on the principle of work or maintenance. Throughout the 1929 Government's tenure of office he was uneasily – sometimes despairingly – aware that he and his ministers were failing to deal effectively with the most important single problem they faced. 'The flood of unemployment flows and rises, and baffles everybody,' he noted privately in February 1930. 'At Chequers one can almost see it and hear its swish.' As the swish grew louder during the next eighteen months, his bewilderment grew more intense. 'Yesterday a baffling day with unemployment,' he noted in July 1930. 'To find work defies everyone.' By March 1931 he was admitting privately: 'I am not happy about our work. It is too much of the onlooker oppressed by circumstances.'[2] This note of despair was echoed by the Government's advisers. In July 1930 Sir John Anderson compared the Government's position to that of 'the captain and officers of a great ship which has run aground on a falling tide; no human endeavour will get the ship afloat until in the course of nature the tide begins to flow'. MacDonald replied that Anderson's letter 'expresses exactly my own frame of mind . . .'.

If the captain was aground, so were the other officers and the vast majority of the crew. In August 1931 the Labour Government was swept from power by the financial crisis. When the National Government which succeeded it met Parliament in September, the House of Commons debated its economy programme. The debate was acrimonious; but although the new administration was bitterly attacked by the official spokesmen of the Labour opposition, the attackers had no alternative to offer. Arthur Henderson, the new Labour leader, went out of his way to stress that he accepted the need to balance the budget; his criticism of the National Government was confined to the subsidiary issue of whether or not it should be balanced by cutting unemployment pay. James Maxton, the leader

54

of the Independent Labour Party, who had been a thorn in MacDonald's side ever since the 1929 Government came into office, asked pertinently how the Government could restore prosperity by 'reducing the purchasing power of the mass of the people'; but instead of following the logic of his own question, found the solution in the total abolition of 'your old capitalist system' and the establishment of a vague and undefined 'new system, in which the whole nation is a planned unity'.

In the whole debate, only one speaker went to the heart of the matter. That was Sir Oswald Mosley. In the circumstances of 1931, Mosley argued, balancing the budget was irrelevant, even harmful. What was needed was a solution to 'the industrial situation'. If that were found the budget could be left to look after itself:

> The continual decline and collapse of the industries of this country makes completely illusory any attempt to balance the Budget. You may balance the Budget on the present basis of revenue, but there is no man in the House who can say with any confidence that this basis of revenue will be long maintained. . . . Revenue rests upon industrial prosperity, and when industry is progressively declining, revenue . . . must progressively decline as well. . . .
>
> Many people seem to think that we are the only country in the world faced with the prospect of a Budget deficit. As a matter of fact ours is the only country in the world which is taking any steps to meet it. Deficits are the fashion nowadays. All the best countries have deficits. . . . There is no collapse of their exchanges, no withdrawal of foreign deposits, no efflux of gold because they have deficits. Why? Because their industrial position is strong. . . .
>
> We . . . should adopt the method of balancing our Budget advocated Mr. Keynes and other economists which is simply to continue to borrow . . . to provide for the Unemployment Insurance Fund, or I would prefer to say, borrow to provide constructive works to give employment in place of it.[3]

Mosley, however, had never had much in common with the rest of the Labour Party. He had first entered the House of Commons as a Conservative, and had not even crossed over to Labour until 1924. By August 1931, he had already severed his connections with it.

By a strange paradox, moreover, the 1931 crisis made it more difficult for the labour movement to come to terms with the problems which had baffled the Labour Government. For the solid mass of Labour loyalists, who had tamely supported that Government until the fifty-ninth minute of the eleventh hour, were the last people to welcome a searching enquiry into the reasons it had failed. MacDonald's so-called 'treachery' in forming the National Government provided them with a perfect explanation for everything which had gone wrong before then, and a perfect alibi for their own inability to put it right. Many Labour people came to believe that he had knowingly and cold-bloodedly plotted his Government's fall – an interpretation which received the imprimatur of such Labour intellectuals as Sidney Webb and Harold Laski. Even those who did not swallow the 'plot theory' generally agreed with its proponents that, in deciding to form the National Government, MacDonald had betrayed the Labour Party. And, if MacDonald was a traitor in August 1931, it was at least plausible to infer that he must have been inclined to treachery before then. That in turn implied that the responsibility for his Government's failures could be laid at his door, and that the only fault attaching to his followers was that they had allowed themselves to be hoodwinked by a treacherous leader.

MacDonald was only one scapegoat. Another was 'capitalism'. The Labour Government had fallen, so many Labour people argued, because the 'capitalists' had engineered its fall. The crisis had not been a real crisis: it had been a 'bankers' ramp', deliberately designed to destroy the Labour Government and do down the working class. Thus, Labour ministers could not be blamed for failing to overcome it. They were to blame, if at all, only for allowing the bankers to bamboozle them into thinking that it *was* a crisis. But if 'capitalism' was to blame, that was one more proof that gradualist tinkering with 'capitalism' led nowhere, and that working-class aspirations could be satisfied only by 'socialism'.

Against that background, it is not surprising that, for most of the 1930s, Marx, not Keynes, was the patron saint of the left-wing intelligentsia. The marriage between Keynesianism and Fabianism, which was consummated with the publication of Evan Durbin's *The Politics of Democratic Socialism* (1940) and Douglas Jay's *The Socialist Case* (1937), and which was to provide the intellectual inspiration for the party leadership in the 1940s and 1950s, did not take place until nearly the end of the decade. Mass unemployment was overwhelmingly the most important domestic problem in British politics between the wars, above all for the working class. Yet the Labour Party failed, not only to offer solutions of its own, but even to appropriate the solutions put forward by others.

Why was it that the party of the working class had so little to say about the most important single economic problem which the working class faced during these years? This is perhaps the central problem of British labour history between the wars, but, by a strange paradox, the intellectual categories which most labour historians have absorbed with their mothers' milk – categories which spring from the governing assumptions of the labour movement itself – stand in the way of a solution.

What might be called 'mainstream' labour historians – historians who share, broadly speaking, the outlook and assumptions of the majority of the labour movement in the period under discussion – do not deny that the 1929 Government failed, but they explain its failure in terms of the difficulties it faced and the personal weaknesses of its leading members, not in terms of the structure of the labour movement itself. We are told more about Ramsay MacDonald's alleged vanity, snobbery and aloofness than about the reasons why he was idolised by the party rank and file: more about Philip Snowden's fiscal orthodoxy and lack of imagination than about the factors which had made it possible for him to be accepted as the party's leading financial expert. In any case, their emphasis is on achievement, not on failure: on the growth of working-class power, not on the ineffective way it was used.

The standpoint of the 'old left' – best exemplified, perhaps, by Michael Foot's *Aneurin Bevan*,[4] as well as by a host of contemporary memoirs – is at first sight diametrically opposed. Writers of this school are only too happy to acknowledge that the working class was inadequately served by those who claimed to speak for it. The party leadership, as they depict it, was not only muddled and incompetent, but cowardly and even corrupt; and its repeated victories at party conferences are interpreted almost wholly in terms of its skill at manipulating the trade union 'block vote'. The same is true of the 'new left', whose standpoint is best illustrated by Ralph Miliband's *Parliamentary Socialism*,[5] now nearly thirty years old, and David Coates's more recent *The Labour Party and the Struggle for Socialism*.[6] It is true that there are fundamental differences between the new left and the old left. Where Foot, for example, is unshakeably committed to parliamentary government, Miliband argues that the British Labour Party has been hamstrung, ever since its formation, by an exaggerated respect for parliamentary institutions. Unlike the old left, moreover, the new left recognises that Labour's failures between the wars cannot be wholly explained in terms of the failure of the party leadership, and that the left deserves at least a share of the blame. Nevertheless, new and old left alike agree on one vital point. The fundamental assumption of both is that the Labour Party would have been more successful if it had been more militant, and that it would have been more militant if only the rank and file had not been bamboozled and beaten down by the leadership. Both, in other words, accept a model of Labour politics ultimately derived from Robert Michels. Both see those politics, first and foremost, as a struggle between a militant rank and file and a conservative leadership; and both take it for granted that the militancy of the rank and file reflects the attitudes of the working class as a whole.

In spite of the differences between these standpoints, they share three related assumptions. In the first place, their exponents all agree that the socialist ideology embodied in the 1918 constitution of the Labour Party was in some sense to the 'left' of, and therefore more 'progressive' than, the ideology of the Conservative and Liberal parties. All of them picture a political spectrum extending from socialism or communism at one end to conservatism or fascism at the other, with liberalism or radicalism in the centre. Thus, all of them see Lloyd George, or Keynes, or the architects of the 'New Liberalism' of the early century as occupying a position somewhere between that of Neville Chamberlain or Stanley Baldwin on the one hand, and Arthur Henderson or even Ramsay MacDonald on the other. It is true that the left – both new and old – constantly berate the Labour Party leadership for being too close to the centre of this spectrum. But the crucial point is that they do not question that the spectrum existed: and that they accept that even the most moderate and pusillanimous of socialists belong, or at least ought to belong, at the 'progressive' or 'left-wing' end of it.

The second assumption follows from the first. If socialism is to the 'left' of Liberalism or Conservatism, it follows that the working class – whose creed socialism is – must be to the 'left' of all other social classes. For neo-Marxists, like Miliband, this assumption is, of course, absolutely fundamental. The proletariat is, by definition, more progressive than the bourgeoisie; if individual proletarians are not, this is because they have not realised what their class interests are and where their historical destiny lies. But even non-Marxists have been curiously slow to question this most pervasive of Marx's intellectual legacies. For them, as much as for the left-wing historians, the working class is, by definition, a force for progress. Sections of it may sometimes be misled, as in 1931 when two million former Labour voters were seduced into voting for the National Government, but its heart is in the right (that is, left) place. All the historians I have mentioned would, of course, accept that large numbers of working men and women voted Conservative throughout the inter-war period, and that even at the height of trade union membership immediately after the First World War only a minority of the working population belonged to trade unions. But although the existence of a substantial working-class Conservative vote was – and remains – one of the characteristic features of British politics, it has received surprisingly little attention from labour historians. For Alan Bullock, or Ben Pimlott, whose biographies of Ernest Bevin and Hugh Dalton[7] respectively are triumphs of 'mainstream' historiography, no less than for Foot or Miliband, the non-unionised working-class Tory is somehow an aberration or an anachronism: a pale and ghostly figure sliding inexorably towards the margin of history, not a robust, red-blooded creature, with at least as much sociological staying power as his Labour-voting, dues-paying neighbours. By the same token, labour historians have not examined the extent to which Conservative and Labour working-class voters shared broadly the *same* values and prejudices: and to which, in consequence, the official ideology of the labour movement failed to reflect the operative ideology of its supporters at the grass roots. The 'secret people of England', Chesterton declared in a famous poem, 'have not spoken yet'. The working assumption of most labour historians appears to be that between the wars the 'secret people of England' spoke through the mouths of those who claimed to represent them. It is a risky assumption to take on trust.

Finally, all three standpoints assume that the central theme of British history between the wars is to be found in a struggle between organised labour and the established order. To some extent, of course, this is inevitable. Labour historians are, after all, primarily interested in the labour moment. Yet if British political history in the 1920s and 1930s is seen first and foremost as a struggle between the labour movement on the one hand and everyone else on the other, and if it is taken for granted that in this struggle the labour

59

movement represented the forces of progress, a number of questions cannot even be asked, much less answered. To take only one example, one of the most remarkable features of British intellectual history in the 1930s is the gradual acceptance of the concept of economic planning. How and why did this happen? If the traditional assumption were right, it would presumably follow that the impetus came from the Labour Party. But, in fact, the concept of planning gained ground in all parties, not only in the Labour Party; and it is at least arguable that maverick Conservatives, like the young Harold Macmillan, or renegade socialists, like Clifford Allen, did more to gain acceptance for it than any member of the Labour Party. Indeed, it is conceivable that Labour's conversion to planning ought to be seen, not as the spur which provoked the conversion of others, but as a response to the measures of rationalisation and *dirigisme* actually introduced by the National Government.

This is even more true of the central issue of how to overcome mass unemployment. Keynes had some partial converts, even in the Conservative Party; if Mosley was his prize pupil in the 1929 Parliament, Lloyd George was second in the class. By the same token, Snowden's fiscal orthodoxy had plenty of adherents in the Liberal Party, as well as on the Conservative and Labour benches, while the Conservative nostrum of protective tariffs won a growing number of converts in the Labour Party. On the central economic questions of the time, in short, the division of opinion cut across the categories of 'right' and 'left', 'capitalist' and 'socialist', 'middle-class' and 'working-class'. Faced with a catastrophe to which past experience offered no guidance, some politicians in all parties groped for new approaches while others stuck to the orthodoxies they had absorbed in the past. If we want to understand why Labour politicians groped so feebly, we must abandon, not only the categories of 'left' and 'right' and 'socialist' and 'capitalist', but the unconscious assumptions which those categories reflect.

Will any other categories serve better? In his now classic study of the economic misadventures of the 1929 Government, *Politicians and the Slump*,[8] R. J. Skidelsky offered a different set. On unemployment, Skidelsky argued, the really important battle was that between 'economic radicals' and 'economic conservatives', and the really decisive event was the defeat of the 'radicals'. Since Labour was in power at the crucial moment, it follows that the struggle must have been fought out inside the Labour Party, and that the reasons for the victory of the 'conservatives' must be found in the internal politics of the labour movement. Skidelsky found it in Labour's commitment to 'a Utopian Socialism which incapacitated it from effectively working the parliamentary system and prevented it from coming to terms with economic reality'. The Labour Party, he wrote, suffered from a form of ideological split personality.

> on the one hand it was committed to constitutionalism; on the other it lacked a social democratic or gradualist programme without which tenure of power was bound to be rather barren of achievement. It thought in terms of a total solution to the problem of poverty, when what it was offered was the limited opportunity to cure unemployment. It was a parliamentary party with a Utopian ethic. It was not fit for the kind of power it was called upon to exercise.
>
> For what was at issue between 1929 and 1931 . . . was not Socialism versus Capitalism. It was interventionist Capitalism versus *laissez-faire* Capitalism. The Labour Party's commitment to a nebulous Socialism made it regard the work of the 'economic radicals' such as Keynes as mere 'tinkering', when in fact it was they who were providing the real choice.[9]

Socialism, in other words, was not merely irrelevant to the struggle between 'economic radicals' and 'economic conservatives'. It was a source of 'conservatism' and a barrier to 'radicalism'.

It is an attractive thesis. To be sure, the notion that Labour's socialism was 'utopian' needs careful qualification. Ramsay MacDonald, with his romantic air and rhetorical ambiguity, may deserve the label of utopian socialist, though in foreign affairs, in particular, he was also a patient and skilled negotiator with an excellent sense of timing. But the label hardly fits the Webbs, whose reputations had been made by the patient and laborious analysis of social problems. Yet, as we have seen, the Webbs were as impotent in the face of mass unemployment as MacDonald himself; and in the fatal dispute over balancing the budget, Sidney Webb, at least, was on MacDonald's side.

But, although Skidelsky overstated this part of his case, there was an important kernel of truth in it. He was wrong in thinking that Labour's ideology was utopian in the sense that the party rejected piecemeal solutions. In fact, both minority Labour governments carried through piecemeal social reforms. Its ideology undoubtedly was utopian, however, in its attitude to the capitalist system as such. For the central premise of Labour's creed between the wars – summed up in the clear implication of Clause Four of the 1918 constitution that the 'workers by hand and brain' could only receive the 'full fruits of their labour' if the means of production were owned in common – was that capitalism was immoral because the profit motive involved the exploitation of man by man. Service, not profit, should be the motive force of economic activity, Tawney declared in *The Acquisitive Society*; and Tawney's doctrine was repeated, with varying degrees of eloquence and emphasis, from a thousand Labour platforms. This doctrine is, of course, inherently at variance with the basic assumptions of Keynesian economics, one of which is that the profit motive is the engine of economic progress. Admittedly, this cannot have been an insuperable obstacle to the spread of Keynesian ideas in the labour movement, for the party leadership was in fact converted to them in the end. But although the obstacle was not an insuperable one, it did exist. Keynes was consciously and deliberately seeking to save capitalism from its own internal contradictions. One reason why British socialists did not follow him was that they were not sure if they wanted capitalism to be saved.

Despite its attractions, however, Skidelsky's thesis no longer seems as plausible as it once did. Like all historians, he was a product of his own time, writing for his own time. When his book first appeared, the 'Attlee consensus', under the aegis of which the welfare state had been consolidated and the mixed economy established, still held sway. The Keynesian revolution was complete, and the erstwhile revolutionaries were in control. Looking back from the vantage point of the 1990s, we can see that the long boom of the 1950s and 1960s was already beginning to peter out. At the time, the problems which presaged its collapse looked like temporary hiccups, which a modicum of good management would soon put right. It was clear, of course, that Britain faced severe problems of economic retardation, and that the Wilson Government's attempts to cope with them had not been particularly successful. But the prevailing orthodoxy suggested that its lack of success was due to a lack of will and intelligence, which had prevented it from applying the remedies which the Keynesian revolution had forged, not to the obduracy of the problems or the inadequacies of a Keynesian frame of reference. By the same token, although the international monetary system created at Bretton Woods was showing signs of disarray, few foresaw its imminent collapse.

In the faintly uneasy, but still rather incurious, climate engendered by this state of affairs, the events of August and September 1931 seemed remote and almost incomprehensible. It was hard to believe that sensible people could ever have believed that the currency might collapse: that the banks might have to close their doors: that the authorities might be unable to borrow enough to cover the budget deficit. It was harder still to believe that their fears might have been justified. In the late 1960s, enlightened opinion, at any rate, assumed that depressions were avoidable, that high levels of unemployment were curable and that currency devaluations were acceptable. The fact that Wilson's Government had struggled as manfully as Mac-Donald's to avoid devaluation only proved that it was not enlightened. Much the same applied to the confusions and fumblings which preceded the 1931 crisis. Most people still assumed that post-war full employment was a child of the Keynesian revolution. Most concluded that, since Keynesian remedies had worked in the 1940s and 1950s, they would also have worked in the 1920s and 1930s, if only governments had had the sense to apply them.

Hence Skidelsky's schema. His heroes – the 'economic radicals' – were Keynesians or, at any rate, proto-Keynesians; his villains – the 'economic conservatives' – anti-Keynesians or, at the best, pre-Keynesians. Virtue lay in anticipating or agreeing with Keynes, vice in ignoring or rejecting him. Twenty years on, that schema looks no more convincing than the older schema of 'left' versus 'right' and 'socialist' versus 'capitalist'. The Keynesian era has ended, and the Keynesian remedies no longer work. We have discovered anew that depressions cannot always be avoided, and that high levels of unemployment sometimes have to be tolerated. We have also discovered that currency depreciation can sometimes be more painful than the deflation needed to halt it, and that international monetary stability is a prize for which it is worth paying a great deal. On a different level, it has become clear that the enlightened, Keynesian governments of the post-war period were no better at coping with the fundamental structural problems of lagging productivity, declining competitiveness and sluggish adaptation than their unenlightened, pre-Keynesian predecessors.

Partly because of all this, Keynes's own claim to economic radicalism no longer seems as self-evident as it did twenty years ago. In the perspective of the 1990s, the similarities between Keynes and the pre-Keynesian 'classics' stand out more sharply than the differences. As strongly as the classics, Keynes believed that the structure and behaviour of the supply side of the economy should be determined by market forces. Government intervention was to be confined to manipulating demand. If the level of demand were right, supply would follow. But the structural weaknesses which lay behind the century-long relative decline of the British economy did not have to do with demand; they had to do with supply. In focusing attention on demand, Keynes diverted it from the really crucial question of how the weaknesses of Britain's supply side could be put right. More damagingly still, he reinforced the fatal 'classical' assumptions that deficiencies in the supply side must, in the long run, be self-correcting: that economic change and adaptation come and can only come from the operation of the free, competitive market; and that, if they are not taking place, it must be because the market is not free and competitive enough. Most damagingly of all, he also reinforced the ancient disdain of the British political class for the humdrum, hands-on 'low politics' through which governments in other systems have tackled the supply side, and its inherited preference for the glamorous generalities of 'high politics'. The Keynesian system was quintessentially a system of indirect rule. The Keynesian managers did not have to dirty their hands in the grubby world where factories are managed, products manufactured and markets captured; they did not even have to deal face to face with those who did. They had only to pull the levers of demand from an aloof sanctum in Treasury Chambers. Looked at in this light, the struggle between Keynesians and 'pre-Keynesians' is a struggle, not between radicals and conservatives, but between one set of conservatives and another. The question is no longer, why did the Labour Party take so long to switch from economically conservative utopian socialism to economically radical Keynesianism? Instead, we must ask, why did Labour remain economically conservative, both in its utopian and in its post-utopian phases?

To that question, Skidelsky's thesis can offer no answer. In spite of these weaknesses, however, it has important strengths. It focuses attention on change, adaptation and attitudes to change and adaptation. It reminds us that men and women live on a number of different levels at once: that a passionate commitment to sweeping and comprehensive change at some time in the future may coexist with a deep resistance to detailed, piecemeal changes here and now. It also encourages us to probe beneath the surface meaning of an ideology to the tacit assumptions and hidden yearnings beneath: to contemplate the possibility that an ideology can face in a number of different directions, and that the obvious directions are not always those most deserving of attention.

What would such a probe reveal in the case of the inter-war Labour Party? As we have seen, there were obvious utopian elements in inter-war British socialism, elements which, as Skidelsky argued, led its adherents to look with disdain on 'palliatives' which might prop up the system they wanted to transform. These, however, ran alongside a rather different element, which cannot be called utopian, which proved, in the end, quite hospitable to Keynesian economics, but which stood in the way of a more thoroughgoing radicalism of supply. To come to grips with that second element, we must look again at the early history of the Labour Party, before it had become a serious contender for power. Pre-war British socialism was, of course, a highly moralistic creed. But it was not exclusively moralistic. It also rested on an analysis of the dynamics of capitalism. At the heart of that analysis lay the assumptions that socialism would be built on capitalism's success and that capitalism had solved the problem of production, leaving it to socialism to solve the problem of distribution. Indeed, these assumptions underpinned much of socialism's moral case. The scandal to which socialists drew attention was that of poverty in the midst of plenty, of a mighty engine of production pouring out wealth in grotesquely unequal heaps. The notion that the engine might be malfunctioning – still more, the notion that some capitalist engines might, for a variety of correctable reasons, function less efficiently than others – was quite alien to this moral critique. Quite apart from morality, moreover, this set of assumptions also underpinned the strategy and tactics of the whole project of gradualist democratic socialism. It was because capitalism had solved the problem of production – because resources were plentiful even if maldistributed – that Marx's prophecy of progressive proletarian impoverishment had been falsified, and the Marxist strategy of class war rendered unnecessary. And it was because revolutionary Marxism was wrong that gradualist democratic socialism was right.

Initially, these assumptions erected a further barrier to the spread of Keynesian or proto-Keynesian ideas. A party whose leaders had spent their youth denouncing the idea that capitalism was doomed to inevitable crisis can perhaps be excused for finding it difficult to come to terms with crisis when it finally appeared. But that barrier proved fairly easy to overcome. On a deeper level, the gradualist assumption that capitalism had solved the problem of production was quite compatible with the Keynesian Revolution. For there is a sense in which Keynes also thought that the problem of production had been solved, in which he too believed that the central issue for the twentieth century was distribution, indeed in which he too was exercised by the scandal of poverty in the midst of plenty. To be sure, the conclusions he drew from his analysis were quite different from the conclusions which gradualist socialists drew from theirs. But the analysis itself was not fundamentally different. By that same token, however, gradualist democratic socialism found it almost as difficult as did Keynesianism to contemplate the possibility that the problem of production had not been solved after all: that supply needed at least as much attention as demand: that the scandal of poverty in the midst of comparative plenty was matched by a scandal of inadequate resources, inefficiently produced in out-of-date plant, by under-skilled workers and under-educated managers. Like the New Liberals, to whose ideology theirs was a sort of counterpoint, the pioneers of British socialism were economic optimists. Though some of the early Fabians flirted with the National Efficiency movement, their flirtations were quite uncharacteristic of the socialist movement as a whole. For most of its adherents, British socialism was a warm-weather creed. The notion that the weather might in fact be turning cold was alien to it.

This, however, is only the beginning of the story. Granted that Labour's ideology was a barrier to 'economic radicalism', it is still necessary to ask why the party should have embraced such an ideology – and why, given that it did, its supporters did not turn elsewhere. In the 1920s, after all, there must still have been a fair number of Labour voters who had voted Liberal before 1914, and whose commitment to the Labour Party might have been expected to be less deeply rooted than that of a staunch Labour voter in our own day. In 1929 the Liberals made a determined effort to persuade such voters to return to their old allegiance. Lloyd George fought the election of that year on a remarkably radical programme, designed, not only to create jobs and mop up unemployment, but to address many of the problems of the supply side through a partnership between the public and private sectors. But it was the Labour Party, and not the Liberals, which emerged as the strongest party in the House of Commons; the Liberals' share of the vote rose by only 6 per cent, and their representation in the House of Commons by only nineteen seats. Even in 1931, despite the failure of the

Labour Government, neither the Liberals nor Mosley's New Party made any inroads on the Labour vote. The 'conservatism' of the Labour leadership, in other words, seems to have reflected a similar conservatism on the part of Labour voters, and it is at least arguable that the 'conservatism' which reigned at the top can only be explained by a different sort of 'conservatism' at the bottom.

This, at least, is the train of thought suggested by W. G. Runciman's celebrated study of social inequality in twentieth-century England, *Relative Deprivation and Social Justice*.[10] Runciman's argument was complex and subtle, but his central thesis was simple enough. It is not actual deprivation which produces social discontent, he argued, but relative deprivation: not the amount of social or economic inequality, but the degree to which those at the bottom of the pyramid feel that they are being treated unequally, and that their treatment is undeserved. But the degree to which people feel that they are being treated unequally depends on their range of comparison – on their 'reference groups', to use Runciman's term. A starving man whose reference group consists solely of other starving men will have fewer complaints against the society which allows him to starve than a wealthy man whose reference group consists of people who are wealthier than he is. But in Britain, at least, working-class people usually have very limited reference groups. They compare themselves, not with people in middle-class occupations, but with other working-class people, and they aspire, not to overturn or destroy the status hierarchy, but to rise modestly within it.

Hence, Runciman argued, the contrast between mass unemployment between the wars and the extraordinary quiescence of the working class which suffered from it. Immediately after the war, working-class discontent was at its height, because the war had widened horizons, extended reference groups and thus intensified the sense of relative deprivation. Thereafter, the sense of relative deprivation grew less acute, as working-class reference groups were 'pared down' by the depression; and working-class discontent declined with it. As Runciman put it:

> The story of the period between the two wars . . . is of a decline or, at least, a considerable easement of relative deprivation among the less fortunately placed; and by egalitarian standards, at any rate, it is a story of a continuing discrepancy between objective situation and the level of relative deprivation which

could . . . have been expected to accompany it. The gap between the promises of the Coalition and its subsequent action is one of the most notorious in the long history of English social reform. Yet this failure, far from arousing a strong and cumulative resentment among those for whom a 'really new world' was to be built, never led to the degree of militant egalitarianism which such failure might be thought bound to evoke. . . .

The Depression reduced rather than heightened the magnitude and intensity of relative deprivation because few of its victims felt it to be obviously avoidable. . . . many of the victims of the Depression, or even the majority, seem to have thought of themselves as victims of misfortune rather than injustice. If redress of hardship is seen to be feasible, then the greater the hardship the greater the sense of relative deprivation. But the less feasible redress appears to be, the less relative deprivation is felt and the more the frame of reference is restricted to such few advantages as might still be obtained.[11]

Mass unemployment, in fact, was seen as an act of God, not of man; as such, it blunted the edge of social discontent instead of sharpening it. Hence, it ceases to be surprising that the labour movement should have failed to spot the significance of Keynes's teaching: if you believe that unemployment is an act of God it is impious to listen to those who claim to know the cure for it.

But if Runciman was right, that is only the beginning of the story. The rise of the Labour Party in the 1920s acquires a very different significance from that usually assigned to it by labour historians. Instead of being a function of the growing maturity and self-confidence of a working class anxious to transform the social order, it becomes a movement of self-defence aimed at preserving existing standards. It is true that, on some occasions at least, the 'conservatism' of the working class was bitterly opposed to that of the middle and upper classes. However limited their ambitions and restricted their reference groups, working-class people were prepared to fight hard for what they believed to be their rights. The general strike, in which the entire trade union movement downed tools out of solidarity with the miners, was, by any standards, a magnificent display of self-discipline and collective self-sacrifice. But the point about the general strike, as about the other great strikes of the 1920s, is that it was seen by those who took part in it as a legitimate act of self-defence, not as a conscious and deliberate assault on the citadels of power.

Similar conclusions are suggested by the well-known study of working-class conservatism by R. T. McKenzie and Allan Silver, entitled *Angels in Marble*.[12] The Conservative Party could not have stayed in power for most of the last eight-five years without the support of a substantial part of the working class, and Professors McKenzie and Silver did a major service to political sociology by examining the attitudes and motives of the working-class Conservative voter in depth. But, although they concentrated most of their attention on the working-class Conservatives, they also had a great deal to say about working-class Labour voters; and their picture of these is, in many ways, more relevant to the theme of Labour's economic conservatism.

What they showed, above all, is that most working-class Labour voters had, at bottom, the same picture of the society around them, and of the proper place of the working class in that society, as did most working-class Conservatives. The two groups differed, not in their values, but in their assessment of the practical capacities of their respective parties, and of the nature of the obstacles which make it difficult to translate the values they share into practice. The ideology, in other words, was the same; only the application was different. As McKenzie and Silver put it:

A basic image that emerges pervasively in responses of both Conservative and Labour working-class voters is that of a society based on a balance of interests. Conservative voters . . . often see the Conservative Party as necessary to hold the balance between competing interests, to regulate conflict, to rebuke greed (whether of capital or labour), and to apportion to all groups in society – including the working-class – their just share of the national product. . . . Many Labour voters, who do not share this beneficient view of the Conservative Party, nonetheless hold a fundamentally similar view of British society. For these people, the Labour Party and the trade unions are defence organisations required to ensure that the working class obtain their 'fair share'. Only a very few see these organisations as means whereby to transform or radically alter present social and economic arrangements. . . .

Both groups see the party they support not as a means to advancing vigorously the competitive claims of the working class but rather as required to prevent an inappropriate division of social goods. Among working-class Conservatives, the belief is widespread that the working class is itself a source of excessive and greedy demands which threaten the delicate balance required. . . . Among working-class Labour voters, many believe that the elite is selfishly prone to press its own interests or to overlook the just demands of the working class; thus, to redress these tendencies, they turn to those who press their claims. . . .

In both cases, this perspective is profoundly in accord with the Conservative view of the balanced, pacific and consensual society – in which no group obtains 'too much', in which the goal of maximising one's own share of social services, goods and resources in a freely competitive struggle is not overly disruptive.[13]

All this has an important bearing on the problems discussed above. McKenzie and Silver were, of course, discussing the working-class voters of the 1950s and 1960s. But their findings fit so well with Runciman's that we can probably assume that working-class voters in the 1920s and 1930s had similar values. This does not mean that the labour movement was wholly 'defensive'. There was a substantial 'aggressive' element in its official ideology and its official ideology – as we have seen – influenced its conduct. Even the most cautious sections of the party wished, in principle, to transform social relationships, to eliminate the profit motive and to establish the common ownership of the means of production. The left wing of the party differed from the leadership, not about the goals to be pursued, but about the speed of the pursuit. Unlike Harold Wilson or Hugh Gaitskell, MacDonald and Snowden were socialists in the same sense that Maxton or Lansbury were. To use the terminology of a later period, they were as 'fundamentalist' as their critics. Although it does not follow that Labour voters shared the ideology of their leaders, there is at least a *prima facie* case for assuming that some of them must have done so, and that one reason for the dramatic increase in the Labour vote after the First World War was that that ideology appealed to an increasing number of working-class people. The question, however, is why it appealed and in what way it appealed; and the picture that emerges from both Runciman on the one hand, and McKenzie and Silver on the other, suggests an extremely complex answer. What working-class Labour voters wanted was a conservative society in socialist clothing. The reason they were prepared to wear socialist clothing was that they saw socialism as the means through which an essentially conservative society might come into being. To put it more simply, they wanted everything to be different, in order that it could stay the same.

More light is needed. How far did the increase in the Labour vote after 1918 coincide with the decline of traditional industries and the collapse of old standards? To what extent did Labour candidates at the grass roots actually appeal to the 'defensive' psychology discussed here, and to what extent to a more 'aggressive' one? How far did their appeals vary from one part of the country to another, and how far can such variations be correlated with variations in the industrial structure and the rate of technological change? These are only some of the most obvious questions, and it would not be difficult to think of others. But these are details. In place of heroic proletarian statuary, Runciman, McKenzie and Silver presented us with recognisable men and women, trying to make the best of a hostile environment, sceptical of the grandiose visions held out in the perorations of their spokesmen, but prepared to fight with stubborn courage for their rights. Their stubbornness and scepticism were the stars by which their leaders had to steer. Perhaps the most surprising thing, in the circumstances, is not how little the leaders achieved, but how much.

Ernest Bevin and the Apotheosis of Labourism

On the surface, at any rate, few contrasts in twentieth-century British history are more striking than that between the confusion and vacillation of the minority Labour Government of 1929 and the confident reformism of its majority successor of 1945. No one deserves more of the credit than Ernest Bevin. More than any other leading figure in the British labour movement, he possessed the quality of creativity in action – of practical imagination in the use of power – which distinguishes the great men of politics from the nearly great. It was that which made him the architect of the Transport and General Workers' Union after the First World War. In government, the same quality enabled him to stretch the potentialities of Labourism further than anyone else has ever done; and in doing so to achieve a kind of apotheosis for it. 'Imagination' and 'create' were the key words of his career, whether as rebellious dockyard organiser, as union boss, as restlessly inventive Minister of Labour or as one of the most dominant Foreign Secretaries of modern times. As his biographer, Alan Bullock, has put it:

'I like to create, brother,' Bevin had told his union delegates, and now at last he had the chance to give expression to the creative side of his nature. It was not a literary or visionary but a practical imagination, best seen in the concern which he showed, even in the middle of a war, for welfare and rehabilitation and his insistence on humanising administration and the exercise of compulsory powers. It was fed, not from books but from talking to people and from reflection on his own experience. He relied on his own memory to store away all sorts of information, ideas and experiences which he had picked up, and would then produce them, often years later and often in unexpected combination.[1]

Bullock's life is a mighty edifice, heroic in scale and depth. The first volume, on Bevin the trade union leader, ran to 654 pages, and the second, on Bevin the wartime Minister of Labour, to 395. The third contained 854 pages of text, covering a little less than six years. Together, the three volumes paint an extraordinarily rich and variegated picture of personal and political growth – the growth of a man, interacting with the growth of a movement. Separately, each volume also recounts in absorbing and compelling detail a crucial chapter in twentieth-century British history.

Thus, the first volume was both the story of the illegitimate, poverty-stricken West Country boy who fought his way to the leadership of Britain's strongest trade union, and the best account we have of the slow, painful, bitterly contested evolution of the trade union movement as a whole into an estate of the realm. The second interwove the story of Bevin's fertile and commanding tenure of the Ministry of Labour with the story of the British war economy, which Bevin did more than any other single person to shape. The third was an affectionate, rounded, occasionally touching picture of Bevin at the apex of his career: breaking the ice at a stiff diplomatic dinner with a rendering of 'Cockles and Mussels'; savaging an absent Winston Churchill during the debate on the repeal of the 1927 Trades Disputes Act (and hammering the dispatch box so hard that his spectacles flew off); fuelling himself with streams of brandy, whisky and champagne and ignoring the protests of 'the old ticker'; reminding his private secretary to be sure to tip the hotel page-boy because 'I was once a page-boy myself'; and ruminating his way to the heart of a problem, like (as one of his staff put it) 'an elephant twitching and pawing the ground during the night'. It is also a masterly study of British foreign policy under the last British Foreign Secretary who really mattered in world affairs and – through that – of the astonishing series of improvisations which created the international order in which we still live today.

The whole trilogy is marvellous history – meticulous, authoritative and imbued with a robust horse-sense reminiscent of Bevin's own. Like all historians, Bullock had to select and, in selecting, to give order and shape to a disordered, shapeless reality. But he had a sense of reality that many historians lack. He knew that order is retrospective and therefore dangerous; that events do not come in neat, easily opened packages, but in great, messy blobs that spill over into each other. He captured the muddle and clutter in which policy is made: the fog of confusion and uncertainty which envelops the policy-makers; the fluctuating mixture of imperfect knowledge, dubious guesswork and inspired intuition on which they have to rely; the laborious, haphazard processes through which they try to translate their policies into action. As a result, we see the episodes he described through the eyes of those who took part in them; and we see the participants not, as so often happens, as marionettes dancing on the historian's string, but as creatures of flesh and blood, groping in the dark and hoping for the best.

More surprisingly, perhaps, it is also marvellous biography. Bevin left no diary, no intimate letters, no tremulous old ladies with memories of distant love affairs, no echoes of long-buried scandals, indeed no evidence of any kind about anything that could be called a private life. Bullock turned this handicap into an asset. Through it, he escaped the malign shadows of Freud and Lytton Strachey. He spared us the keyhole gossip and amateur psychologising that trivialise so many biographies, and proceeded on the refreshing basis that men of action realise themselves in action. Lacking evidence about the private Bevin – who would almost certainly have turned out to be a figure of monumental insignificance if such evidence had been found – he concentrated on the public Bevin, who really mattered. The result is a wonderfully fresh and authentic picture of one of the most creative men of his time, engaged in the business of creation – pushing, bullying, cajoling, dominating, persuading, horse-trading through the endless, dreary committees and occasional angry meetings which were his raw material.

The picture is built up, like a mosaic, from masses of detail; and no brief summary can possibly do justice to it. All the same, one or two themes emerge, each of enduring significance. The first is the theme of interdependence, of partnership, in the deepest sense of power-sharing. On one level, it must be admitted, that description is so paradoxical as to be almost perverse. Whatever else he may have been, Bevin was not, in his own career, a power-sharer. On the contrary, he was a power-hogger, ruthlessly and sometimes brutally expanding the frontiers of whatever empire he happened to rule, until he came up against another empire which was too strong for him to fight. The Transport and General Workers' Union, which is his most enduring monument, was not a planned structure, designed to achieve a defined purpose. It was an octopoid growth, reaching out wherever there were members to be won, a kind of conglomerate of the working-class movement, with no organising principle save the will and appetite of its founder. The wartime Ministry of Labour never quite became the TGWU of Whitehall, but one cannot help suspecting that, if the war had lasted another six years, it would have come close to doing so.

Nor, for that matter, does the theme of power-sharing square easily with Bevin's treatment of opponents. Bullock thought that his instinct when confronted with opposition was to 'flatten' it. Even that is a rather coy way of putting it. The truth is that Bevin loathed and detested opposition, and did his best, not merely to flatten, but to expunge it. On such occasions, the ruminating elephant remembered by his staff became a wild, roaring, warrior elephant, mercilessly trampling down anything and anybody standing in its way. Indeed, if there is a criticism to be made of Bullock, it is that he did not paint this side of Bevin in quite the gory colours it deserves. We get, so to speak, the mahout's-eye view, the view from the top of the elephant's head. We do not get the view from under its feet – the view of a George Lansbury, for example, brutally savaged for his pacifism, or of a Dick Crossman, accused of stabbing his Government in the back because he had the temerity to speak for himself over foreign affairs.

But although Bevin loved power, amassed power and hoarded power, he knew, on a much deeper level, that in the complex, interdependent society in which he lived, and which his own actions were making ever more complex and more interdependent, power-sharing was the price of survival. Like the contemporary business tycoons who were building up the amalgamations with which he negotiated, he realised instinctively that the old, nineteenth-century world of perfect competition had vanished; and that the great combinations of capital and labour which had destroyed it would have to share power with each other and the state, or drag society down in a Hobbesian war of all against all. Like all really good negotiators, moreover, he also realised instinctively that the point of negotiation is not to defeat the other side, but to find a common interest with it, so that the whole notion of victory and defeat will be transcended.

As a raw, young trade-union organiser in pre-1914 Bristol, one of his first actions, after organising the carters, was to organise their employers, so that he could persuade them to set up an Arbitration Board to regulate future disputes. That was the *leitmotiv* of his career, not only as trade-union leader, but as Minister of Labour and Foreign Secretary as well. *Organise, negotiate, compromise.* If possible, create a structure which will make it easier to negotiate and compromise in future. If necessary, even create the structure which you will face across the negotiating table. That was the Bristol story in a nutshell. It was also the story of the 'Triple Alliance' of miners, railwaymen and transport workers in the early 1920s, of the Mond-Turner talks between the TUC and the employers which followed the general strike, of the OEEC two years after the war, and of the North Atlantic Treaty two years after that. Interdependence and power-sharing within a society, in short, complemented by interdependence and power-sharing between societies.

This theme runs through the whole of Bevin's career, but with markedly different variations. At first the emphasis was less on sharing power than on building it up: less on the diplomacy of interdependence than on a hard, and sometimes brutal, struggle against dependence. To some extent, that was inevitable. You cannot share power if you do not have it: before organised labour could become a partner in the quasi-corporatist triangle of state, employers and unions, it had to develop the muscle to compel the other putative partners to take it seriously. But I suspect that there was more to it than that. Bevin, the deft and conciliatory Labour statesman, emerged out of the chrysalis of Bevin, the truculent and class-conscious union militant, only after the defeat of the general strike. Before 1926, he had kept his eggs in two baskets – class co-operation, but also class war. Then came the humiliating nine days when the brave talk of an industrial alternative to politics was put to the test and failed: when the union leaders, having looked into the revolutionary abyss which their own actions had opened up, discovered that they would rather surrender than jump. The class-war basket collapsed; and only co-operation remained.

One cannot help suspecting that, for Bevin, co-operation – or, at any rate, the unequal co-operation which was all that was available to him – was a second-best. 'We are imbued with the idea', he told his union conference in 1927, 'that we are the last great class to march onward, to rise to power and equity.' Power and equity for the working class: that was Bevin's aim in a nutshell. If he could have achieved it through class war, he would have done so. Since he had to settle for corporatist co-operation, he made the best of it. But he did not settle eagerly or easily.

Once embarked on the corporatist second-best, however, he became a past-master of its arts. From the mid-1920s onwards, he played a central part in the slow, often grudging and only half-acknowledged evolution of the triangle of power around which

Britain's political economy revolved from the 1930s to the 1970s. But, in the end, it was also a rather sad part. As yet, the triangle was lop-sided. Though organised labour belonged to it, it was still very much a junior partner. In grasp and flair, Bevin towered above most of the employers and civil servants with whom he dealt, but he had too little leverage to make his insights bite. As a member of the famous Macmillan Committee on finance and industry, Bevin was quicker than anyone else to see what his fellow member, Keynes, was driving at: in some respects, indeed, he ventured further along the Keynesian path than Keynes was willing to go himself. But, although this was a remarkable achievement, it was also a negative one. When Labour's moment of truth came in 1931, Bevin played a crucial part in stiffening the TUC's resistance to further deflation, and thereby in making it impossible for MacDonald and Snowden to carry their economies through the Labour Cabinet. His reward was the fall of the Labour Government; the formation of the National Government; and the most crippling electoral defeat in Labour's history. With all his creativity and drive, and his massive influence on the labour movement, Bevin could play only a marginal part in the decisions that shaped the 1930s; and the approach of war found him with his powers under-used and his promise unfulfilled.

His entry into Churchill's War Cabinet in 1940 changed all that. At last power and equity were within reach; and he strained every nerve to attain them. He had nothing to do with grand strategy, but as Minister of Labour he had everything to do with raising the armies without which no grand strategy would have been possible, and with mobilising the labour force which kept those armies supplied. Once the period of phoney war was over, manpower was the country's scarcest resource; and control of manpower inevitably became the key tool of economic management. Whoever determined the allocation of manpower would dominate the commanding heights of the war economy. As a result, Bevin's Ministry of Labour took over the Treasury's traditional role as the most important economic department. From that vantage point, he did as much as any single person to win the war. In doing so, he also left an indelible imprint on the post-war settlement. Thanks to wartime full employment, the balance of economic power had, in any case, shifted massively in labour's favour. But the shift might have been temporary. Bevin's achievement was to make sure that it would last – not, as things have turned out, for ever, but at any rate for more than thirty years.

On the purely political side of a minister's life, Bullock's touch was a little unsure. One suspects that his attitude to the House of Commons, with its mysterious changes of mood and its unpredictable swings between frivolity and grandeur, was as suspicious as Bevin's own. But he was a superb guide through the labyrinth of interdepartmental committees, consultations with officials, minutes and agenda which form the framework of ministerial action. Administrative history, it is true, is not usually thought of as a subject to stiffen the sinews or summon up the blood. During the Second World War, however, it was a different matter. Ministers and civil servants were grappling with problems which had never been faced before; and they were doing so in a crisis situation in which they knew that failure could mean not merely the defeat, but the total destruction of their country. Squabbles over the conscription of women, the organisation of the coal mines and even the wages of the catering industry were, at east potentially, matters of life and death; and the struggle between the Ministry of Labour and the Ministry of Aircraft Production over the allocation of skilled manpower seemed to matter as much as the battles fought in North Africa and Greece.

This particular struggle was given extra bitterness by the fact that Bevin's opponent happened to be Lord Beaverbrook. The two men were opposed by temperament and philosophy as well as by departmental interest. As Bevin himself put it, Churchill's attitude to Beaverbrook was that of a man who has married a whore. 'He knows she's a whore, but he loves her just the same.' In fact, there was a strong element of the courtesan in Beaverbrook, which came out in his fascination with personalities, his frivolity about issues, and his lack of staying power in the face of determined opposition. He was no match for Bevin: and the struggle between them ended with Bevin in undisputed control of the field.

Behind these rivalries lay issues of more general importance, some of which continued to preoccupy decision-makers for as long as the post-war settlement endured. True, the problems of economic management were both simpler and more acute during the war than they later became. Bevin and his colleagues in the War Cabinet could concentrate on one overriding goal: they did not have to worry about the balance of payments or the rate of private investment. But the crucial problem of any managed economy is, after all, how to reconcile management with freedom: how to ensure that the managers do not trample on those in whose name they act, while preventing their being pushed aside by organised minorities who wish to trample on the interests of the majority.

During the war this problem presented itself most insistently in the arguments over manpower policy. Given that manpower was the nation's scarcest resource, and given that manpower could not be allocated by the free market without an intolerable degree of inflation, what other method of manpower allocation should be used instead? Should there be a system of industrial conscription, or was there some halfway house between the traditional free market for labour on the one hand and outright compulsion on the other?

This was the central issue which faced Bevin on his arrival at the Ministry of Labour in 1940, and it continued to face him in one form or another until his departure in 1945. Bevin's answer to it was to seek a compromise – but out of conviction, not out of weakness. As Bullock put it:

> He started with the question: how could a country with the democratic institutions of Britain hope to match the degree of organisation in Germany? Not, Bevin answered himself, by discarding its own traditions and trying to copy the totalitarian methods it was fighting against: this was the mistake of those who wanted to treat the whole nation in wartime as if it were an army and organise it on military lines. The right way was to stick to the basic principle of democracy, government by consent, and rely on the willingness of the people in an emergency to make greater sacrifices than they could be dragooned into making by compulsion.[2]

In the new era of organised, quasi-corporatist interdependence, as in the old era of atomistic, free-market capitalism, voluntarism was to be the hallmark of British industrial relations. Not surprisingly: voluntarism in industrial relations has always been the ark of the covenant of British Labourism. But there was an irony here, which Bevin would not have appreciated. In the short term, his faith in the voluntary principle was justified. His version of voluntarism did not rule out resort to law in all circumstances. It implied that the law should be called in only as a last resort, as the essential underpinning of a voluntary system. Thus, he acquired powers which he did his best not to use; and when he used them in the end, he did so sparingly. As a result, he was able to use them, in Bullock's words, 'upon a basis of consent': in effect, to get the best of both worlds.

But it was one thing to operate a voluntaristic system in the extra-ordinary conditions of total war, when all concerned could see that victory depended on co-operation, or, for that matter, in the immediate aftermath of war, when wartime solidarity still lingered. It was another to do so in a mass-consumption peacetime society, driven increasingly by individual self-interest. Whether Bevin could have kept his own system going in these conditions can never be known. What is clear is that the generation which followed him could not. It is clear too that its breakdown in the 1970s was the chief cause of the collapse of the post-war settlement, and of the repeated catastrophes which Labourism has suffered ever since. A law-based system would have been harder to install, but it might have proved more enduring.

Much the same applies to his response to international interdependence. In many ways, Bevin the Foreign Secretary had more in common with Bevin the trade union leader than with Bevin the Minister of Labour. After 1945 as before 1940, his hand was weaker than his masterful playing suggested. He had to persuade, cajole, above all bluff: he could very rarely command. Indeed, his position after 1945 was, in some ways, weaker than before 1940. Then, his union had been on a rising curve: now, his country was on a falling one. Given all that, his achievements were remarkable. His imprint lay as heavily on the post-war system of international relations as on post-war Britain's system of industrial relations. But here too there was a limit. What he sought – and helped to build – was a system of voluntaristic collective security, reminiscent of his system of voluntaristic corporatism: of sovereign states freely co-operating in their own defence like employers and union leaders freely co-operating to maximise output. When Jean Monnet and Robert Schuman gave him the opportunity to transcend sovereignty in their Coal and Steel Community, he shied away.

Bullock defends him, partly on the ground that the time was not yet ripe for Britain to join a European Community of the kind Monnet and Schuman wanted, and partly on the ground that failure to join in in the early 1950s did not preclude entry in the mid-1950s, when the time *was* ripe. On one level, the argument is valid. As Monnet almost certainly realised, no conceivable British Government would have accepted Schuman's invitation in 1950. On another level, arguments about timing are beside the point. There is nothing in Bullock's account to suggest that Bevin would have reacted differently in the mid-1950s from the way he reacted in the early 1950s.

80

The real point is that Bevin, like most of us, was a product of the tradition into which he had grown up. No one in his generation did more to adapt his inheritance to changing conditions, but even he could not escape its limitations. If he had, he might not have achieved what he did.

This is where the second theme – the theme of solidarity or group loyalty – interacts with the first. Bevin's ruthless ways with opponents sprang, no doubt, from the depths of his character. But they also reflected his experiences as an organiser and negotiator, and were implicit in the ethic which made those experiences possible. Successful negotiation demands discipline; and the best kind of discipline is self-discipline. The union members must come out when the negotiator judges that it is time for a strike. They must go back when he decides that he has made the best deal he can get. They cannot be forced, but they can be led; and leadership depends on loyalty. There is no room for the free-wheeling conscience, the sacred heart of Protestant individualism and all the varieties of liberalism that derive from Protestant individualism. 'The plural of conscience', Arthur Henderson once said, 'is conspiracy.' Bevin did not phrase the doctrine as epigrammatically, but he practised it even more strenuously. The union was bigger than the member, the movement than the individual. Those who forgot that – the Mosleys, the Ramsay MacDonalds, the Stafford Crippses, the Kingsley Martins, the Richard Crossmans – were untrustworthy at best and treacherous at worst.

It was a hard, rough, very masculine ethic, not unlike the public-school ethic of the Foreign Office officials with whom Bevin established what seems at first sight an extraordinary rapport. But there is no doubt that it was Bevin's ethic. It was, of course, a convenient ethic from his point of view. Since he controlled the biggest of the big battalions which determined what the majority decision would be, an ethic extolling loyalty to majority decisions had no terrors for him. I doubt, however, if that is the whole story, or even an important part of it. Bevin did not merely preach the ethic of group loyalty, he lived it; and he lived it because it was in his blood. For him it was the key, the only conceivable key, to the success of the movement, which was the only conceivable vehicle for the rise of his class.

In this, he was right. Group loyalty *was* the key, not perhaps to the rise of the working class, but certainly to the rise of the working-

81

class movement. As such, it was also the key to the emergence of the interdependent society, which the rise of the working-class movement helped to bring about. Yet there is a paradox here, of which Bevin and his contemporaries were not conscious. The ethic of group loyalty, which is fundamental to the interdependent, power-sharing society which they created, runs counter to – or is, at any rate, in acute tension with – the ethic of individual freedom and self-realisation, which is central to that same society's political values and perhaps also to its economic needs. In Bevin's day, the problems raised by that paradox seemed remote and academic, of no concern to practical men. They have loomed larger and larger since his death. How do you square group power with the right to dissent, the need for a consensus between capital and labour with the need for industrial flexibility, corporatist power-sharing with parliamentary government? These are the questions for the Bevins of the 1990s. The present sad state of the reforming tradition is eloquent testimony to the fact that no new Bevin has yet come forward to answer them.

7

Hugh Dalton:
The Progressive as Bounder

Hugh Dalton was a Member of Parliament for thirty-five years, a minister for twelve, a front-bencher for thirty and member of the Labour Party National Executive for twenty-five. In the 1930s, he played a central part (after Bevin, *the* central part) in dragging the Labour Party out of the semi-pacifist isolationism of the 1920s into a grudging acceptance of rearmament and, when necessary, the use of force. As President of the Board of Trade in the wartime coalition, he laid the foundations of the post-war Labour Government's regional policies. As chairman of the policy sub-committee of the National Executive, he did more than anyone else to shape the economic strategy on which the Labour Party fought the 1945 election. He wrote twelve books, one of which ran to five editions over thirty years, and edited two others. He was an assiduous, not to say relentless patron of bright and, if possible, handsome young men, counting among his protégés Hugh Gaitskell, the most impressive leader the Labour Party has ever had, and Tony Crosland, one of its two or three most important theorists.

Yet, in talent and personality, Dalton never quite belonged to the front rank of politics. To be sure, he was a robust and formidable party warhorse – a kind of William Harcourt or Roy Hattersley, say – with enormous energy, considerable administrative drive and a powerful debating style. But he captured no imaginations, lifted no horizons and inspired no disciples. He left worthy memorials – the National Parks, for instance, and the spread of light industry to the depressed North – but he did not change the political or intellectual landscape.

As Keynes implied when he nicknamed him 'Daddy', there was something faintly ludicrous about his gnawing hunger for advancement, his insatiable appetite for intrigue, and his odd mixture of self-importance and self-doubt. He was a fusser, a buttonholer, a clasper of shoulders, a pacer of lobbies, at least metaphorically a listener at keyholes, endlessly obsessed by the narcissistic gossip and jockeying for position of the Westminster stock-exchange of reputations. As a minister he was also, and less forgivably, an appalling – in James Meade's phrase, a 'paranoid' – bully, shouting at civil servants who could not answer back, insulting senior officials in the presence of their juniors, and displaying an astonishing incapacity to understand the ethic of public service or the requirements of team management.

Sometimes, he got his come-uppance. The best of the rich store of anecdotes collected by his biographer, Ben Pimlott, concerns Dalton's stormy relationship with Sir Frederick Leith-Ross, his Director General when he was Minister of Economic Warfare.

> Dalton, it was alleged, had issued a peremptory order for Leith-Ross to attend on him instantly. When a Private Secretary explained that Sir Frederick was not available, the Minister merely repeated the command. Tracking down the Director General to the lavatory, the embarrassed Secretary passed a note under the door. 'Tell him', came the reply, 'that I can only deal with one shit at a time.'[1]

Other anecdotes show Dalton in a more endearing, though still rather ridiculous light. A favourite one, of which there were several versions, describes his technique for building support in the Parliamentary Labour Party. Roy Jenkins's version is probably the neatest: 'Once, as we were entering the Chamber, Hugh called cheerfully to a working-class member: "Hello, Fred!" Turning to me, he said: "You know, Roy, you'll never get on in politics until you learn to call that chap Fred." I pointed out gently that in fact the man's name was Bert.'[2]

As all this implies, he makes a fascinating psychological study. Beneath the bluster and showmanship, Dalton was an unusually tormented member of a species more than usually prone to torment. At first sight, he seemed the ruling-class renegade *par excellence*: Old Etonian; Kingsman; son of a canon of Windsor who had once been tutor to the future George V. But he was not quite as ruling class as he looked and sounded. He belonged to the clerisy, not to the baronage: to the exam-passing classes, rather than to the order-giving ones. To use Harold Macmillan's classification, he was a 'gownsman', not a 'swordsman'. Unfortunately, he did not pass his exams well enough to be a really confident gownsman. He was an

Oppidan at Eton, not a Colleger; a closed exhibitioner at King's, not a scholar. Though he got a good Second, it was, after all, a Second. He never made 'Pop', and was not elected to the Apostles. In the 'homoerotic' culture of pre-1914 Cambridge, he was again an also-ran. He was obviously in love with Rupert Brooke. As obviously, Rupert Brooke soon found him a tiresome bore. His marriage seems to have been a disaster, and his emotional life a desert. His daughter – bundled off to a residential home at the age of four and shamefully neglected by both parents – died in early childhood.

The strong implication is that, for Dalton, socialism was a kind of revenge. Like the seventeenth-century puritans who hated the bear-baiters more than they loved the bears, he hated the ruling class more than he loved the ruled. In his case, the tired Tory jibe that egalitarianism is about levelling down rather than about levelling up contained a distinct element of truth. As Pimlott put it:

> De Freitas saw him as the 'first of the upper-class renegades', who liked nothing better than the shocked faces of those who kept the old social code. He took pleasure in being a bounder and a cad, the kind of chap you itched to duck in the school pond or blackball from the club. Once, dining at the House, he interrupted his own monologue to boom in the direction of a Tory MP: 'What's that suburbanite looking at me for!' The MP looked unhappy. 'Come on, let's show him how we in the Labour Party behave!' Dalton started to shovel peas into his mouth with a knife.[3]

All this adds to the gaiety of nations, but it hardly bears the weight of a major historical study. Dalton the man, even Dalton the Opposition politician and wartime minister, would deserve, at most, an extended essay. The justification for a 700-page biography lies in Dalton's position as a member of the 'Big Five' – the inner circle of key ministers who dominated the Attlee Government in its initially exuberant but subsequently hagridden first two years. To be sure, he was personally, and in some ways politically, the fifth of the five. Bevin and Cripps, the first two, were men of genius – ruthlessly egocentric, no doubt, and sometimes catastrophically wrong, but towering above their colleagues in force and will. Dalton was not remotely in their class. Attlee and Morrison, the second two, were not in their class either. Both, however, outgunned Dalton – not in intellectual ability, but in resilience, in political nous and, on a deeper level, in inner toughness and self-confidence.

As Chancellor of the Exchequer from 1945 to 1947, however, Dalton's ministerial position was pivotal – more so, in some ways, than he seemed to realise himself. During the war, at any rate in its later stages, the Treasury did not count for much. So long as the Americans footed the bill for Britain's over-extended war machine, the constraint that mattered was manpower, not money. Bevin's Ministry of Labour was then the key economic department, not the Treasury. Peace changed all that. For the 1945 Labour Government, the central, overriding, by the end almost all-encompassing issue was how to squeeze a quart out of a pint pot – how to marry the humane and generous aspirations of the party of the bottom dog with the cold realities of inadequate resources, excessive commitments and the pressures of an economic system run by top dogs. The key figure in squaring that circle was bound to be the Chancellor of the Exchequer; and the abiding significance of Dalton's political career lies in the way he responded to its challenge.

Judged by results – and results are as good a test for Cabinet ministers as they are for the rest of us – he did not respond very skilfully. The circle was not squared. Aspirations and resources did not marry. The convertibility clauses of the American loan agreement, accepted with so many heart-searchings in 1945, had to be suspended in August 1947, only a month after they had come into force. The continuing drain of gold and dollars was halted only by a deflationary autumn budget two and a half months later. The 1945 Government, in short, followed essentially the same cycle – though on a higher level, so to speak – as those followed by its successors of 1964 and 1974. An ebullient upswing, when new hope seemed momentarily to triumph over old experience, was suddenly cut short by a crisis, when the constraints of the external world drew in. Then came a long downswing of austerity, wage restraint and public expenditure cuts, accompanied by pangs of guilt and cries of betrayal. Dalton presided over the key economic department during the upswing, and took no action to avert the crisis before it broke. It may or may not have been his fault. The fact remains that, after two years in the Treasury, the basic assumptions underlying his management of the economy were in ruins. His unnecessary resignation after a trivial breach of budget secrecy merely set the seal on what was clearly an agonising moral and psychological defeat.

Pimlott entered a vigorous plea for the defence, which sometimes read like 'not guilty', but which really amounted to 'guilty with extenuating circumstances'. Unfortunately, the one weakness in an otherwise splendid book was that his argument in this crucial section was a bit muddled, and I may therefore have misunderstood it. The essence seems to be that the 1947 crisis could have been avoided only by greater austerity at an earlier stage, and that greater austerity at an earlier stage would have imperilled the Government's all-important social policies. 'Arguably,' Pimlott wrote, ' "self-denial" on a scale necessary to avert a crisis would have meant postponing Labour's social programme *sine die*.' And he added, in a later passage: 'A social revolution was undertaken between 1945 and 1947. Such a revolution required, not only courage and determination, but an element of blind faith.' Dalton, he implied, had more blind faith than the rest of the inner circle. But for this, but for his refusal to sacrifice Labour's welfare objectives to the requirements of the external balance, the achievements for which the 1945 Government has gone down in history might never have happened.

It is a clever defence, but it is also a specious one. Blind faith is not the ally of radicalism. It is its most insidious and destructive enemy. Radicalism, radicalism in government at any rate, is about choice. Again and again in the history of the British left, blind faith has provided excuses for postponing or avoiding choice. The incoming 1964 Government, faced with a choice between devaluation and deflation, preferred faith, and ended by having to devalue as well as deflate. The 1974 Government, faced with a choice between unemployment and an incomes policy, put its faith in a loose, unenforced social contract, and ended with no social contract, no incomes policy and an unemployment rate twice what it had been when it came into power. The 1945 Government was incomparably more successful than these, of course, but if it had been a little less blind in its first two years, it might have been more successful still. It was, after all, the 1947 crisis which revived the credibility and restored the morale of the Conservative Opposition, and began the long process of Labour self-questioning and self-doubt which ended in the Bevanite split in 1951. If it had been avoided, even at the cost of slower progress in the first two years, the left might have kept the political initiative, and the whole history of post-war Britain might have been different.

Half-hidden by the doctrine of blind faith, however, a much better defence can be detected between the lines. The social services were not the sole – perhaps not even the chief – contributors to the quart which Attlee and his colleagues were trying to squeeze out of their pint pot. Another – and, with hindsight, a much less respectable contributor – was the Government's unflinching determination to maintain Britain's role as a world power. As Pimlott points out, the real function of the American loan was to buy time. The Government undoubtedly spent part of the time it bought on the social revolution of 1945 to 1947. It spent another part on a doomed attempt to cling to a great-power status which had gone for ever. Its critics were right in thinking that it was piling excessive burdens on a shattered economy. They were wrong in thinking that the burdens were solely the fruit of soft-hearted socialist egalitarianism. Robust, old-fashioned patriotism and a high-minded sense of responsibility to the rest of mankind were at least as much to blame. Like the Wilson Government twenty years later (though, it must be admitted, with better excuses) the Attlee Government took it for granted, not only that Britain should remain a great power, but that she could. If the laws of arithmetic said otherwise, then the laws of arithmetic should be ignored. Here Dalton ranks with what must, from the vantage point of forty years later, be cast as the angels. Pimlott makes it clear that he fought for cuts in overseas commitments and military expenditure, and endorses Dalton's own judgement that it was the 'mulish resistance' of the Foreign Office and the defence departments which stopped him from having his way. He also concedes, however, that Dalton's inability to make his will prevail on what was, after all, the central issue facing the Government and party was the symptom of a fatal political weakness. High politics is a rough game; there are no prizes for honourable defeat. Dalton's defeats were honourable enough. They were defeats all the same.

In the end, moreover, defeat on military expenditure and blindness towards the economic implications of the welfare state went together. In retrospect, the really striking feature of the Attlee Government is that – for all the talk of sacrifice, austerity, the export drive and the dollar gap – no one grasped the full significance of the wartime revolution in the balance of world economic power. No one saw that, materially though hardly morally, Britain belonged with the vanquished, not with the victors: that she had escaped defeat and occupation, not through her own merits, still less through her own strength, but through her good fortune in being allied to the two superpowers which were now busily dividing the world between them: and that her industrial base was as weak as, in some important respects weaker than, that of devastated Central Europe. By the same token, no one realised that the social revolution she needed was not the benign and kindly revolution of consumption foreshadowed in a decade and a half of Fabian summer schools, but a much harsher, almost Jacobin revolution of production, designed to smash the structures and root out the habits which had already produced more than half a century of relative economic decline. Excessive welfare commitments at home and excessive military commitments abroad were different sides of the same coin. Both were symptoms of, and at the same time contributors to, the inability or unwillingness of a proud old country to see how far it had come down in the world. As Chancellor of the Exchequer, Dalton was in a better position to see this than any other minister. He failed to do so. In that, he was a child of his time – no less, but also no more.

8

Sir Stafford Cripps:
The Progressive as Moralist

'Annus Horrendus'. For the Labour Government as whole, as well as for the chancellor of the Exchequer as an individual, Hugh Dalton's description of the year 1947 could hardly be bettered. It began with a fuel crisis, which momentarily crippled the industrial recovery programme and put nearly two million people out of work. Four months after the fuel crisis had ended, the country staggered into the so-called convertibility crisis, in which 700 million precious dollars were lost in a month. The crises were painful enough, and the logic behind them was more painful still. In 1945 Britain had emerged from the war as one of the 'Big Three', bankrupt but unbowed, and she had elected a government pledged to carry through a social revolution. By 1947 it was becoming clear that her status as a great power was no more than a polite fiction, that her loss of strength had created a power vacuum which others would fill, and that she faced a desperate struggle for solvency, in which the Government's social aims might have to be sacrificed. It was in 1947 that British troops left Greece, that India became independent, and that the Marshall Plan was launched. It was also in 1947 that Sir Stafford Cripps was appointed Chancellor of the Exchequer in Dalton's place.

His appointment was, of course, the result of an accident. No one could have foreseen Dalton's fall, for it was due to momentary indiscretion rather than to any difference of principle with his colleagues. On the afternoon of 12 November 1947, Dalton was on his way to the chamber of the House of Commons to deliver his fourth budget, when he stopped for a few minutes' conversation with the lobby correspondent of the *Star*. The two men discussed the speech which Dalton was about to make. Later that afternoon, the *Star* published an accurate forecast of some budget proposals, in an edition that reached the streets a short time before the proposals themselves were officially announced in the House. Next day, Dalton resigned; and that evening it was announced that Cripps was to succeed him.

There was, however, a kind of logic about the accident. Dalton's blunder came at an opportune time for the Government. The two great crises of 1947 had produced little in the way of scapegoats; and Dalton's indiscretion made him an ideal candidate for the role. Yet neither crisis can fairly be laid at his door. The fuel crisis of January and February was due in the main to acts of God. As for the summer crisis, its true authors were the convertibility clauses of the American loan agreement of 1945. In order to obtain a loan at all, the British Government had been made to promise that, a year after the agreement came into force, sterling would be made freely convertible for all current transactions. No one on the British side liked this commitment, but after six years of war, in which over £1,000 millions of assets had been sold and over £13,000 millions of external liabilities had been incurred, Britain was in no position to bargain. No matter that her losses had been incurred in the common cause, nor that her efforts had been proportionately far greater than those of the United States. Now that peace had come, the Americans were in no mood for sentiment. It was made plain to the British negotiators that no convertibility clause would mean no loan – and they had taken it for granted all along that no loan would mean national disaster.

President Truman ratified the loan agreement on 15 July 1946. On 15 July 1947, the convertibility clause came into effect. The result was what might have been expected. Already the British gold and dollar reserve had been ebbing away at an alarming rate, partly because of the effect of the fuel crisis on British exports and partly because of the rise of American wholesale prices. Convertibility turned the drain into a flood. During the second quarter of 1947, the average weekly drawing rate had been $75 millions. In July it was $115 millions. In the four weeks before 23 August it was $150 millions. On 6 August, the Government announced a programme of cuts and austerities. The miners were to work an extra half-hour a day; food imports from hard-currency areas were to be cut by £12 millions a month; the basic petrol ration was to be reduced by one-third. On 20 August, full convertibility was suspended, having lasted for little more than a single disastrous month. On 23 August, the meat ration was cut, public dinners were restricted, foreign travel was suspended, and the basic petrol ration was abolished. Dalton's emergency budget in November was designed to cut down internal spending still further.

Even before Dalton's fall, the growing sense of *malaise* in the country had been reflected in a minor political crisis and a major Government reshuffle. Towards the end of July, Cripps and Dalton (with the former very much in the van) had tried to persuade Bevin to depose Attlee and become Prime Minister himself. Their blandishments were rebuffed. The end result of a tortuous series of negotiations between leading members of the Cabinet, in which Attlee showed once again that he was a much wilier politician than he was sometimes given credit for being, was that Cripps became Minister of Economic Affairs, taking over the co-ordinating and planning functions previously discharged by Herbert Morrison. Cripps's appointment was popular, but it was not popular enough to prevent the Government from losing 652 seats in the municipal elections on 1 November, or to remove a widespread impression that tougher measures and stronger men were needed at the Treasury. As Charles Curran once remarked, the British people like their leaders to resemble either bishops or bookies. Dalton was a bookie. Cripps was pre-eminently a bishop; and as the economic climate grew colder a bishop was what was required. His appointment as Chancellor of the Exchequer was greeted with enthusiasm. Even Osbert Peake, speaking for the Opposition, congratulated the Government on having sent for the plumber who was needed.

In 1947, these sentiments seemed natural, almost conventional. Ten years earlier, coming from either front bench, they would have seemed proof of mental disorder. In January 1934 a meeting of the constitutional sub-committee of the Labour Party National Executive was held to consider the latest pronouncements of Sir Stafford Cripps. Afterwards, Hugh Dalton noted in his diary:

> Cripps seems quite unable to see the argument that he is damaging the party electorally. It is all 'misreporting', or picking sentences out of their context. He has become very vain and seems to think that only he and his cronies know what Socialism is or how it should be preached. His gaffes cover an immense range – Buckingham Palace – League of Nations – 'compelling' Unions to declare a General Strike – prolonging Parliament beyond five years, unless . . . 'seize land, finance and industry'

(without compensation?) – Emergency Powers Bill in one day, giving 'all necessary powers'. . . .

I make a violent – perhaps too violent – speech asking that this stream of oratorical ineptitudes should now cease . . . It is the *number* of these gaffes which is so appalling. Our candidates are being stabbed in the back and pushed onto the defensive. Tory HQ regard him as their greatest electoral asset. . . .

Attlee says I am like a pedagogue addressing a pupil. I wish the pupil were a bit brighter.[1]

By the end of the decade, the pupil had become even more obstreperous, and the pedagogue even more contemptuous of his ability. In January 1939, Cripps launched the campaign for a Popular Front which culminated in his expulsion from the Labour Party. Shortly before the denouement Dalton reflected:

This conduct is . . . utterly intolerable. The broadcasting of the opinion that we cannot win the next election will tend to spread a miasma of defeatism and discouragement all over the country, particularly in constituencies where the fight is difficult. . . .

To start this hopeless campaign just at this moment is to invite Chamberlain to take an election while the Labour Party is engaged in a bitter and weakening controversy. The thing is perfectly timed to create the maximum embarrassment and weakness in the Party. . . .

The man has the political judgement of a flea.[2]

Dalton was not alone. Cripps's aunt, Beatrice Webb, thought her nephew had 'sufficient personality – physical and mental – for leadership', but complained that he was 'oddly immature in intellect and unbalanced in judgement: a strange lack of discrimination and low standard of reasoning in picking up ideas . . . He does not *know* his own limitations: he is ignorant and reckless in his statements and proposals.'[3] Herbert Morrison, who had been largely instrumental in bringing him into the Labour Party, thought him 'invincible' in private discussions, but added: 'We would argue to a point where my case could no longer be argued, yet I knew in my bones that he was wrong and I was right – which subsequent events usually proved to be so.'[4] Even Attlee, who thought highly of Cripps's 'intellect, integrity and debating skill', suspected his practical judgements,[5] and complained of his propensity to 'seek martyrdom'.[6]

These comments date, of course, from a period when Cripps was in rebellion against the leadership of his own party. But Cripps the rebel had a long innings – longer, as a matter of fact, than Cripps the Chancellor; and Cripps the Chancellor is comprehensible only against the background of his stormy political past. The first fact to notice is that he came into politics late. He was born in 1889 of an old and wealthy family. His father and grandfather were both distinguished lawyers; and he himself was called to the Bar in 1913 after a scientific education. Until the late 1920s most of his energies went on his successful and lucrative legal practice. The remainder was spent, not on politics, but on the Anglican Church. It is true that his father, Lord Parmoor, was Lord President of the Council in the Labour Government of 1924. But although Cripps himself was attracted during the 1920s by the moderate socialism of Ramsay MacDonald and the Labour Party leadership, he delayed some time before taking the plunge into active politics. At thirty-nine he was not even a member of the Labour Party; at forty he was Solicitor-General in the second Labour Government. The election of 1931, in which he was one of the few Labour ex-ministers who held their seats, thrust him still further into a precocious prominence. From then on, he was one of the leading members of the Labour Party, and one of the idols of the rank and file.

From the point of view of the leadership, at any rate, its idolatory could hardly have been more damagingly focused. In the 1930s the divisions which had been endemic in the party from its foundation were particularly acute. MacDonald's alleged treachery in 1931 had created a bitter suspicion of leadership as such. What MacDonald had done, other leaders could do. Better, then, to have no leaders at all – or, if there must be leaders, at least subject them to searching and incessant scrutiny. It is doubtful whether Cripps was ever completely carried away by this reasoning, though he certainly profited from it in his conflicts with the party leadership. He undoubtedly did accept, however, another and equally embarrassing ideological legacy of the 1931 crisis. This was the widespread belief that the fall of the second Labour Government had been engineered by the 'capitalists'; that any future Labour Government would face equally nefarious 'capitalist' plots; and that in order to defeat them it would be necessary to by-pass, or at least to overhaul, the entire parliamentary and constitutional machine. The lesson of 1931, he insisted, was that 'the ruling classes will go to almost any length to defeat parliamentary action'. The first decision of a newly elected Labour

94

government must therefore be to arm itself with an Emergency Powers Act, giving itself semi-dictatorial powers. Sometimes he stressed the moderation of his proposals. 'Emergency Powers', he told the 1933 conference of the Labour Party, 'have no relation to dictatorship whatsoever,' they were needed only to scotch the machinations of 'financial strikers'. But that was an untypical note. More characteristic was the curious mixture of imprecision and menace of his notorious 'Buckingham Palace' speech, in which he warned that, as well as dealing with the City and the House of Lords, an incoming Labour government would have to 'overcome opposition from Buckingham Palace and other places as well'.[7]

His stand on foreign and defence policy was similarly imprecise. In the great debates on sanctions and rearmament which divided the labour movement in the mid-1930s, there were two logical positions: Lansbury's and Bevin's. According to Lansbury, war was wrong and therefore sanctions and rearmament must be wrong. According to Bevin, sanctions and rearmament were necessary as the only way to stop fascism before it was too late. Cripps hovered between these two arguments in a state of dialectical schizophrenia. He was not a pacifist; he did not underestimate the fascist threat; he was prepared in principle to resist fascism by force. But, although he wanted fascism to be resisted, he was not prepared to give the British Government the wherewithal to do so. Cripps objected to sanctions against Mussolini if the price were to strengthen Baldwin. 'There is no man in this Conference who more cordially detests Mussolini and all his acts than I do,' he told the Labour Party conference in 1935. 'If I could feel that British imperialism had turned over a new leaf . . . then my difficulties and doubts would largely disappear.' Unfortunately, this was not the case. The driving force behind the British Government, 'overpowering all humanitarian and liberal sentiment is, and must be, the urgent necessities of the capitalistic economic system itself'.[8]

Far more bitter than these battles over policy, however, were the battles over structure and organisation with which they were muddled up. Cripps's real sin, in the eyes of the party leadership, was not that he wished to change the party's policies. It was that he was prepared to work outside the party framework: that he so obviously disdained the rituals of party unity, and appealed, quite deliberately, to a wider constituency, beyond the party's boundaries. The sin had two manifestations – the united front campaign for an alliance between the Labour Party, the Communist Party and the recently

95

disaffiliated ILP; and the Popular Front campaign for an alliance covering the whole spectrum of anti-Government opinion. The first was intended to resist the imperialist designs of the National Government and the rearmament plans which those designs had entailed. To its supporters, the victory of socialism at home was an indispensable prelude to the defeat of fascism abroad. The second was intended to promote collective security abroad, at the price of postponing socialism at home. The analysis behind the first was rigidly Marxist: fascism was a form of imperialism and imperialism of capitalism; therefore only the workers could be trusted to resist fascism. The assumptions underlying the second, despite its obvious communist associations, were well within the tradition of British radicalism: men and women of goodwill, irrespective of class or party, were to unite in a cause transcending the divisions of everyday politics. Yet it was on the second, not on the first, that the breaking point came. In January 1939 the Labour Party executive rejected Cripps's memorandum on the Popular Front by seventeen votes to three. Cripps proceeded to circulate it to Labour MPs, constituency parties and affiliated bodies. The executive ordered him to withdraw the memorandum and reaffirm his loyalty to the party, on pain of expulsion. He refused, and was duly expelled. In May the party conference upheld his expulsion by a majority of more than 1,500,000. He was out of the party for almost six years.

Cripps's character can be understood only in the light of his activities in the 1930s. Yet the light they shed is singularly ambiguous. To his trade union colleagues on the Labour Party executive he was the quintessential intellectual; to the general public, he was the sea-green incorruptible of British Labour, at best a semi-revolutionary and at worst an undiluted one. It is clear that, except in the most superficial sense, the first of these descriptions is almost wholly misleading. Cripps had little of the intellectual's passion for ideas, and showed no interest in penetrating beneath the surface of an argument to the assumptions beneath. Three characteristics marked his conduct in the 1930s: a rigid absolutism of doctrine, a notable lack of intellectual subtlety and a lonely obstinacy which was, according to taste, either heroic or pig-headed. But these do not qualify him for the title of revolutionary. Revolutionaries are politicians too. Like all politicians, they have to have a grasp of political forces: an ability to smell the way the wind is blowing, to sense shifts in public opinion, and to gauge the weight of the different groups with which

96

they have to deal. Cripps was not so much deficient in these qualities as contemptuous of them.

Interpreted flexibly, Marxism might have furnished a more accurate guide to European politics in the 1930s than that provided by any other political creed. But Cripps's Marxism was not interpreted flexibly. For much of the time he was more Royalist than the King: more doctrinaire than the Communist Party. His central assumptions in the 1930s were that the logic of capitalism was bound to drive the National Government into imperialism, and that therefore Britain must not rearm until she had 'a Workers' Government, as they have in Russia'. It was the kind of reasoning which had led the German communists in the Weimar Republic to regard the Social Democrats as a greater menace than the Nazis. The strange thing is that in the 1930s the Comintern showed a greater willingness to abandon it than Cripps did.

The clue to his behaviour lies in his education, his profession and his religion. He was above all a distinguished lawyer and a devoted churchman, with a scientific education. Scientists, trained in the exact measurement of quantifiable data and engaged in a search for Truth with a capital 'T', are apt to make heavy weather of the uncertainties and ambiguities of political life. The same applies, in a different way, to lawyers. The skills of a trial lawyer, adept at manipulating a jury, are not far removed from the skills of a politician. But Cripps was not that kind of lawyer. He shone at the precise and lucid presentation of legal arguments, and the handling of expert witnesses. He was a lawyer's lawyer: more at home with a judge than with a jury. On that level, legal skills consist chiefly in the application of general principles to particular cases. It is a skill akin, in some ways, to that of the theologian. The framework is taken for granted; and great ingenuity is devoted to fitting the facts into it. And there is the most important clue of all. To Cripps himself, the most significant and valuable part of his life was not politics or the law but the Christian Church. He went into politics in the first place primarily because he was convinced that it was through politics that God's work could best be done. Christians, he believed, must fight the forces of evil and complacency in this world, and not wait passively for the next. Socialism, for him, was the practical expression of Christianity; and it is in the light of this belief that the complexities of his politics can best be understood.

There is nothing new in a British politician, above all a British politician of the left, trying to do what he believes to be God's work. For generation after generation, British radicalism has been enriched by the nonconformist conscience. But Cripps did not belong to that tradition. He came of a different and more esoteric line: that of the Anglican conscience. The distinction is difficult to describe, but important to grasp. Nonconformity, in Britain, is on the whole democratic and plebeian; the Anglican Church is patrician and in an important sense authoritarian. In recent years, at least, the non-conformist conscience has stressed works and adopted a rather robust and unsubtle attitude to the intricacies of faith. For the Anglican conscience (though doubtless not for the average member of the Church of England), doctrine seems to have had a greater emotional significance. The difference is the difference between John Bright and Gladstone – or between Arthur Henderson and Cripps.

Cripps's religious temperament manifested itself in two ways. In the first place, it helps to explain the sweeping extremism with which each successive change of heart was expressed. It is a commonplace that a doctrinaire in one faith can become a doctrinaire in another. Cripps was no exception; only in his case there were two changes of doctrine, not one. In the early 1920s, he was first and foremost a churchman, with little interest in conventional politics. Hugh Gaitskell, then a schoolboy at Winchester, remembers Cripps telling him, the first time they met, that the 'only hope' for the world was the union of Churches. By the 1930s, the prescription had changed; but the single-mindedness of the dispenser remained. Now the 'only hope' was the destruction of capitalism, and the purging of reformism from the labour movement. After the war, the prescription changed again. Now it was national unity and class co-operation. The second manifestation was less obvious, but in the long run more significant. For Cripps, the calculus of the ordinary politician was almost irrelevant. He was a fiercely ambitious man, of course: no one gets as far as he did without ambition. But he disdained the arts of the conventionally ambitious; and, because of this, he had a kind of force which the conventionally ambitious lack. No doubt, it would have been better for the Labour Party if ordinary members had not idolised him in the 1930s. The fact remains that they did so; and they did so, not just because of what he said, but of what he was.

The last of Cripps's three prescriptions worked. One of the biggest gaps in the historiography of post-war Britain is that we still lack a full-scale biography of Cripps, based on his own papers and the records of the Government in which he served. In its absence, it is impossible to be sure how far he deserves the credit for the economic performance over which he presided. The austerity programme which dominated his reign as Chancellor was started by Dalton, not by him. The economic recovery of Western Europe, which was a prerequisite of Britain's economic recovery, was the product of forces far beyond the control of any British government. Marshall Aid, which provided an indispensable cushion for British policy-makers, came from the United States. What cannot be disputed are the broad outlines of the economic record. Resources were poured into the balance of payments, transforming the country's external position. Consumption was reined back, but – to the dismay of some officials – spending on the social services was maintained. The fiercely egalitarian taxation policy of the wartime coalition was continued. Military spending, the burden which had done so much to wreck Dalton's economic policies, was steadily reduced until the Korean War. For a surprisingly long time, a voluntary wage freeze – arguably the most successful incomes policy of the entire post-war period – contained the inflationary pressures inevitable in an over-extended economy with virtually no unemployment. To be sure, the deep-seated structural problems which had made themselves felt as long ago as the late nineteenth century, and which were to become far more obvious in later years – above all, the comparatively low rate of productivity growth – were not overcome. But it is hard to see how they could have been overcome in the lifetime of a single government. In their own terms, Cripps's policies succeeded; had they been continued, the deeper problems might have been overcome over a longer time-scale. As Sir Alec Cairncross summarises it,

All in all, the early post-war years presented the government with a much more difficult task of economic management than the two decades that followed; and its mastery of that task entitled the government to all the more credit. It pointed the economy in the right direction, rode out the various crises that the years of transition almost inevitably gave rise to, and by 1951 had brought the economy near to eventual balance. No doubt there were false starts, concentration on secondary issues, a slowness to react, an unwillingness to act with sufficient firmness, and at the end a serious error over the scale of rearmament that was feasible. There was, too, little success in changing long-standing attitudes in industry that slowed down innovation and expansion. But whether one tries to look forward from 1945 or backwards from forty years later, those years appear in retrospect, and rightly so, as years when the government knew where it wanted to go and led the country with an understanding of what was at stake.[9]

Most of that achievement was registered while Cripps was at the Treasury.

It was, in many ways, a paradoxical achievement – at any rate by the yardstick of his earlier career. Cripps came into office in 1945 a planner, perhaps the most convinced planner in the Government. It was on the ticket of more effective planning that he conceived the abortive *putsch* against Attlee in the summer of 1947; it was as a planner that he took over Morrison's economic functions when the *putsch* failed. But planning is, of course, a coat of many colours. As Cairncross points out, there were two different conceptions of planning in the post-war period – 'a socialist, egalitarian approach which saw planning as a purely organisational activity akin to the planning that goes on within a productive enterprise, an army or, for that matter, a political party; and a liberal, Keynesian, approach which saw planning as a corrective to the operation of market forces and dwelt particularly on the need for a level of effective demand adequate to maintain full employment'.[10] The story of the post-war Labour Government is, in large part, the story of the victory of the second approach over the first. And Cripps was both the chief exponent of the first in the Government's early days, and the chief vehicle of the second in its later ones. His last budget speech was the 'requiem' of the former.[11] He may not have appreciated the full significance of the change. Like most socialists of his generation, he was instinctively suspicious of the price mechanism – one of the reasons, perhaps, why he resisted the necessary devaluation of sterling in 1949 longer than he should have done. Robert Hall, the head of the economic section of the Treasury at the time, paid him the slightly double-edged compliment that 'He did not really understand the basis of economic planning as we developed it under his regime, but he was entirely responsible for its development'[12] – meaning, presumably, that he accepted the advice of his officials and pushed it through with all his characteristic intellectual power and moral authority.

In the end, it was these which mattered most. For Cripps there was a link between Cairncross's 'socialist, egalitarian' and 'liberal, Keynesian' forms of planning. The link was persuasion. A democratic government, he wrote in the 1947 *Economic Survey* – the high-water mark of the Government's attempts at the first kind of planning – could not possibly direct as large and complex an economic system as Britain's. 'Events can be directed in the way that is desired in the national interest only if the Government, both sides of industry, and the people accept the objectives and then work together to achieve the end.'[13] Perhaps it is an impossible ideal. Certainly, it presupposes a degree of civic solidarity hard to conceive in the Britain of the 1980s. But during Cripps's tenure of the Chancellorship it came nearer to realisation than ever before or since in peacetime. One reason, no doubt, was his spartan lifestyle: up at 4 a.m; three hours' work before breakfast; a cold bath; a walk in the park; and then the gruelling day. Everyone could see that, in the battle for national solvency, he was leading from the front; as time went on it was equally plain that he was slowly killing himself in the process.

But there was more to it than that. Cripps's confidence in the rightness of his own cause, and his sublime indifference to the constraints of party, did not make for easy relations with his colleagues. They did make him an inspiring leader, who managed to appeal, as he hoped he would, to the best to his listeners. No one since the later Gladstone has embodied the progressive conscience – with all its strengths and weaknesses – more fully. Churchill's jibe is well known: 'There but for the grace of God goes God.' Hugh Gaitskell made essentially the same point in a rather different way:

> Most of us, I think, are cowards in the sense that we are always counting the political difficulties and probably tending to exaggerate them. You feel with Cripps that almost nothing is politically impossible. He sails on simply concerned with what is the best solution from every other point of view and ignoring all the rocks which lie ahead. . . . [T]he courage is not obvious as courage; one does not feel there is a tremendous moral struggle because of this great confidence. Perhaps it has something to do with his religion. Perhaps too it has something to do with the martyr complex.[14]

It is hard to believe that it is a complete coincidence that he should also have been the most successful Chancellor of the Exchequer since the war.

Herbert Morrison: The Socialist as Consolidator

In 1910, the twenty-two-year-old Bert Morrison, formerly a member of the extreme revolutionary wing of the Social Democratic Federation, joined the Brixton branch of the more moderate Independent Labour Party. A year later, he stopped calling himself Bert and became Herbert instead: his landlady had persuaded him that 'Bert' sounded common.

It is a trivial detail, but it throws a vivid shaft of light on an aspect of labour history which is too easily forgotten. Partly because it is, in any case, easier to romanticise the past than to understand it, and partly because a romanticised past can often be a useful weapon in battles about the present and future, the labour movement is often tempted to deceive itself about its origins. Everyone remembers the leonine integrity of Keir Hardie; few recall that he owed his seat in Parliament to a pact with the Liberals. Labour activists celebrate the heroic struggles of the dockers or the miners: who waxes sentimental about the railway clerks or the shop assistants? *The Ragged Trousered Philanthropist* can bring a lump to the throat. It is easy to forget that, to become a force, Labour also had to win support from Mr Polly.

Morrison never forgot: and this was the source both of his achievements and of his ultimate failure. He was rooted in the lower-middle class of South London – as much as Jim Griffiths, say, was rooted in the mining villages of the South Wales coalfield, and probably a great deal more than Ernest Bevin was rooted anywhere. The street where Morrison was born was classified in Charles Booth's great survey as 'fairly comfortable'; his father was a policeman, with strong Tory prejudices; he himself started life as a shop assistant. The 'folk from whence he came' were not disinherited proletarians, with nothing to lose but their chains. They were the highly skilled owner–occupiers of Woolwich, which he represented on the London County Council: the black-coated workers of Eltham, where he lived for most of his life. He knew them better than any other leading British politician has ever done, and he knew them because he was one of them. He understood their craving for respectability, their uneasiness in the face of emotional display, their distaste for demagogic slogans. He understood also their common sense, their respect for facts, their instinctive decency and their belief in fair play. On that understanding he built the most effective municipal political machine since the Chamberlain machine in Birmingham. It also enabled him to contribute more than any other single Labour politician did to his party's sweeping victory in 1945.

For Labour's victory in 1945 was, in at least three senses, Morrison's victory. It was Morrison's victory in the sense that he had done more than any other single member of the party leadership to shape the programme and image which the party presented to the electorate, partly through his activities on the party executive and partly through his speeches in the country. Less obviously, it owed almost as much to his personal and political triumph as leader of the London County Council. As has often been pointed out, Labour's participation in the wartime coalition was almost certainly a prerequisite of its election victory once the war was over, for only experience could kill the canard that Labour was unfit to govern. Morrison's leadership of the LCC had a similar significance. If Labour could run the capital with competence and flair, why could it not run the country? Last, but by no means least, 1945 was Morrison's victory in a deeper, sociological, sense as well. It was Morrison's England – the England of the clerks, the shop assistants, the school teachers, the technicians; the flat, unheroic, determinedly unproletarian England of the lesser suburbs – which gave Labour its massive majority and Morrison his opportunity.

Then why the failures and disappointments afterwards? In 1945 Morrison and Bevin were easily the most outstanding Labour politicians in the eyes of the general public. In the eyes of party activists and of the parliamentary party, Morrison almost certainly stood higher than Bevin did. Many influential figures in the party – not only those in Morrison's bustling and over-zealous entourage, but left-wingers like Laski, Cripps and apparently even Bevan – thought that Morrison would make a better leader than Attlee, and some tried unsuccessfully to make the change. Yet, when the party left office in 1951, Morrison's reputation was already sagging badly. In 1952, he lost his seat on the National Executive, to which he had first been elected in 1920. In 1955, when Attlee at last retired, he received only a humiliating forty votes in the election for party leader. What went wrong?

His decline began much earlier than either he or his enemies realised; in one crucial sense, it began at the very moment when the Government was formed. Immediately after the 1945 election, he made a clumsy and surprisingly irresolute bid for the leadership. Attlee foiled it by the simple expedient of accepting the King's commission to form a government and announcing that he had done so. Having tried and failed to get rid of him, Morrison could hardly expect to be in Attlee's good graces. Nor was he. Instead of the Foreign Office or the Treasury, Attlee gave him a vague and ill-defined overlordship over the entire home front as leader of the House of Commons and Lord President of the Council. He was deputy Prime Minister, but the trappings of status were no substitute for the realities of departmental power.

He was supposed to be in charge of economic planning and chaired the Lord President's Committee, which, in wartime, had settled the key issues of domestic economic policy. But in wartime, when manpower had mattered more than money, the Treasury had occupied a subordinate place in the Whitehall scheme of things. In peacetime, this was no longer true. The Treasury was in any case determined to reassert its ancient centrality in the machinery of Government; and, once the matters for which it was responsible had become central to the management of the economy, it was virtually bound to succeed. Morrison's empire did not include the Treasury and he had no solid base from which to defend his authority against the Treasury's inevitable assaults on it. Like a whole succession of economic co-ordinators, from J. H. Thomas in the 1929 Government to George Brown after 1964, he found himself exercising wide and highly controversial responsibilities without the power to back them up. When the convertibility crisis came in 1947, he was the scapegoat. He remained deputy Prime Minister and continued to chair the Lord President's Committee, but he lost his economic overlordship to the relentlessly advancing Cripps. He still played a central part in the Government's inner circle and did so until the 1950 election. For the last few months of Attlee's short-lived second Government, he was Foreign Secretary, albeit an unhappy and unconvincing one. But after 1947 the curve of his career went steadily, if slowly, down.

His biographers, Bernard Donoughue and George Jones, have told this part of the story with great insight and skill.[1] Equally full of insight is their shrewd and sympathetic picture of the streak of diffidence which lay at the core of Morrison's character and which also contributed to his political decline. Morrison's private life, they show, was profoundly unhappy; his frantic public life, with its neurotic obsession with politics, its continual over-work and its endless bustle and rush, was an attempt to paper over a deep crack of personal emptiness. Though there can be no proof, their narrative strongly suggests that private emptiness also reinforced – may even have been responsible for – the insecurity which caused Morrison to shrink from wielding the knife which others so eagerly put into his hands, and which made him so fatally ready to give up the substance of power provided he could hold on to the shadow. For, in spite of his ambition, flair and mastery of the arts of party management he lacked the ultimate hardness without which few reach the top of the greasy pole.

In a titillating aside, Donoughue and Jones suggest that his inability to hold his own in the jungle of high politics may have been due to his lack of a public-school education. As it stands, the judgement will not do: if ever there was a successful predator in the high-political jungle, it was the working-class Bevin, while the public-school Dalton was considerably less successful than Morrison. All the same, there is an instructive contrast between Bevin and Morrison on the one hand, and between Cripps and Morrison on the other. Bevin and Cripps were both supremely confident, not just intellectually but existentially; one reason was that neither was a prey to the nagging inner doubts of the upwardly mobile and socially insecure. Both were indifferent to status because neither needed it: because both had a robust, unquestionable authenticity – Bevin as proletarian and Cripps as patrician – that Morrison lacked. How and to what extent Morrison's personal insecurities, yearning for recognition and unwillingness to take risks were linked to social insecurity, no one can say. It is hard to believe that there was no link at all.

Yet I doubt if Morrison's decline can be explained in these terms alone. His inability to hold his own in the Whitehall in-fighting which gave economic primacy first to Cripps and then to Gaitskell owed more to a confusion of purpose and doctrine which was common to the whole party than to personal insecurity or the lack of a departmental power base. If it stood for anything, Labour stood for planning. It wished to subordinate the anarchic and wasteful higgling of the market to social control; to substitute rationality, order, social responsibility for the greed and confusion of profit-seeking private enterprise. That was presumably what Aneurin Bevan meant by the gnomic assertion that the language of priorities was the religion of socialism. It was because these aspirations chimed with the mood of a nation in arms that Labour had won. But although Labour believed, on principle, in a planned economy, it soon discovered that it did not know what it meant by the term. Plainly, it did not mean a command economy on the Soviet model. Nor, however, did it mean systematic, long-term *dirigiste* economic restructuring – coupled, as it would have had to be, with a radical reconstruction of the machinery of government – of the sort that Jean Monnet pursued in France.

The record suggests that, in practice, it meant little more than a generalised suspicion of the price mechanism and an instinctive preference for administrative, as against market, allocation – scarcely a satisfactory basis from which to manage the transition from total war to uneasy and resource-starved peace. Slowly, but inexorably, this intellectual vacuum was filled by a strange, though characteristically British, doctrinal *mélange*, made up of the traditional anti-interventionism of the Whitehall machine, the neo-classical assumptions which the Government's economic advisers shared with the rest of the economics profession, and the teachings of Keynes. Ministers stuck to the slogan of economic planning, but gradually reinterpreted it to mean Keynesian demand management. The chance for a radical reconstruction of the supply side of the economy was lost. Instead, the scene was set for the easygoing, arm's-length manipulation of the 1950s. Ironically, it was Cripps, the left-wing puritan, not Morrison, the right-wing compromiser, who presided over the crucial later stages of this shift of emphasis. All the same, the ambiguities and uncertainties which were responsible for it were as apparent in Morrison's conduct as in that of Cripps. Even if he had had a clear conception of the purpose and nature of the economic planning for which he was supposed to be responsible, Morrison would have found it hard to make a success of his vaguely defined and inadequately serviced role. He might, however, have had a chance. As things were, he had no chance. He was toppled from his perch because he did not know what to do with it. The fact that those who toppled him did not know either only underlines the irony of the whole story.

The irony does not end there. Apart from the National Health Service, the socialism of the 1945 Government was, above all, Morrison's socialism – the socialism of the great public corporation which he did more than anyone else, if not to invent, then at least to patent. That socialism has few defenders now, but in 1945 it had important advantages. It enabled Labour to marry the old dream of a New Jerusalem, in which production for use would replace production for profit, with the less exalted, but electorally more appealing, promise of technical competence and economic efficiency. The Morrisonian corporation was to be publicly owned, but run as though it were privately owned. There would be no nonsense about workers' control and not much about parliamentary accountability. Its managers would manage in the public interest instead of in the private interest, but they would be the same people, operating in the same way. Like planning, all this chimed with the mood of wartime Britain – particularly with the mood of the intermediate, black-coated, 'useful people' who figured so prominently in Morrison's rhetoric. Well before the end of the Government's term of office, however, Morrisonian socialism was beginning to lose its non-partisan glitter. The slow demise of planning had removed one argument for it, while the Government's much trumpeted success in persuading the private sector voluntarily to co-operate with it had removed another. The extension of public ownership from mining and the public utilities into the rest of the economy was hard to justify on any but ideological grounds. But those grounds were hard to square with the structure and conduct of the defiantly non-ideological Morrisonian corporation. Worse still, they had little appeal to the 'useful people' who held the result of the next election in their hands and who were now beginning to drift away from the party. Ever sensitive to shifting public moods, Morrison spotted this sooner than most of his colleagues. He did his best to stop the nationalisation of steel, and although he lost that argument he won the more important argument over Labour's approach to the future. Largely under his influence, 'consolidation' became the order of the day.

But there was a further irony in store. Just as Morrison the planner had not known what he meant by planning, so Morrison the consolidator gave only vague and negative intimations of what he meant by consolidation. A time came, he told the 1948 Labour Party conference, when 'advance must be followed by detailed consolidation, and by exploiting the territory that has been gained. That is the state we are now reaching. And if we go on always stretching out our hands for more and not making good the gains we have claimed, only disaster can follow.'[2] No doubt intentionally, that formulation was ambiguous. It could be read to mean that socialism should make a temporary halt on its onward march, the better to move forward once the period of consolidation was over. But there were at least two other possible readings – that the march should stop altogether, and that it should change direction.

In practice, Morrison's version of consolidation meant stopping, or at any rate halting for as far ahead as anyone could see. Though some of the younger Labour intellectuals were beginning to search for a new direction, the results of their searchings did not become apparent until Morrison's star had waned. Labour fought the 1950 and 1951 elections on profoundly conservative platforms: a ragbag of petty and rather apologetic nationalisations; defence of the welfare state; full employment. It offered no new ideas, yet seemed unwilling to take its old ones any further. The contrast with the Asquith Government, which repeatedly turned the flanks of its opponents with adventurous new initiatives, only tenuously connected with the traditional ideology of the Liberal Party, could hardly be more striking. Yet the Britain of the 1950s offered plenty of scope for radical reform, in areas to which the 1945 Government had been indifferent as well as in areas into which it had ventured. The tragedy was that Morrisonian consolidators and their enemies on the left of the party were equally blind to the opportunity. Perhaps it is a backhanded compliment to Morrison that they should have been so. After all, both took it for granted that socialism meant Morrisonian socialism; that the house which Morrison had built was the only house on offer. It was a tragedy even so.

Aneurin Bevan: The Progressive as Socialist

The British working-class movement has so far produced three leaders of undoubted greatness – Ramsay MacDonald, Ernest Bevin and Aneurin Bevan. Of the three, Bevan was the most attractive, the most brilliant and intellectually the most original. Yet his achievements did not match his talents. Unlike many left-wing socialists he knew that politics is, in part, about power. But judged by the harsh test of power, he was himself a failure, although a magnificent one. In the National Health Service, he had one huge constructive achievement to his credit. Sadly, it was the only one: a monument to abilities under-used, not the precursor of a long series. Out of a political career of more than thirty years, less than six were spent in office. Most of the causes he championed went down to defeat. The United Front campaign in the 1930s failed. The Popular Front campaign led to his expulsion from the Labour Party. His attacks on Churchill's wartime strategy appealed only to the converted. The Health Service charges were imposed in 1951 in spite of his opposition. His campaign against German rearmament was defeated. His bid for the leadership of the Labour Party was unsuccessful.

According to his enemies on the right wing of his own party, there was nothing surprising in this catalogue of failure. 'Don't ever trust that man, he is wicked,' Herbert Morrison warned his secretary when Bevan passed them on the Terrace of the House of Commons.[1] Told that Bevan was his own worst enemy, Ernest Bevin gave the immortal reply: 'Not while I'm alive, he ain't.'[2] At the party meeting immediately after Bevan's resignation from the Cabinet in 1951, Hugh Dalton passed a note to Herbert Morrison comparing him to Oswald Mosley. Afterwards he noted in his diary that Bevan had been 'sweating and screeching and seemed on the edge of a nervous breakdown'. Ten months later, he recorded another party meeting at which Bevan 'made a violent speech, of nauseating egoism and sweating with hatred'. In 1955, when Gaitskell and Morrison hoped to expel Bevan from the party, Dalton differed from them only over tactics: instead of expelling him, he thought, the leadership should provoke him into resigning. At the height of the crisis he complained in his diary of Bevan's 'increasingly evil face, both when silent and when speechifying'.[3] Others went further. According to Dalton, Roy Jenkins described Bevan's performance at the party meetings following his resignation as 'sub-human'.[4] If Crossman's diary is to be trusted, Gaitskell even saw 'extraordinary parallels between Nye and Adolf Hitler. They are demagogues of exactly the same sort.'[5]

Of course, it would be a mistake to take all this at face value. Moods are evanescent, and politicians' moods are more evanescent than most. The Palace of Westminster is a theatre of the emotions; in the glare of its footlights, loyalties and hatreds, friendships and jealousies loom larger than life, waxing and waning with bewildering speed. Even if Gaitskell did tell Crossman that there were parallels between Bevan and Hitler (and we only have Crossman's word for it), that was a momentary spasm, not a considered judgement. Earlier, he had shocked Frank Pakenham by telling him he thought Bevan would one day be leader of the party and Prime Minister.[6] By the same token, Dalton's loathing for the 'evil' in Bevan's face sometimes ebbed. On a happier occasion, he was able to record, 'Long and affectionate talk with Nye. . . . He said he and I had always got on very well when I was Chancellor of the Exchequer. I said I had backed him for *National* Health Service when Morrison wanted it only municipal.'[7] Yet, when all the qualifications have been made, there is no doubt that the bile of the Labour right was real. In its eyes, Bevan – at any rate when he was alive – was at best an egocentric prima donna, unable to work in a team, and at worst a destructive demagogue, corroded by class bitterness, incapable of constructive political activity and dominated by personal ambition. Only after his death did its judgements mellow.

A generation later, it is hard to see how normally sensible people could have formed such a view. Bevan was a captivating platform speaker, perhaps the best of his generation, but he was not a demagogue. He relied on wit rather than passion and aimed to persuade, not to carry away. His record as Minister of Health makes nonsense of the charge that he was incapable of constructive activity and, for that matter, of the charge that he could not work in a team. He was, of course, ambitious: few people get as far in politics as he did without the spur of ambition. But, if ambition could be weighed, it is doubtful if his would register more on the scales than Morrison's

110

or Dalton's or Gaitskell's. The true explanation for his repeated political failures must lie deeper. What is it, and what light does it throw on the dilemmas of Labourism, then and since?

What might be called the 'official' answer is set out with characteristic exuberance and literary skill in the two volumes of Michael Foot's massive biography.[8] On one level, they constitute a biographical *tour de force*. Foot approached his subject as a self-confessed hero-worshipper. Perhaps because of this he managed to convey something of the magic of Bevan's personality, and something of the wayward genius that lay behind it, with a warmth and insight which few political biographers can equal. In his pages, Bevan came tumultuously alive, sprawling superbly through thirty years of British history, scattering a golden shower of epigrams as he went. Foot's warmth and insight were directed almost exclusively to Bevan, Bevan's admirers and Bevan's heroes. The idea that Bevan's opponents may also be worthy of sympathy, or at least of a serious attempt at understanding, scarcely seems to have entered his head. For Foot, Bevan was an idol who could do no wrong, who rarely made mistakes, whose judgements were almost invariably borne out by events, and whose defeats were engineered by the trickery and intrigues of smaller, meaner men – who somehow contrived to find themselves in control of the party machine whenever a decisive moment came. Thus, the first volume wrote Attlee off as the Lepidus to Lansbury's Antony and Cripps's Octavius, and failed to examine the qualities which enabled him to remain leader of the Labour Party for twenty years. Bevin was depicted as an autocratic and intolerant union boss (which, of course, he was), but the constructive patience, negotiating ability and political judgement which made him the greatest union boss in British history are hardly mentioned. Morrison and Dalton are dismissed with even smaller ceremony.

Yet these four, with all their shortcomings, were the dominant figures in the Labour Party for some twenty years. No one who reads through the annual conference reports for the 1930s can doubt their pre-eminence in Labour's councils. To dismiss them as intellectual and moral pygmies is to turn the movement they led into a movement of pygmies, and to make the history of the British left in the 1930s and 1940s incomprehensible. For the fact is that in almost all the major conflicts between the Labour Party leadership and its left-wing critics during the 1930s, it was the leadership which won. If the leadership was as mediocre as Foot implied, how can its victories be explained? Only two answers are possible. Either the left was equally mediocre – or the rank and file of the labour movement were themselves so mediocre that they failed to perceive the mediocrity of their leaders. Neither answer does much credit to Bevan's activities at the time.

But in fact, of course, the dilemma is imaginary, since the party leadership was not mediocre. The conflicts between left and right in the 1930s (like those in the 1950s, for that matter) were not epic battles in which a handful of intellectual and moral Gullivers contended against battalions of Lilliputians. Both sides had a fair share of ability, integrity and courage, as well as of stupidity and self-seeking; neither had a monopoly of wisdom or folly. On the crucial issues of foreign policy and defence, and the related issues of political strategy, both made a number of appalling mistakes. The left justified its opposition to rearmament on the grounds that the National Government in Britain was little better than fascist itself, and might therefore misuse the weapons it obtained for its own imperialistic purposes. In fact it would be hard to imagine anyone less likely to engage in imperialistic ventures than Stanley Baldwin. But, on the Spanish Civil War, the rights and wrongs were reversed. The British policy of non-intervention had no justification in international law since the Republican regime was the legal Government of Spain, and as such perfectly entitled to purchase arms abroad. Even today it is hard to read the speeches on this issue delivered by the party leadership at the Edinburgh conference without wincing.

In the same way, the left's position on the United Front seems in retrospect incredibly naive – while the right's position on the Popular Front seems hopelessly obtuse and inflexible. The United Front was to be an alliance of the 'working-class' parties against capitalism. Its champions failed to see that in Britain the working class was already united, for all practical purposes, in the Labour Party. The communists and the ILP commanded no substantial segments of working-class support, and if the Labour Party had joined a United Front with them it would have lost the support of other classes, without making any compensating gains. But, on the Popular Front, the positions were reversed. Now the left was proposing an alliance of all anti-Chamberlain groups, whether 'capitalist' or not; and the right denounced the project as a betrayal of socialist solidarity. It is arguable that such an alliance would have failed to work, but it seems astonishing that the Labour Party leadership should have refused even to attempt the experiment – and worse than astonishing that it should have expelled Cripps and his followers from the party for trying to convert it to their view.

But, if the rights and wrongs were evenly balanced in this way, why is it that the left consistently lost? Foot did not ask this question directly, but even so his book contains a clue to the answer. In almost all the major conflicts between the Labour Party leadership and its left-wing critics in the 1930s, one fundamental issue was at stake. At bottom, all the major conflicts were conflicts about the implications for the labour movement of British parliamentary democracy. To the right-wing leadership, those implications seemed obvious. The Labour Party was the heir of the old Liberal Party. In 1929 it had almost won an absolute majority of the seats in the House of Commons. In 1931, it was true, most of its parliamentary strength had been swept away – but that was solely due to the incompetence, cowardice and wickedness of Ramsay MacDonald, Philip Snowden and Jimmy Thomas. Freed of the incubus of pusil-lanimous and treacherous leaders, the Labour Party would soon recover, and indeed surpass, the position it had enjoyed in 1929. All that was necessary was to play the parliamentary game by the familiar rules, to fight elections at the appropriate times in the approved manner, and by the display of statesmanship and moder-ation to win over a sufficient proportion of the floating vote to gain a parliamentary majority.

These propositions suffered from a number of defects. In the first place, they totally failed to account for the débâcle of 1931. The Labour Party leadership in the 1930s occupied a position *vis-à-vis* Ramsay MacDonald similar to that occupied by Khrushchev *vis-à-vis* Stalin. The more they protested their disgust and contempt for their late leader, the harder they found it to account for their own behaviour under his leadership. It was easy enough to make Mac-Donald the scapegoat for the failure of the 1929 Government, and this was rapidly and effectively done. But a number of nagging doubts remained. Had MacDonald suddenly become a traitor to socialism in 1931, or had he been one all along? And if he had been one all along, how was it that his ministers had failed so signally to notice the fact? And if they had noticed it, how was it that they had flinched from doing anything about it? These doubts nurtured others. The political strategy of the Labour Party leadership in the 1930s was not substantially different from that followed by MacDonald and Snowden in the 1920s. But, if the MacDonald–Snowden strategy had led to 1931, what guarantee was there that the Morrison–Dalton strategy would lead to a more inspiring destination? Dalton had declared, at the meeting of the Parliamentary Labour Party held after the formation of the National Government, that whereas the first Labour Government had been dismissed by a 'Red Letter', the second had been dismissed by a 'Bankers' Order'. But, if the first two Labour governments were so easily dismissed, why should a third prove more resolute? Because Dalton said so? But no one could have *sounded* more resolute than MacDonald.

These doubts were reinforced by the course of events in Europe. The constitutionalist creed of the party leadership, and the parliamentary strategy which derived from it, seemed hopelessly inadequate in face of the spread of fascism. The Labour Party leadership refused to take part in joint action with the communists – yet across the Channel it seemed that the communists, almost alone in the working-class movement, were prepared to kill Hitler with something more deadly than their mouths. Where the Labour Party leadership concentrated sagely on winning elections (with small success) the fascists won bloodier victories, without opposition from this country. The leadership argued that its orthodox parliamentary strategy might lead to a Labour victory in the general election of 1939 or 1940. But in the meantime what would become of the Spanish Republicans? And, in any case, what guarantee was there that Labour *would* win in 1939 or 1940? Its performance in 1935 was nothing to be proud of, and the by-elections that followed did not point to a sufficient swing to guarantee a Labour victory in the next general election. It is true, of course, that Baldwin had won the election of 1935 on a platform which he later repudiated. But, if the Conservatives could steal Labour's clothes in 1935, they could do the same in 1939 or 1940.

Such were the doubts of the left, and Foot did full justice to them. But he failed, as the left failed at the time, to suggest a credible alternative to the orthodox strategy of the right. The left saw the weaknesses in the narrowly constitutionalist position of the leadership. But it shrank from a thoroughgoing revolutionary alternative and failed also to construct a theoretical halfway house between revolutionism and constitutionalism. Most of the left-wing leaders of the 1930s had imbibed fairly heavy doses of Marxism. But they failed to draw the appropriate Marxist conclusions from their Marxist premises. Thus Cripps opposed the rearmament programme in

1935 on the grounds that the British Government was not 'a workers' government', and that it would therefore be driven, by the inexorable logic of capitalism, to embark on imperialist ventures on its own account. But, if this was in fact the case, surely the left should have given a more emphatic reply than a campaign of speech-making and pamphlet-writing? The same applies to the arguments over the United Front. As we have seen, the United Front made no sense in the context of a parliamentary strategy, since the ILP and the communists had no actual or prospective parliamentary strength to offer. It might have made sense in the context of a revolutionary strategy – but no revolutionary strategy was devised to accompany it.

It seems clear, then, that what the left really wanted in practice was not an alternative to parliamentarianism, but a more aggressive, and above all a morally more intransigent, form of parliamentarianism. Powerful arguments could be adduced to support such a demand. In the 1930s, as in the early 1950s, the Labour Party leadership often seemed unable to distinguish between caution and cynicism, and forgot that if a left-wing government is to come to power in this country the politics of interest must be supplemented by the politics of moral protest. The Labour Party had become the major progressive party in the state largely because the virulent personal antagonisms which divided the Liberal Party after 1916, and still more the squalid performance of the Lloyd George Government in Ireland and over the sale of honours, appeared to demonstrate the moral bankruptcy of orthodox Liberalism. After his fall from power in 1922, Lloyd George tried to rebuild a position on the left. He failed, in part at any rate, because he could never entirely throw off the memory of the Black and Tans. But in the 1930s the Labour Party leadership often seemed to ignore the lesson of Labour's rise in the 1920s. The way in which it maintained internal party discipline was scarcely calculated to appeal to liberal-minded voters; its domestic policy could be represented – unfairly, but that is beside the point – as sectional and unpatriotic; its foreign policy failed to offer a compelling moral challenge to the Government's. The left was justified in sensing this, and in demanding a more inspiring moral posture. Where it failed was in clothing that demand in *marxisant* phrases, the logic of which contradicted the logic of the demand itself. What left-wing members of the Labour Party really wanted was a twentieth-century version of Gladstone's Midlothian campaign. By saying so in accents reminiscent of Lenin at the

Finland Station they misled their listeners and confused themselves. It would be anachronistic to condemn them. Their confusions were the confusions of their time. But it is one thing to sympathise with their predicament, and another to slide over its consequences.

Much the same is true of Foot's second volume, which takes the story from 1945 to Bevan's death in 1961. Once again, Foot succeeded triumphantly in bringing his subject to life. Once again, there are marvellous vignettes: Nye plunging into the role of farmer at his Chilterns retreat and staying up all night to tend a sick calf; Nye at Stratford, exuberantly laying down the law on Shakespearean criticism to 'an astounded audience of theatre directors'; Nye captivating a hostile delegation of doctors by explaining that, while they were experts, he was a 'comparative virgin' and being reminded that comparative virginity was a condition unknown to medical science; Nye, in a 'silvery Welsh baritone', serenading the leaders of the Italian Socialist Party on the Grand Canal in Venice. The reader sees the world through Bevan's eyes, shares Bevan's triumphs and suffers Bevan's disappointments. This, one feels again and again, is what it must have been like to be Aneurin Bevan. And to make the reader feel that is a large part of what biography is about.

Unfortunately, it is not all that biography is about. The historian's task does not end with bringing the past to life. He also has to understand it – in its terms rather than in his own. To do that, he has to try to drain himself of his own sympathies and prejudices (knowing, of course, that he can never succeed completely) so as to enter imaginatively into sympathies and prejudices which are alien to him and of which he may disapprove. Few people have the imagination and humility to do this, but all historians have to try. Foot's view was different. He saw himself, not as a historian, but as a kind of historical advocate pleading Bevan's cause, or perhaps as a kind of historical adjutant fighting Bevan's battles. He fought them with superb literary skill and great emotional power. Almost always he won. But there were times when one could not help wondering if victories won over the dead were worth winning at all.

As in the first volume, Morrison and Attlee emerge as cardboard villains, characterless, convictionless, motivated only by unsleeping ambition in the first case and by a desire for a quiet life in the second. Gaitskell, Bevan's successful rival in a struggle for power which consumed the energies of both men for several years, emerges as a petty, joyless technocrat, whom no one with any pretensions to political nous could conceivably have supported and whose victory is therefore incomprehensible. It is true, of course, that Bevan frequently talked in this way himself. Gaitskell as depicted by Bevan (or to put it more precisely, Gaitskell as depicted by Bevan to Foot) *was* little more than a jumped-up, dry-as-dust Treasury official, with no roots in the labour movement and no understanding of the aspirations which had given birth to it. But Bevan's inability to understand his rival – to realise that the finicky Wykehamist exterior concealed a driving will and a political commitment as fierce as his own – was one of his greatest weaknesses.

It is a much greater weakness in his biographer. For, although Foot saw that Gaitskell had more steel in his character than Bevan was prepared to admit, he could not bring himself to face the possibility that Bevan's picture of Gaitskell's views might have been as much of a caricature as was his picture of Bevan's personality. Still less could he face the possibility that the struggle between them might have been a struggle between two opposing, but equally honourable, conceptions of the party's mission rather than a struggle between conviction and opportunism. Of course, it would have been wrong for him to have concealed Bevan's dislike and disapproval of Gaitskell and of what he thought Gaitskell stood for. But, by failing to make it clear that there can be two views of whether that dislike and disapproval were justified, he came dangerously near to turning the struggle which took up the lion's share of Bevan's energies in what might have been the most creative years of his life from a tragedy into a melodrama. And, in melodrama, the heroes are as unconvincing as the villains.

Yet there is a paradox in Foot's account of which Foot himself was not – could not have been – aware. Between the lines of his strenuous and therefore unconvincing advocacy, the attentive reader can detect the faint outlines of a much bigger and more complex man. If Bevan's enemies saw him as a vain and over-sensitive prima donna, his friends saw him as the Sir Galahad of socialism, fighting for the historic verities of the movement against the machinators of Transport House and the more insidious revisionists of the Hampstead Set. Foot easily demolished the first, and never very convincing, legend, above all in his account of the establishment of the National Health Service. No doubt unintentionally, he also threw doubt on the second. For what his book showed most clearly of all was that Bevan was, at most, half a Bevanite. He shared his followers' opposition to the Attlee–Morrison leadership of the early 1950s. According to Foot, he also shared their suspicion of Gaitskell's leadership in the late 1950s and their determination to prevent the party from turning its back on its traditional commitment to public ownership. But, in spite of his opposition to 'revisionism' as the term was then understood, there are intriguing signs that he was – or at any rate half-wanted to be – a kind of revisionist himself. One sign was the famous 'naked into the conference chamber' speech at the 1957 party conference, in which he brutally, even contemptuously, savaged the orthodox *Tribune* case for unilateral nuclear disarmament. Another was his uneasy, but nevertheless fruitful, partnership with Gaitskell in the years before the 1959 general election. A third was the subtle and flexible credo at the end of his book, *In Place of Fear:*

> The philosophy of democratic Socialism is essentially cool in temper. It sees society in its context with nature and is conscious of the limitations imposed by physical conditions. It sees the individual in his context with society and is therefore compassionate and tolerant. Because it knows that all political action must be a choice between a number of possible alternatives it eschews all absolute prescriptions and final decisions. Consequently it is not able to offer the thrill of the abandonment of private judgement which is the allure of modern Soviet Communism and of Fascism, its running mate. Nor can it escape the burden of social choice so attractively suggested by those who believe in *laissez-faire* principles and in the automatism of the price system. . . .
>
> Democratic socialism is a child of modern society and so of relativist philosophy. It seeks the truth in any given situation, knowing all the time that if this be pushed too far it falls into error. It struggles against the evils that flow from private property yet realises that all forms of private property are not necessarily evil. Its chief enemy is vacillation, for it must achieve passion in action in pursuit of qualified judgements.[9]

The man who wrote that was not, in 1950s parlance, a 'fundamentalist' – or not, at any rate, by nature. The tragedy was that nature and circumstance were at war with each other. Bevan, the generous and imaginative 'child of relativist philosophy', who might have contributed more to the evolution of the progressive tradition in

British politics than any other politician since the war, was encased in the armour of Bevan, the rugged and unswerving socialist hero of Bevanite legend. The first Bevan rarely managed to escape from the second. He could not afford to: the Bevanites who hemmed him in were also his praetorian guard. And so his (and his party's) energies were consumed in a faction fight which he only half-wanted to win.

Foot, chief bard and embellisher of the legend, could hardly have been expected to explore the gap between circumstance and nature or to probe the tensions to which it gave rise. John Campbell, Bevan's most recent biographer, comes closer to doing so.[10] He has rescued his subject from the hagiographic mausoleum which Foot constructed for him and replaced the edifying statuary of the authorised version with a fallible mortal whose enduring fascination lies in his fallibility. The unswerving socialist hero has disappeared. In his place is a confused, sometimes almost tormented figure, thrashing about uncertainly in a world which is becoming progressively more alien. The terrible blood feud which convulsed the party for most of the 1950s, leaving a legacy of bitterness and suspicion which haunted it for a generation, ceases to be melodrama and becomes the tragedy it was.

Campbell emphasises that part of the responsibility for the feud was Bevan's. Whatever the rights and wrongs of his decision to resign in 1951 he carried it out with astonishing clumsiness. Having resigned, he behaved with a petulant arrogance that poured salt into all the wounds he had inflicted. More was Gaitskell's. The rearmament programme which he was determined to finance was inflated and unnecessary. Even if it had not been, there was no need for him to insist on health charges which he knew Bevan would resist. The sum they raised was insignificant and the escalating health costs which they were supposed to contain were already beginning to level out. If the right had justice in its complaint that Bevan's post-resignation behaviour wrecked Labour's electoral prospects, the left could reply with equal justice that the right had forced him to resign. But in the end such calculations are beside the point. The point is that both sides were swept towards a common doom by events which both had helped to unleash, but which neither could control. As Campbell puts it in an eloquent summing up:

First there was the long rumbling build-up leading to a false climax and the protracted, unheroic conclusion after the crisis

119

had apparently been passed. Then there is the sense of remorseless inevitability working itself out through a combination of quite minor historical accidents. At the heart of the matter was a real clash of political philosophies; but it found expression in a petty argument over budgetary priorities, based upon assumptions which were afterwards shown to be unfounded. Above all there was the rivalry of two contrasting personalities, with the turbulent hero brought down by his antagonist's cool exploitation of one fatal defect of character: in this respect Bevan's is a personal tragedy to compare with Antony's or Othello's. Finally, there is the consequence: the Labour Party riven in two, doomed to waste itself in fractious opposition for half a generation, until both the principal protagonists were dead. Bevan's defeat was scarcely Gaitskell's victory. Between them they practically destroyed the thing that in their different ways they loved.[11]

In some ways, however, the tragedy went even deeper than that. Campbell was right that the quarrel over budgetary priorities reflected more profound differences of principle, but the differences were much less clear-cut than they seem at first sight. In retrospect, it is easy to see that the Labour right of the early 1950s had, in practice, begun to abandon socialism for social democracy. Its policies were no longer governed by the central socialist assumption that social justice is impossible without common ownership of the means of production; it was content to run a mixed economy, as different in character from the socialist commonwealth envisaged by the founding fathers as from the market economy of the past. But, although this is easy to see now, the Labour right itself did not see it then. Even Gaitskell was not yet a fully-fledged Gaitskellite. Still less were Attlee, Morrison, Dalton and the other right-wingers of the pre-war generation. Like nineteenth-century Oxford fellows suppressing their doubts about the Thirty-Nine Articles, they practised social democracy on weekdays while continuing to worship at the old socialist shrines on Sundays. This, of course, made them all the more indignant with the old socialist left. The fury with which they pursued the Bevanites was the fury of a heretic who cannot bring himself to acknowledge his heresy. But their heresy was implicit, not explicit: a heresy of deed, not yet of faith.

The irony is that similar heresies were to be found on the left. Some Bevanites were and remained old socialists, of course, Foot among them. Bevan himself was a horse of a much less obvious colour. Campbell depicts him as a kind of parliamentary Marxist, and argues that the key to his politics lies in the Marxist intellectual formation which he never outgrew. In Campbell's view, the moral of his career is therefore a simple one. He was a magnificent anachronism, a whale floundering on the beach of history, left behind by a receding tide. 'For all the wonderful vigour of his mind; for all the seductive plausibility of his theorising; for all the democratic inspiration with which he humanised and sophisticated the crude Marxism which he imbibed in the South Wales of his youth, sadly it cannot be said Bevan read correctly the lessons of the twentieth century.' He died a failure because the socialism to which he had given his life had failed.

Unquestionably, there is something in it. But I am not convinced that it is the whole truth, or even a large part of it. Bevan certainly absorbed many of the Marxist assumptions which were spreading through the South Wales coalfield when he was a young man. Even in later life, he often used Marxist categories when he turned from day-to-day politics to philosophical system-building. But, whatever else he was, he was not a systematic thinker. *In Place of Fear* – the closest he came to system-building – is full of haunting phrases and illuminating *aperçus*, but it is the reverse of systematic. It is a messy, unorganised bran-tub of ideas, some original and thought-provoking, others second-hand and second-rate. In practice, its author's Marxism amounted to little more than a vague sense that History, with a capital 'H', ought to be moving towards socialism, coupled with a nostalgic attachment to the rhetoric of the class struggle. The rigour and discipline of systematic Marxism were alien to him, as were the narrowness and inflexibility that so often accompany them. Campbell berates Foot for trying to annex Bevan to his own tradition of nonconformist Liberalism. Here Foot is a better guide than Campbell. If we want to understand Bevan we should see him, not as a philosophical Marxist, but as a wonderfully articulate, though distinctly opportunistic, dissenting radical, dressed sporadically and unconvincingly in Marxist clothes.

He thought of himself as a socialist, of course, but for him socialism was not a project: it was an ethic, or perhaps an instinct; a matter of feeling and intuition, not of analysis or strategy. As Crossman's backbench diaries make clear, the most striking features of his behaviour after he resigned were his distaste for policy-making and his refusal to plan ahead. The last thing he wanted was an alternative

Bevanite programme behind which to mobilise the party rank and file, and by which he would then have been bound. He wanted to keep his hands free to take advantage of new developments as they occurred. One of his main complaints against Gaitskell was that the latter was forever dotting 'i's and crossing 't's which would have been better left in uplifting obscurity. When his followers tried to tie him down – as Crossman, in particular, was constantly trying to do – he slipped away. No doubt one reason was a romantic's distaste for bureaucratic routine. ('Poor man,' he once said of Walter Citrine, 'he suffers from files.') A more important one was that, as Crossman realised after an early meeting of the Group, 'Nye didn't want to be a Bevanite at all.'

What he disliked about the right of the party was the character of its revisionism, not the fact that it was revisionist: the moral and emotional logic of its arguments for embracing the mixed economy, not the fact that it had embraced it. After all, he was in favour of a mixed economy himself; in *In Place of Fear* he said so in so many words. But his mixed economy would have been an economy shaped by communal purposes and informed by a communal morality: an economy imbued, like the National Health Service, with the values of the South Wales mining communities of his youth. He saw the revisionism of the Labour right as a surrender to the rising tide of acquisitive individualism which was gradually overwhelming those values and destroying the culture from which they sprang; he resisted it, not because he was shackled anachronistically to the past, but because he dreamed of a richer and more generous future. His resistance failed, but that does not prove that history was against him or that he had failed to learn its lessons: Gaitskellite social democracy has worn no better than Bevanite socialism, partly because, as Bevan sensed, the view of human nature on which it was based was curiously thin and two-dimensional. His real failure was that he never managed to hammer out a coherent alternative; that his tentative and uncertain gropings for a different kind of revisionism never got further than the occasional mordant insight. Had they done so, the subsequent history of the British left might have been much happier. As things are, we can only mourn what might have been.

Hugh Gaitskell:
The Social Democrat as Hero

Hugh Gaitskell died more than twenty-five years ago. Few under forty are likely to remember him; few under fifty can have fallen under his spell. He was formed intellectually and politically in the 1920s and 1930s; he earned his place in British history as a champion of the now vanished post-war settlement. But, although most of the controversies which surrounded him have faded, the underlying issues are still alive and so are the passions which they aroused. Unilateral disarmament, membership of the European Community, the relationship between public and private ownership and between the state and the market – these questions divided the Labour Party of the 1980s as bitterly as they divided it in the 1960s. So did the deeper and more explosive questions of how the party sees itself and its constituency: of how it is to relate to the mass electorate on which it depends for victory and to the progressive intelligentsia on which it depends for ideas.

Gaitskell's answers were blunt and uncompromising. Partly because of that, however, his legacy and reputation have been in contest ever since his death. For some, his leadership of the Labour Party provides a model of what democratic leadership ought to be. Others – including some who agreed with him on policy – condemn him for failing to understand the history and ethos of the movement to which he devoted his life. Harold Wilson, his successor as party leader, took an essentially Gaitskellite line on most issues of policy, but went out of his way to adopt a non- (even an anti-) Gaitskellite leadership style – the chief reason for the otherwise inexplicable support he received from Gaitskell's old enemies on the left. Gaitskell's biographer saw him, with some justice, as 'a natural hero for social democrats'.[1] Not long after the biography appeared, however, the relationship between social democracy and the labour movement was called into question. The Labour politicians who left the party in the early 1980s to set up the SDP mostly saw themselves as

Gaitskell's heirs. Yet his widow remained in the Labour Party, as did his closest political friend. If willingness to jettison traditional socialism is the test, Neil Kinnock could claim to be a better Gaitskellite than Gaitskell, but it is a safe bet that he would be embarrassed by the compliment. In his most famous speech, Gaitskell promised to 'fight, fight and fight again' to save the party he loved. To judge by its conduct since his death, the emotion he felt for it was not reciprocated.

What are we to make of all this? The facts are easily summarised. Gaitskell was born in 1907 into a rather conventional upper-middle-class family, with a strong record of conventional public service. He was educated at Winchester and at New College, Oxford. At Oxford, he was taught by G. D. H. Cole; under Cole's influence, he became involved in the labour movement at the time of the general strike. After a spell as an adult education tutor in the Nottinghamshire coalfield, he became an economics lecturer at London University. During the war, he was a temporary civil servant. He was elected to Parliament in 1945; appointed Minister of Fuel in 1947; and in 1950, at the age of forty-three, succeeded Sir Stafford Cripps as Chancellor of the Exchequer. In opposition, he was the Labour shadow Chancellor from 1951 to 1955. In 1955 he was elected on the first ballot as Attlee's successor as leader of the Labour Party. Just over seven years later, he died, having led his party into a serious defeat in the 1959 general election and having then presided over a period of tumult and schism in which it seemed conceivable that the party might be torn to pieces.

On the surface, it is not a particularly impressive record. Gaitskell was plainly an outstanding administrator, as is shown by his rapid rise in the wartime civil service, but the qualities that make an outstanding administrator are quite different from – indeed, in some ways antithetical to – the qualities needed for political leadership. In the 1945 Government, it is true, he was a competent, and perhaps more than competent, departmental minister. More significantly, he played the key part in persuading the economically 'tone-deaf' Attlee that the run on the reserves which developed in the summer of 1949 should be halted by devaluing sterling rather than by the orthodox methods which had destroyed MacDonald's Labour Government in 1931 and which were to be followed by Wilson's between 1966 and 1967. But, when all is said, it would be absurd to claim that his record as Minister of Fuel deserves more than a page or two in the history of one of the greatest reforming governments of the century.

Certainly, it does not begin to equal Aneurin Bevan's as Minister of Health – or, for that matter, Churchill's or Lloyd George's records as departmental ministers before 1914.

His record as Chancellor of the Exchequer is more controversial, but here too it would be wrong to claim too much. The central problem he faced as Chancellor was how to finance the enhanced rearmament programme on which the Government embarked under American pressure in early 1951. Whatever the technical merits of Gaitskell's solutions, it is clear now that the rearmament programme was impractical and probable that it was damaging. It is clear too that Gaitskell deserves a substantial share of the blame for the Government's decision to embark upon it. In a brilliant memoir, Douglas Jay wrote that, on becoming Chancellor, Gaitskell was:

> faced by the menace of an aggressive Stalin. . . . Here undoubtedly the deep conviction which Hugh had formed in the Munich years played a dominating part in his mind. He did not make the crude mistake of confusing Stalin or Mao with Hitler. But he did believe that military dictators were usually arbitrary and often expansionist; and that military weakness among the democracies . . . invited disaster. For this reason, he became convinced that, as in 1938–40, we must take some deliberate economic risks to defend basic freedoms.[2]

Douglas Jay was one of Gaitskell's closest friends as well as a colleague; his account leaves little doubt that Gaitskell shared the Government's responsibility for embarking on a rearmament programme which could not be carried out, both in the technical sense that he was a member of the Cabinet which approved it, and in the much more important sense that he thought it was right. He was also responsible, of course, for insisting on the health charges which provoked Aneurin Bevan's resignation and which, in doing so, helped to procure one of the most damaging splits in the party's entire history.

Even Gaitskell's record as party leader was by no means dazzlingly successful in the terms by which party leadership is conventionally assessed. He was elected leader in November 1955. In October 1959 his party suffered its third successive election defeat. Gaitskell then embarked on a campaign to rewrite the party's statement of aims and, after a period of furious theological exegesis and ideological hair-splitting, was, for all practical purposes, defeated. This unhappy episode was followed by a furious battle over nuclear disarmament, in which the party conference and the parliamentary party were briefly, but unmistakably, at loggerheads. By the time Gaitskell died in 1963, passions were cooling and Labour's chances of winning the next election seemed to be improving. If he had lived, Labour would probably have won the election – perhaps more decisively than it actually did in 1964 – and he probably would have become a great reforming prime minister. But there can be no certainty: history is littered with the corpses of ex-future-great-prime-ministers who never lived up to expectations. If party leaders are to be judged by their skill at avoiding conflicts with their followers and at winning and holding office, the record shows that Gaitskell was at best a mediocre one.

Then why all the fuss? Why waste time on a dubiously successful Chancellor of the Exchequer who then became a rather unsuccessful Leader of the Opposition? Why did it make sense to talk of 'Gaitskellites' in the way that men once talked of 'Peelites' or 'Bevanites' and now talk of 'Thatcherites', but did not talk of 'Heathites' or 'Wilsonites'? Is there something more to the record than I have suggested so far?

I believe that there is, but I also believe that it is more elusive and more paradoxical than appears at first sight. The answers lie in the last three years of Gaitskell's life – in the period between the 1959 election defeat and the standing ovation which he received from the 1962 Labour Party conference for his speech on the Common Market. It was during that period that the divisions in the Labour Party were at their height. Gaitskell's leadership came under sustained and sometimes virulent attack. In October 1960 he was defeated, narrowly but decisively, at the party conference, on the central issue of the moment. Soon afterwards, Harold Wilson stood against him in the annual election for the party leader. It was the first time an incumbent Labour leader had been challenged in that way since Ramsay MacDonald had challenged Clynes in quite different circumstances nearly forty years before. But, although these were in many ways the blackest years of Gaitskell's public life, it was then that his qualities of passion and will, which had been familiar for a long time to his own circle, first became apparent to a wider public and that his conception of political leadership was put to the test.

For the controversies which convulsed the Labour Party between 1959 and 1962 reflected the unwillingness of many people on the

126

left to adapt themselves to the changes which had taken place in British society – and to the even more disturbing changes which had taken place in Britain's relationship with the rest of the world – since the heroic days of the Attlee Government. Since 1951, a marked improvement had taken place in working-class living standards, and a style of life which had formerly been the prerogative of the middle class began to spread to at least a section of the working class as well. At the same time, thanks partly to the wartime coalition and partly to the Attlee Government itself, a revolutionary change had taken place in the relationship between the state and the private sector of the economy; as a result, governments of both parties accepted – and seemed, in practice, able to fulfil – the commitment to maintain full employment which had first been made during the war. Meanwhile, Britain's power *vis-à-vis* the outside world shrank steadily as Europe recovered from wartime devastation and as technological change made it more and more difficult for any but a superpower to defend itself by its own efforts.

The impact of these changes on the British people was bound to be disorientating. For a variety of reasons, the impact on the British left was particularly so. In retrospect, it is clear that the social changes that took place in the 1950s were often misunderstood. The 'affluent society' was not as affluent as it looked. The comfortable assumption of those days that rising prosperity would lead to greater equality later proved to be, not merely untrue, but in many ways the reverse of the truth. As the general standard of living rose, a growing minority fell behind; though absolute deprivation diminished, relative deprivation increased. But although contemporaries may have misunderstood them there is no doubt that important social changes did take place, or that their implications for the Labour Party were deeply disturbing.

The Labour Party had never accepted the Marxist doctrine of the class struggle in its pure form. All the same, it had seen itself as a working-class party, committed, above all, to the defence of working-class interests. Though it had many middle-class supporters, and a proportionately larger number of middle-class Members of Parliament, its electoral base had traditionally consisted, in the last resort, of the organised manual working class. Now it was beginning to look as if a working-class party of the kind which the Labour Party had been for most of its history might suffer a steady erosion in its support. To those brought up on the notion that the working class was, by definition, the chief agent of social progress, this conclusion was deeply – and shockingly – unpalatable.

The implications of the change which had taken place in the relationship between the state and the private sector of the economy were more unpalatable still. Since 1918, the Labour Party had been committed to the 'common ownership of the means of production, distribution and exchange'. Between 1945 and 1950, the Attlee Government had passed a great series of nationalisation measures. In the leadership, few wished to go further, but most ordinary party members had seen these measures as the first wave and had assumed that they would one day be followed by a second wave. Now, ten years later, it looked as if one of the chief intellectual assumptions on which the party's commitment to public ownership was based had been exploded. Before the war, it had been universally assumed – by the right wing of the party as much as by the left, by Ramsay MacDonald as much as by James Maxton – that the cycle of boom and slump and the mass unemployment associated with it were incurable without public ownership. There were other arguments for public ownership as well, but this was overwhelmingly the most potent. Now the argument had been disproved. It seemed that governments could iron out the swings of the trade cycle and maintain full employment whether they had a large public sector or not. More alarming still, Conservative governments seemed as able – and as willing – to do this as were socialist governments. Public ownership could still be advocated on moral grounds. But it could no longer be argued seriously that capitalism was doomed to an endless series of economic crises, from which public ownership provided the only escape.

The implications of the change which had taken place in Britain's relationship with the rest of the world were equally unsettling, though in a more subtle way. Unlike some continental socialist parties in the heroic age of classical social democracy, the British Labour Party had never been, in any sense, an anti-national party. Most of it, for most of its history, had been as deeply and conventionally patriotic as were most of its working-class supporters. Even those who were not conventionally patriotic were more often 'little England' radicals in the nineteenth-century sense than socialist internationalists; and most of them had inherited the assumptions, as well as the values, of their radical ancestors. They could, and frequently did, protest violently against what they saw as the abuse of British power, but they took it for granted that Britain had power to abuse. As strongly as Charles James Fox or Richard Cobden or John Bright, they believed that Britain should give a moral lead to the rest of the world; as unshakeably as Fox or Cobden or Bright, they assumed that when Britain spoke, the rest of the world would listen. Now that assumption too was beginning to crumble at the edges. As George Orwell once pointed out, the 'Little England' radicalism of the nineteenth century was a product of the *pax Britannica*, guaranteed, in the last resort, by the Royal Navy. Now the Royal Navy could no longer even guarantee Britain's own security. In the last resort, her security was guaranteed by the United States strategic air force.

This, then, was the condition of the Labour Party immediately after the 1959 election. It had just been defeated for the third time by an even larger majority than before. Technical change was narrowing its traditional working-class base, while social and economic changes were loosening its hold on the loyalty of that base. The central assumption of its traditional ideology had been undermined. Its most cherished assumptions about Britain's place in the world and about the nature and purposes of British foreign policy had been called into question. It is hardly surprising that it should have embarked on a series of internal controversies, unequalled in passion even in its stormy history.

There were, in fact, three controversies: over the party's commitment to public ownership, enshrined in Clause Four of the 1918 constitution; over unilateral nuclear disarmament and British membership of NATO; and, last but by no means least, over British entry into the European Community. In different ways, these three controversies all reflected the changes I have just described: and it was because the changes were so disturbing that the controversies were so passionate. Thanks to the passion they engendered, moreover, they in turn raised still more disturbing questions about the nature of the Labour Party and, on a deeper level, about the nature of left-wing politics in a modern mixed economy and of political leadership in a modern mass democracy. It is in the answers he gave to this last set of questions that Gaitskell's true legacy lies.

It would be absurd to claim that the line he took in the three controversies over the Common Market, nuclear disarmament and public ownership has, in every detail, stood the test of time. His great speech on the Common Market at the 1962 Labour Party conference contained a rather perfunctory attempt to weigh up the economic pros and cons of entry, but it was not the economic analysis which won him a standing ovation then or which echoes in the memory now. The reason why his speech evoked such enthusiasm from the audience was that he appealed, with all the passionate conviction he could muster, to precisely that 'Little England' nationalism which had always been so deeply embedded in the labour movement; and the reason he was able to appeal to it is that he shared it himself. When he evoked 'a thousand years of history' he meant what he said; it was because they could see that he meant what he said that his audience responded as they did. The economic historian Michael Postan, who knew Gaitskell well between the wars, painted a revealing picture of his political attitudes in the 1930s.

[H]e invariably placed his own socialist ideas and his visions of the future in a purely English setting. In one of our conversations with Tawney in 1933 we got him to describe his social work in the slums of pre-1914 Manchester, and heard him say all through that time he felt humiliated by the sight of 'his fellow Englishmen' in their abject condition. Later, when left alone with Hugh, I commented on the words used – fellow Englishmen, not fellow human beings – but Hugh, after a brief pause, confessed that he would have used the same words. He had reasoned himself into international socialism, but his vision of the future was one of England's Jerusalem. During his sojourn in Vienna he soon established contacts with the local party, formed close personal links with one or two individuals and was drawn into the actual business of the Socialist risings. But on the whole his residence abroad brought home to him his Englishness, his dependence on the English milieu, and his preference for English ways. On the day of his return to London, Eileen Power and I met him at the Russell Square Underground and took him out for a meal to a grill room in Southampton Row. Once inside he eagerly sniffed the air and his face lit up. 'English sausages, how much I missed them in Vienna!'[3]

A liking for English sausages is not, of course, incompatible with support for British membership of the European Community. Europeanism can and perhaps should go hand in hand with a respect for national differences: the Community is not, and cannot be, an American-style melting pot. But that is not the point. The point is that what Postan referred to as Gaitskell's 'Englishness' extended from sausages to politics. Unlike many of his younger followers, he was not stirred emotionally by the vision of an ancient continent transcending national statehood and burying national hatreds while cherishing cultural diversity. What stirred him was the Churchillian vision of the open sea: the vision of a Britain (or perhaps an England) with worldwide ties and a worldwide vocation, more splendid than that available to any merely European state. It was, of course, a common vision in his generation. Unfortunately, it blinded him to the new international realities which had already led Macmillan's Conservative Government to apply for Community membership and which were shortly to lead Wilson's Labour Government to do the same. Had he lived to experience these new realities in office, he might, of course, have changed his mind as so many of his contemporaries did. The fact remains that, on this issue, he led his party firmly towards the past.

On nuclear disarmament and the Labour Party constitution, matters are more complicated. The first raised two questions, not one. One was whether Britain should possess nuclear weapons herself. The other was whether she should remain in a North Atlantic alliance that possessed nuclear weapons. On the British deterrent, Gaitskell was prepared to compromise. He was unwilling to abandon the ageing, but still functioning, British force of V-bombers, but after the failure of the Blue Streak missile tests he was ready – if with misgivings – to accept that the days of a genuinely independent British deterrent were numbered. As for the notion that Britain might preserve the fiction of nuclear independence by taking an American delivery system, that seemed to him 'a rather dishonest verbal trick'.[4]

British membership of a nuclear-armed NATO was another matter. On that he staked his political life. It is, of course, impossible to prove that he was right. In this, as in most great political battles, questions of fact and questions of value were inextricably confused. Even the former cannot be answered with any certainty. We cannot know what would have happened if the Labour Party had committed itself to leaving NATO; still less can we know what would have happened if a Labour Government had actually left it. What is clear is that, in fighting for British membership of NATO, Gaitskell was fighting for the sheet anchor of post-war British foreign policy: that the battle over nuclear disarmament was, at bottom, a battle over the international dimension of the post-war settlement of which the post-war Labour Government had been the chief architect. Though they did not always admit or even realise the fact, the unilateralists were trying to unpick the seams laboriously stitched by Ernest Bevin to reopen the debate which the crises and contingencies of the 1940s had closed. There was a case for doing so. The structure of international relationships which Bevin had bequeathed to his country and party was not the only possible one, and it is not self-evident that it was the best. Gaitskell's assumption that it was may have been mistaken then, and cannot be taken for granted now. But, to make the case, it would have been necessary to propose an alternative structure, based on an alternative assessment of the facts of power. The Labour unilateralists were too divided, too preoccupied by the imperatives of party faction-fighting and, above all, too unwilling to come to terms with the role of power in international affairs to do anything of the sort. The choice before the party was not a choice between one foreign policy and another. It was a choice between a foreign policy and a new version of the old radical dream of a world in which foreign policy would be unnecessary. It is hard to see how any party leader with a hope of holding government office could have chosen differently.

On nuclear disarmament, Gaitskell fought for the party status quo. On Clause Four, he fought against it. To be sure, he did not believe that public ownership should never be extended or that the Labour Party should never fight an election on a proposal to extend it. He did however, believe that it should cease to be regarded as the essence of socialism; that it should be seen as a means to an end, to be used as and when circumstances might dictate; and that the Labour Party should declare openly and explicitly that its fundamental commitment was to certain moral values – above all, to the values of equality and fraternity – to which public ownership was subordinate and might be irrelevant. Here too some of the assumptions underlying his argument have worn thin. He was trying to marry socialism with Keynesianism: to revise Labour's traditional ideology in the light of the full employment and rising living standards which the Keynesian revolution was believed to have made possible. A generation later, the Keynesian era no longer seems the unquestioned success that it seemed in the 1950s and early 1960s, and it has become clear that, in an increasingly interdependent world economy with intensifying international competition, even the best-intentioned British government may be unable to follow Keynesian policies if other governments do not. Above all, it has become clear that we can no longer look forward indefinitely to a steady improvement in the material standard of living, as measured by the familiar criterion of *per capita* GDP. Because of all this, the revisionism of the 1950s – the doctrine which was set out at its most persuasive in Anthony Crosland's *The Future of Socialism* and which provided the intellectual underpinning for Gaitskell's attack on Clause Four – is now a candidate for revision.

But that is not what the argument was about in 1959 and 1960. Gaitskell's opponents in the Clause Four battle were not trying to revise revisionism; they were trying to defeat it. They were trying to defeat it, moreover, not because they did not intend to practise it but because they did not want to say they would practise it. No one was then proposing big extensions of public ownership. To use Henry Drucker's distinction, Clause Four encapsulated the ethos of the party rather than its doctrine.[5] It told party members that, in a changing and in some ways disturbing world, they still belonged to the same old Labour Party, rooted in the experience and culture of the working class; that no matter what the party did or failed to do, its heart was still in the right place. No implications followed for the policies of a future Labour Government. The battle was about symbols, not about policies. That, of course, was what many of Gaitskell's opponents (including some who normally supported him) objected to. Why fight over symbols, the argument ran, when policies are what matter? And why attack cherished symbols, in an inevitably divisive fashion, when there is no need to do so? Gaitskell was fighting the wrong battle at the wrong time, later critics have echoed: he brought his defeat on himself.

So, in a sense, he did. On nuclear disarmament, he was the defender, but on Clause Four the aggressor. He was under no obligation to rewrite the party's aims. He could perfectly well have lain low. Had he done so, he would have been better placed to resist – perhaps even to deflect – the unilateralist tide a few months later. Yet these calculations miss the point. Gaitskell cannot have known that he would lose, but he must have known that he was running big risks. He did so for two reasons. During the row over the health charges in 1951, his old patron, Hugh Dalton, in general a warm, not to say bigoted, admirer, complained that 'H. G. thought too little of the Party and too much, relatively, of the general body of the electorate.'[6] On the face of it, it is almost inconceivable that one democratic politician could have seen that as a ground for complaint against another, but in the hermetic world of the Labour Party the charge made ominous sense. In Gaitskell's case, it was deserved. In

Labour Party terms, he *did* think too much of the wider electorate outside the walls of the traditional Labour fortresses; that was what his critics meant when they accused him of failing to understand the labour movement. The truth was that he understood it only too well, and wished to change it. He also understood that the things he wanted to change had to do with ethos rather than with doctrine and therefore with symbols rather than with policies. It was not policy that had caused Labour to lose in 1959; it was image and impression. Though he would not have put it in this way, he wanted to transcend Labourism: to turn the Labour Party into the natural, instead of an occasional, home of the non-Labour constituency which it had captured in 1945, but lost thereafter. He sensed rather than saw that this could not be done without a dramatic, visible and almost certainly painful cultural transformation. To procure such a transformation, to shock his party into changing the way in which it saw itself and the society around it, he had to take the offensive. Defeat undoubtedly weakened him and his cause. Not only did Clause Four stay in the party constitution; the fact that it stayed there in spite of the leader's attempts to remove it reinforced the walls which he had wished to knock down. But if he had been unwilling to join battle he would have lost anyway.

The second reason goes deeper. In 1953, at the height of the Bevanite row but well before the Clause Four conflict, Gaitskell described the political approach which he and his friends had tried to follow in the 1930s.

The most fundamental ideal of those who shared this outlook was social justice – but it was an ideal in no way inspired by class hatred. They were equally devoted to democracy and personal freedom. They believed in tolerance and they understood the need for compromise. They were for the rational and practical and suspicious of large general ideas which on examination turned out to have no precise content. . . .

They were realistic in politics and critical of armchair politicians who, not understanding what the British electorate was really like, were forever making bad political judgements. Above all, while accepting the ultimate emotional basis of moral valuation, they had great faith in the power of reason, both to find answers to social problems and to persuade men to see the light. They were for the pursuit of truth to the bitter end, through the patient and unswerving application of logical thought. They wanted no barriers of prejudice to obstruct the free working of the mind or to blunt the sharp edge of intellectual integrity.[7]

'For the pursuit of truth to the bitter end': 'to persuade men to see the light'. Rhetoric, no doubt, but revealing rhetoric. In Peter Clarke's terminology, Gaitskell was a moral reformer, not a mechanical one. Intellectually, he was a Fabian utilitarian, imbued with the positivist rationalism which was coming into fashion in his early manhood. That was the source of Bevan's famous jibe, 'the desiccated calculating machine'.[8] Beneath the rationalist carapace, however, was a turbulent and passionate political romantic, a latter-day Gladstonian. In his early years as party leader, the rationalist was mostly in control. After 1959, perhaps because he reckoned that he now had nothing to lose, the romantic broke free. He *would* now pursue truth to the bitter end: he would no longer allow barriers of prejudice to obstruct the free working of the mind: putting his faith in the power of reason, he *would* try to persuade his party to see the light. In doing so, he breathed new life into the internal schism which had begun in the closing years of the Attlee Government. But the schism would have continued whatever he had done. It sprang from the very nature of the party; and it grew wider, not narrower, under his more conciliatory successor. The choice did not lie between schism and no schism. It lay between open debate about the party's nature and mission, and elite manipulation.

For, in raising the question as he did, Gaitskell brought the whole party face to face with it. For the first time since 1918, party members were invited to determine, not merely what should be in the next election programme, but what their party should stand for. Party ideology was treated, not as the property of the leadership, to be changed by pragmatic accommodations when in office, but as the property of the party as a whole, to be changed (or not changed) through a process of discussion and debate. Whatever its short-term disadvantages – and they were many – the whole exercise was a profoundly democratic one, for it was based on the assumption that ordinary, rank-and-file members of the Labour Party were rational adults, who could understand a rational argument and who deserved to be treated as such. Gaitskell may have been unwise to make that assumption, but it is hard to see how democratic politics can proceed on any other basis.

It would be wrong to idealise him. Gaitskell was no plaster saint of participatory democracy. His path to the Labour leadership was smoothed by the block votes of heresy-hunting right-wing trade union leaders looking for a hammer to crush the left. Having become leader with the aid of the block vote, he was then sustained by it – at any rate until the Clause Four conflict. There is no evidence that he had any qualms about the way in which it was used, or any wish to banish it from the party's affairs. He emerges from his diary as a bit of a prig, with more than a touch of the school prefect about him. All too often, his private charm and grace went hand in hand with a curiously unimaginative inflexibility. What his supporters saw as courage and determination, his opponents had some justification in seeing as rigidity and stubbornness. Yet, when all the qualifications have been made, his conduct during the three stormy years before his death remains an inspiration for all who believe that representative democracy depends on trust between representatives and represented, and that trust is built on telling the truth. Not the least of the reasons why the progressive dilemma remains unresolved is that the same can be said of no other leader of his party.

Richard Crossman:
The Progressive as Gadfly

The post-1918 effort to apply the principles of Lockeian Liberalism to the building of a machinery of international order has
failed as decisively as the Conservative struggle to return to pre-
War 'normalcy'. The belief in national governmental organisation as the instrument of positive good is also undermined.
In short, the economic and social conditions which rendered
Liberalism so palatable have gone, and we are at last aware
that they have gone. For the first time since the era of Hobbes
we are faced by problems which demand a radical solution, and
which cannot be shelved by kindly compromise and 'muddling
through'. At last we too have reached a crisis where the only
practical course open to us is to become philosophers and under-
take a radical analysis of the fundamental postulates of our
society.[1]

So the thirty-year-old Richard Crossman, Hugh Gaitskell's scintil-
lating and unruly Winchester contemporary, a few years before the
Second World War. The passage is taken from an essay on 'The
Theory and Practice of British Freedom', written when the author
was still Dean of New College, Oxford and leader of the Labour
Group on Oxford City Council, and reprinted in a collection of
theoretical writings in 1965, shortly after he had become a member
of the first Wilson Cabinet. Set in the context of the essay from
which it comes, it provides an ideal vantage point from which to
assess one of the most engaging and least easily classified figures in
the recent history of the British left.

In 'The Theory and Practice of British Freedom' Crossman argued
that the Englishman's notorious aversion from political philosophy
as it had been understood on the continent was due, not to innate
incapacity and still less to innate intellectual virtue, but to a historical
accident which had come to an end. From 1688 Lockeian Liberalism

reigned unchallenged in England, not because of its intellectual merits but because there was no good reason to challenge it. Englishmen saw no point in speculating on the fundamental questions of political philosophy, not because such speculation was in fact worthless, but merely because the questions had already been answered by the Revolution Settlement, in a way which continued to satisfy the holders of economic and political power. But, Crossman went on, that happy state of affairs had now come to an end. Since 1931, the traditional Lockeian answers had been exhausted. Because of this, the traditional questions, which had been evaded for 250 years, would have to be asked and answered anew.

But what should the answers be? This, of course, was the crucial question; and it is here that the enduring significance of the essay lies. For Crossman gave no answers. Like most left-wing intellectuals at the time, he recognised the inadequacies of traditional liberal pragmatism and 'muddling through'. But unlike many of his contemporaries he also recognised the inadequacies of the alternatives most commonly accepted at the time, and avoided the Marxist fire as carefully as the empiricist frying-pan. He regarded Marxism – and, for that matter, pacifism – as 'emotional reactions' to the crisis he had diagnosed, not as 'positive contributions' to its solution. But having exposed the inadequacies of traditional liberal pragmatism, and dismissed Marxism and pacifism as dogmatic pseudo-solutions, he offered no alternative of his own to put in their place. His essay was a magnificent intellectual demolition job: brilliant, exciting and carried through with exhilarating zest and power. But when the demolition was over, the site was left vacant.

That was to be the *leitmotiv* of the author's career. Richard Howard Stafford Crossman was born in 1907 in a comfortable upper-middle-class professional family of the utmost conventionality. His father, Charles Stafford Crossman, was a cautious and industrious Chancery barrister – according to his son, the 'very paradigm of the judicial mind' – who rose to the bench in 1934. Like his father, Crossman won a scholarship to Winchester at the age of twelve. He ended his school career by becoming prefect of hall and winning a scholarship to New College, Oxford where he won a double First in 'mods' and 'greats'. At twenty-three, he became a Fellow and Tutor of New College, having spent a year in an increasingly strife-torn Germany, but knowing nothing else of the world beyond the confines of the southern English mandarinate of which his father was an ornament.

Father and son both had first-class academic minds. In every other way, they were poles apart. The neat, dry, bewigged father peers apprehensively from his official court photograph at a world he obviously finds disordered and disconcerting. The son was a big, powerful, untidy, bear-like man, with the physique of the second-row Rugby forward he had once been, radiating physical and intellectual vitality and coruscating with mischief. He was one of the best lecturers I have ever heard – lucid, exuberant, sometimes gloriously perverse and, above all, unfailingly exciting. He was also a superb journalist, with an economical, unpretentious, captivating style. He had the reputation of being an intellectual bully, and he certainly showed no mercy to the dialectically meek. Unlike the true bully, however, he wanted to get as good as he gave; the purpose of the exercise was not to trample on others but to provoke them into standing up for themselves. From his adolescence onwards, he was in passionate revolt against his father and all the dusty things that seemed to him to symbolise his father: the legal profession, bourgeois morality, cautious pedantry, conservative politics. As he wrote years later, a life lived 'within the confines of the law' had turned his father's natural caution into:

> a conformity so intense that he was scared in the end of any kind of moral or intellectual innovation. In my case, the rough-house of political warfare and political journalism has enlarged the priceless bump of irreverence I inherited from my mother, and has made me feel that, in a country where free thought and action are almost smothered under sheer respectability, the most useful contribution I can make to public life is to expose the cowardice of conformity wherever I detect it, and challenge the organised hypocrisy of the Establishment.[2]

Yet, for all the bump of irreverence, there was a curious strain of diffidence in his make-up, only half-concealed by the minatory finger and challenging voice. He was a rebel against authority, but he half-wanted its approval; as his former parliamentary private secretary has pointed out, he was born into the 'epicentre of the establishment'[3] and, in spite of his oft-expressed contempt for it, he never quite threw off the legacy of his early indoctrination in its values. He was fascinated by power, contemptuous of sentimentalists who ignored the realities of power and anxious, as any ambitious politician is bound to be, to wield power. But his diaries give the impression that he did not really enjoy power or find it natural. Whitehall was, for him, an alien, forbidding place. His minister's room, he wrote in the immortal opening paragraph of his ministerial diary, 'is like a padded cell, and in certain ways I am like a person who is suddenly certified a lunatic and put safely into this great, vast room, cut off from real life and surrounded by male and female trained nurses and attendants'.[4] Later he got used to its ways, but he was never fully at home there. The same strain of diffidence emerged in his relations with his prime ministerial patron, Harold Wilson. By any reckoning he was a far more considerable figure than Wilson, and he soon realised that Wilson's inveterate unwillingness to think ahead was doing great damage to the Government and party. But, in spite of continual grumbling, he continued to think of himself as a loyal lieutenant to Wilson, influential only insofar as he could influence Wilson, rather than as the possessor of an independent power base of his own.

His first big challenge to 'the organised hypocrisy of the establishment' was a magnificent exercise in *haute vulgarisation* called *Plato Today*.[5] His Plato was a 'respectable', change-fearing, life-diminishing and establishment-upholding moderate conservative, who sounds remarkably like a rather superior, but possibly more menacing, version of Mr Justice Crossman. Against him he pitted a democratic and subversive Socrates, 'incorruptible, intolerant of sham, greedy for every variety of human experience, insatiable in discussion, ironic and yet serious' – condemned to die because 'such a spirit is generally intolerable to any well-organised community'.[6] This was followed by a panoramic survey of the history of political thought from the Renaissance to the 1930s, called *Government and the Governed*.[7] But academe could not hold him for long. He was the leader of the Labour group on Oxford City Council at twenty-seven, Labour candidate for West Birmingham at thirty and assistant editor of the *New Statesman* at thirty-one. After five years helping to run Britain's wartime propaganda against Nazi Germany, he entered Parliament at the age of thirty-eight. Despite his talents, he was denied preferment; Attlee, a close friend of his parents, had been shocked by his rebellious behaviour as a young man, and he had compounded his crime by leading a backbench revolt against Ernest Bevin's Palestine policy. Gradually, he drifted to the left. In the early 1950s he acted as a rather mutinous, though intermittently influential, chief of staff to Aneurin Bevan; though the inner circle of Bevanites viewed him somewhat askance after he supported Wilson's decision to take

Bevan's place in the shadow Cabinet when Bevan resigned from it in 1955, he was much more suspect to the party loyalists on the right.

His role in the incessant internal party manoeuvres of the period is, however, less significant in retrospect than his contribution to the developing debate over Labour's philosophy and stance. It was a characterisically paradoxical one. In 1951 he edited a volume of 'new' Fabian essays, which was explicitly intended to do for the socialism of the post-war world what the original Fabian essays had done for that of the late nineteenth and early twentieth centuries. It was a remarkable volume, containing essays by Anthony Crosland, Roy Jenkins, Denis Healey and John Strachey, pointing the way to the 'revisionist' social democracy which was to give the party leadership its governing philosophy for the best part of twenty years. Even in this company, Crossman's introduction stood out. It promulgated, with exhilarating eloquence and emotional power, a programme for socialist theory in opposition. The reforms of the post-war Labour Government, Crossman argued, had not really been socialist after all. The transformation of empire into Commonwealth was 'essentially liberal'; the welfare state was essentially 'the adaptation of capitalism to the demands of modern trade unionism'. They were important achievements, but the road which led to them had now come to an end. 'Buffeted and battered', the Labour Party was 'travelling in strange country, exposed to climatic rigours it had not anticipated and against which its traditional equipment gave little protection'. It could recover only if it ceased to rely on mere ' "hunch" and empirical experience' and turned instead to fundamental thinking. For pragmatism was bankrupt: and 'philosophy begins where pragmatism fails'.

But what should the new philosophy be? Here Crossman was more cautious. Marxism was as irrelevant as ever; and the fashionable political quietism of the 1940s was worse than irrelevant:

> Facing the century of totalitarianism we can choose between two philosophies, symbolised by the figures of Buddha and Prometheus. Buddha represents the withdrawal from the struggle for freedom. For the Oriental Buddhist and for the Western defeatist, intellectual humility is the greatest virtue; the good man is not involved, but detached; he accepts this world as a vale of woe and seeks realisation in a transcendental eternity. The other philosophy, that of the sceptical humanist, is symbol-

141

ised by Prometheus, chained to his Caucasian peak, with the eagle pecking out his liver. Prometheus stole fire from the Gods in order to help his fellow man. He did not believe that any law of nature or divine purpose would automatically give them freedom and happiness. . . . So too the humanist today knows that we are surrounded by misery and injustice, and that it is quite possible that all we have achieved in Western Europe may be destroyed. But he also knows that it is man's destiny to struggle against this natural process, and that there is no more justification of pessimism in politics than there is for a gardener to say, 'I'll give up weeding because it's a wet summer.'[8]

In itself, however, 'freedom' is a negative ideal. If it is to be a guide to positive action, it must be set against the background of the concrete restrictions on freedom which are to be removed or resisted. For Crossman, there were three restrictions which mattered most. The welfare capitalism of the post-war Labour Government fell short of socialism, he argued, because the concentration of capital and economic privilege remained unchanged; because profits, wages and salaries were still determined, not by considerations of social justice or the national interest, but by old-fashioned *laisser-faire*; and above all, because effective industrial and political power still remained in the hands 'of a small managerial and civil service elite'. The real enemy, in fact, was the Managerial Revolution; and the main task of socialism was 'to prevent the concentration of power in the hands of *either* industrial management *or* the state bureaucracy – in brief, to distribute responsibility and so to enlarge freedom of choice'.

It would be unreasonable to cavil at Crossman's failure to elaborate these three points in more detail at the time when they were first made. They were, after all, explicitly designed as tentative signposts to the uncharted terrain which lay ahead, not as maps to be followed without further argument. But, as time went on, the uncharted terrain slowly began to be charted. The fundamental thinking which Crossman had called for was in fact begun. In 1956 John Strachey published the first volume of his attempt to revise traditional Marxism in the light of modern democracy. In the same year Anthony Crosland published *The Future of Socialism*, which consisted essentially of an equally ambitious attempt to revise traditional Fabianism in the light of modern economics and sociology. They were followed by Douglas Jay and – outside the ranks of professional politicians

— by Raymond Williams and the new left. By the early 1960s, in fact, the really striking feature of British socialism was no longer the absence of theory, but the plethora of theoreticians: not the end of ideology, but its vigorous revival and growth.

In this Great Debate, however, one voice was conspicuous by its absence. From time to time Crossman continued to produce sudden flashes of illumination — but in the manner of a revolving lighthouse, whose rays dazzle for a moment, and then leave the darkness even blacker than it was before. Just as he had rejected the Marxist alternative to traditional liberalism in the late 1930s, so now he rejected the revisionist alternative to traditional Labourism. But his rejection was oddly defensive and unconvinced. In the early and mid-1950s, after all, he had himself been a pioneer of revisionism. The starting point of his argument in the *New Fabian Essays* was that the traditional attitudes of the labour movement provided no guide to the problems it would face in the future; and in 1956 he had argued, with characteristic force and emphasis, that until socialists had abandoned their old assumption that capitalism was inherently unworkable, they could not even 'begin to think sensibly about the next stage of socialism'.

Yet, by the end of the decade, he had come perilously close to the traditional 'catastrophic' argument, albeit in a different form. True, the catastrophe was no longer economic. Instead, it was political. It lay in the 'inherent' inability of an Affluent Society to achieve an adequate level of investment and generate an adequate rate of economic growth.

we can predict with mathematical certainty that, as long as the public sector of industry remains the minority sector throughout the Western world, we are bound to be defeated in every kind of peaceful competition with the Russians and the Eastern bloc. It is not that our workers are less skilful and energetic, that our managers are less competent, or even that our politicians do their job any worse. The truth is that, whatever our intentions, wishes or individual capabilities, the nations of the Western world will be unable to strengthen themselves by developing adequate public services until the public sector becomes the dominant sector in our economies.[9]

Thus, the Labour Party should refuse to come to terms with the

Affluent Society, as the revisionists allegedly demanded. Instead it should concentrate on warning the nation against the 'coming crisis'.

It was a paradoxical destination for the sceptical humanist of eight years before. Yet the real paradox of Crossman's later essays lies less in such aberrations than in his failure to pursue the argument he began in *New Fabian Essays* and follow it through to a conclusion. For, the more one considers it, the more perceptive and illuminating that argument seems, and the more relevant to the real needs of our time. It was not true that the post-war Labour Government had left the concentration of capital and economic privilege untouched. It was, however, true that the free play of the market was an unsatisfactory (and, on any reasonable definition, unsocialist) basis for the determination of wages, profits and salaries. Above all, it was true that the inveterate economism of the British labour movement had become obsolete – that the oligarchic tendencies endemic in all modern societies ran counter to the humanistic values of democratic socialism; and that these tendencies could be overcome only by giving much higher priority to political and institutional reform. Yet, on that last point, Crossman's was a voice crying in the wilderness. The trade union leadership was unmoved by his suggestion that Britain might have something to learn from the West German experiment with *Mitbestimmung*; the party leadership ignored his plea to 'found our socialist case not only on economic arguments about increased productivity and improved living standards, but also on the defence of personal freedom and personal responsibility in a managerial society'.[10] And, as he feared, Labour's indifference to the classical issues of power, responsibility and democratic control eventually helped to bring about a backlash against the interventionist state, imperilling the social and economic achievements to which the party had given priority.

Then why did he not do more to break through that indifference? Why were his warnings against oligarchy and his trumpet calls for participatory democracy confined to occasional journalism? Why did his introduction to the *New Fabian Essays* remain a prologue without a play? One answer, of course, it that there are only twenty-four hours in a day and seven days in a week: that the demands of popular journalism and active politics left him no time for sustained thinking and writing. Another is that he did considerably more than any other leading politician of the day. As a publicist and backbench rebel in the 1950s, he did at least sound the alarm. His lucid, characteristically overstated but inescapably telling introduction to the Fontana Press edition of Bagehot's *The English Constitution* in 1963 – in which he annexed John Mackintosh's theory of prime-ministerial government to his own earlier concern with oligarchy and responsibility – took the analysis a stage further. When Labour returned to office in 1964, he found himself in the Cabinet as Minister of Housing and Local Government; as such his energies were fully absorbed in the remorseless routine of a departmental minister. But in 1966 Wilson promoted him to be Leader of the House of Commons; and from that citadel of tradition he launched the experiment in specialist investigatory parliamentary committees which has done more than any other single development in the post-war period to open the workings of the executive to democratic scrutiny. On a different level, his decision to publish his ministerial diaries – originally kept as the raw material for the modern Bagehot he hoped to write – was a direct contribution to democratic education, of immense value. His death from cancer at the comparatively early age of sixty-six cut him off with his work uncompleted.

But none of this disposes of the central question. Crossman was a man of immense gifts and restless energy. Had he been driven to develop the tentative, exploratory hints of the early 1950s into a systematic analysis on the scale of Crosland's or Strachey's, he would have made the time to do so. The reason no such analysis appeared is that he was not so driven. Part of the explanation may lie in the strand of diffidence I mentioned earlier. *Plato Today* and *Government and the Governed* were a young man's books, brilliant with promise. That achievement could not be repeated. Perhaps Crossman feared that a sustained treatise was beyond him, or flinched in anticipation from the criticisms it would have attracted.

But I do not think that can be the whole story. As Crossman himself pointed out in 'The Theory and Practice of British Freedom', political theory is the product of social demands, hammered out in a dialogue between the theorist and his audience. Crosland and Strachey both had audiences. Both ran with the grain of the times. Both preached an essentially complacent message to a society exuding complacency: Marx had been proved wrong; Keynesian welfare capitalism had resolved the crisis which loomed so large before the war; slow and gradual incremental change would deliver the goods. Crossman's message would have been deeply disturbing. He would have had to run against the grain, to challenge the conventional pieties of the British state, to demolish and reconstruct the conventional view of politics and political man which underlie them, to undermine what in *Plato Today* he had called the 'dogmatism of inertia'. In the cosy, introverted Britain of the 1950s and early 1960s, steeped in its own version of the Platonic noble lie, there was no audience for a message of that sort. Crossman fell through the gap between two historical worlds. He came too late for the constitutional ferment of the years before the First World War, and too early for the institutional crisis of the 1970s. He was condemned to remain a gadfly – a marvellously provocative, hugely life-enhancing gadfly, no doubt, but not the philosopher of the democratic revolution he had dreamed of as a young man.

The Tortoise and the Hare

After a decade and a half of decline, the old, Fabian right of the Labour Party is now so chastened that it is hard to remember it was once the dominant tradition of British left-wing politics. Two volumes of autobiography[1] bring back its greatest days: in doing so, they also throw a good deal of unintentional light on the reasons for its fall. Michael Stewart and Douglas Jay were both awarded Firsts at Oxford in the 1920s, entered Labour politics in the 1930s, held junior office in the Attlee Government in the 1940s, supported Gaitskell in the battles of the 1950s and were appointed to Wilson's Cabinet in the 1960s. Both served their country and party honourably, faithfully and as selflessly as anyone can reasonably be expected to do. Both exhibited, to an almost alarming degree, the characteristic Fabian virtues of rationality and reliability. Both were so obviously fish out of water in the Labour Party of the 1980s that the reader could almost hear them gasping for breath. Neither had the remotest idea why.

Douglas Jay belongs to the aristocracy of Fabianism; Michael Stewart belonged to its bourgeoisie. Jay is a quintessential mandarin: old Wykehamist, scholar of New College, Fellow of All Souls. At twenty-nine, after spells on *The Times* and the *Economist*, he was appointed City editor of the *Daily Herald*. At thirty, he was an Assistant Secretary in the wartime Ministry of Supply, and at thirty-eight economic adviser to the Prime Minister. He went from the Prime Minister's office to a safe Labour seat in South London, and after only a few months on the back benches was appointed Economic Secretary to the Treasury. When Labour left office in 1951, he had been near the centre of power for the best part of ten years.

Michael Stewart had it harder: from Brownhills Road Elementary School in South London to Christ's Hospital, and from Christ's Hospital to St John's. After Oxford he became a schoolmaster; during the war he rose from lance-corporal in the Intelligence Corps to captain in the Education Corps. While Jay was using the City page of the *Daily Herald* to make propaganda against appeasement, Stewart was teaching economics to sixth-formers; while Jay was helping to set up the Development Areas, Stewart was lecturing to the troops in the Middle East. His ministerial apprenticeship was drabber too. Like Jay, he reached the front bench almost immediately after reaching the House of Commons. But whereas Jay was appointed straightaway to the most powerful and prestigious department in Whitehall, Stewart started as a Whip, the lowest form of ministerial life, and progressed to the Labour Party's equivalent of a Mongolian power-station, a parliamentary secretaryship at the War Office.

In the end, of course, the tortoise beat the hare. Michael Stewart joined the Cabinet in 1964 as Education Secretary, but within a few months he had been promoted to Foreign Secretary. He headed the Foreign Office for a total of three and a half years, and the Department of Economic Affairs for eighteen months. After 1970, it is true, he went to the back benches, but only after five years as one of the central figures in the Wilson Government. The curve of Jay's career, on the other hand, flattened out after the fall of the Attlee Government in 1951. Having climbed steadily, and without apparent effort, for most of his twenties and thirties, he spent his late forties and fifties trudging along a kind of parliamentary plateau – well above the ruck of ordinary backbenchers, but well below the peaks. He was a loyal and courageous Gaitskellite, but his most celebrated intervention on Gaitskell's behalf – an article in the right-wing Labour weekly *Forward*, implying that the Labour Party would never win another election unless it changed its name – did his cause more harm than good. He published another reassessment of socialist theory, but it lacked the sweep and depth of Crosland's and Strachey's contributions on the same side of the ideological divide, and the glitter of Crossman's on the opposite side. In Parliament, he was overtaken by younger men – George Brown, Jim Callaghan, even Denis Healey. When Labour returned to power in 1964, he was given the important, but hardly central, office of President of the Board of Trade. Three years later, he was brutally and unceremoniously sacked. For years he hung on as a backbencher – indomitable, incorruptible, but increasingly isolated, estranged from his natural allies on the right of the party by his detestation of the EEC, and from anti-Marketeers on the left by his loyalty to the revisionist social democracy he first preached forty years ago. Now he sits in the Lords.

Their memoirs redress the balance of their careers. Michael Stewart's is a classic Privy Councillor's autobiography – bland, decorous, full of long descriptions of visits to distant continents, firmly committed to the principle of *nil nisi bunkum* and about as personal as a Cabinet minute. The enormous decency and fair-mindedness of the author come through, but only just. His ideas and feelings, hopes and fears, loves and hates are rigidly suppressed. He tells us that he joined the Labour Party as a schoolboy of sixteen, that insofar as he belongs to any school of socialist thought he is a Tawneian, and that he still accepts the Tawneian thesis 'that capitalist society, based on the principle of individual acquisitiveness, is bound to encounter Nemesis'. Because he tells us, we believe him. But we do not feel the belief. Tawneian socialism, or rather Stewart's conception of Tawneian socialism, remains an abstraction: the schoolboy of sixteen who was converted to it, even the elder statesman of seventy-four who still professed it, remain shadowy and unreal. As a back-bench Labour MP in the late 1960s, I admired Stewart more than almost any other senior minister. On the rare occasions when I encountered him socially, I either froze into a shaming, gawky silence or (even more shamingly) found myself talking much too loud and much too fast. His book had the same effect. One sensed that one was in the presence of that rare animal, a good man. One then stood about, staring at the carpet and wishing that someone would say something.

Jay's, by contrast, is one of the most revealing political autobiographies of the last twenty years. In the first place, he is almost free of bunkum. Even he could not resist long accounts of EFTA ministerial meetings, but these are a small price to pay for his splendidly unedifying inability to think well of his opponents and his robust capacity to pursue old rivalries beyond the grave.

> I never found I could harbour warm sympathy with those who were deeply opposed to my convictions on fundamental issues such as appeasement, or the EEC, which affected the whole future of this country. To maintain amicable relations with people who disagree on minor arguable controversies, including some in other parties, is certainly a refreshing part of democratic life. But tolerance is one thing, and friendship another. It is hard in my experience to feel personal affection towards those who are actively working to destroy, however unconsciously, something for which one cares deeply.[2]

149

Later passages make it clear that that is an understatement. Not only was Jay unable to like or sympathise with his opponents: he wilfully refused to make the slightest effort to understand them. Thus he attributed Roy Jenkins's support for British membership of the European Community to his friendship with the Bonham Carter family and his consequent assimilation into the 'Liberal way of life', Lord Longford's to his membership of the Roman Catholic Church, Michael Stewart's to the influence of the Foreign Office, the Foreign Office's to 'departmental empire-building' and the Conservative Party's to its 'age-long desire' to reimpose taxes on food. The presence in the pro-Market camp of non-Liberal, non-Catholic, non-food-taxing, non-empire-building non-friends of the Bonham Carters was not even acknowledged, much less explained. As a contribution to history this is laughable. Without the support of mainstream Labour social democrats – without the Bill Rodgerses, the Willy Hamiltons, the Vic Feathers and the Roy Granthams – the pro-Market cause would never have triumphed. But what would be inexcusable in a historian can be an advantage in an autobiographer. Jay's resolute refusal to assume a mellowness he did not feel gave his book spice it would otherwise have lacked. It also helps his readers to understand why he acted as he did.

The same is true of his strange, half-envious, half-disapproving relationship with Richard Crossman, a Winchester and New College contemporary. After they left Winchester, Crossman was Jay's closest confidant. But he let him down over an arrangement to share digs, and the shock to Jay was so 'stunning' that they did not speak again for some years. Looking back, Jay evidently saw Crossman as a kind of fallen angel, personifying the anti-Fabian (and anti-Wykehamist) principle of Unreliability. Crossman is for ever blurting things out when they ought to be kept secret, allowing himself to be captured by ephemeral enthusiasms for the fashionable and the meretricious, unsettling everybody by changing his mind for no good reason and, above all, making a fool of himself by allowing his unreliability and frivolity to be detected by others. At Winchester, he competes for the English poetry prize with 'an elaborate and rather unintelligible composition in the latest fashionable style of T. S. Eliot'. He is beaten by Jay, who has the sense to play safe 'with a series of sonnets in the manner of Matthew Arnold, Wordsworth and Keats'. At Oxford, he loudly proclaims his intention of competing for the Chancellor's English essay prize, only to forget all about it. As a new backbencher in the House of Commons, he 'recklessly'

moves a critical amendment to the Address, and then fails to vote
for it. As a fellow Cabinet minister, he makes his colleagues wonder
whether his prime object is 'to carry out the Government's policies
or to collect material for his diaries'. For all this, there is a simple
explanation. Not only was Crossman's mother half-German, but
one of his maternal grandfathers was wholly German. That fact,
Jay writes darkly, 'contributed, I realised in later years, to a fair
understanding of Dick'.

Jay's interpretation of it contributes even more to a fair understanding of Jay. He saw himself, above all, as British patriot (or
perhaps as an English one: significantly, he uses the words interchan-
geably, as though the Scots and Welsh did not exist) – in love with
British ways, practising, as best he can, the solid, unpretentious
British virtues and defending the British heritage from the slick, the
glib and the cosmopolitan. The tastes which enabled him to beat
Crossman in the competition for the poetry prize at Winchester
remained with him at Oxford. There, Jay tells us, D. H. Lawrence
and *The Waste Land* 'attained almost the status of cults'. However,
his own 'lifelong distaste for fashion led me, I fear, somewhat to
undervalue them. It was Hardy, Yeats, Matthew Arnold, Housman
and above all Shakespeare's Sonnets which to me rang truest and
struck deepest.' In a moving passage at the end of the book, he
wrote that, as he grew older, he became more attached to the values
of Athens as against those of Sparta:

> It may seem paradoxical to add that for that very reason my
> admiration for the spirit and institutions of this country grew
> incomparably stronger in the years 1939 and 1940, when I
> suppose the British showed the greatest fidelity in their history
> to the Spartan virtues. But in those years the British people also
> seemed to me to believe that they had something precious to
> defend, and wished to establish something even more civilised
> thereafter. What other country, after all, has preserved an
> unbroken record of constitutional government for nearly 300
> years, and fought right through the two Great Wars, without
> attacking anyone else or being first attacked, to eventual vic-
> tory? In a morass of transient controversies, let us not forget
> that. It is one reason why I can conceive of no better fortune
> when the time comes to cultivate private rather than public
> aspirations, than to live, love, garden and die, deep in the
> English country.[3]

There is, of course, no logical connection between a love of Housman or the English countryside – or, for that matter, an admiration for Britain's stand in 1940 – and opposition to membership of the EEC. In Jay's case, at any rate, the emotional connection is so obvious that it scarcely needs pointing out: to him, being British meant, among other things, not being European. Less obviously, his attitudes to England, English literature and English history also help to explain his otherwise baffling inability to understand his opponents on the opposite side of the argument. For the pro-Marketeers were patriots too: but with a different sort of patriotism. For them, Britain was part of Europe, culturally, socially and politically as well as geographically. British history was a theme in European history, incomprehensible apart from the other European themes which were interwoven with it. To stand aside from the European union developing on the other side of the Channel would have been to deny, not perhaps Hugh Gaitskell's tendentious 'thousand years of history', but the two thousand years since the Roman legions first set foot on British soil. Thus, for Jay, the pro-Marketeers' victory was an emotional affront as well as a political defeat. He could not bring himself to find out what the pro-Marketeers really thought, because he could not bring himself to admit that he was defeated by the forces which in fact defeated him. He could not do so because the very existence of those forces – or, at any rate, their existence in sufficient strength to win – denied both his view of the world and his image of himself.

None of this was true of Stewart. Like most Labour politicians, he was sceptical about British membership of the Community in the 1950s. But he changed his mind in the 1960s; thereafter he was one of the staunchest pro-Marketeers in the Labour Party. On domestic policy, too, his attitudes were by no means identical with Jay's. Though a right-winger, he was usually closer to the 'centre' of the Labour Party than Jay. Had he not become Foreign Secretary, he would probably have been one of the most egalitarian Education Ministers in British history, a role which Jay would have found hard to fill. Despite these differences, however, it is the similarities between the two that strike the reader most, and it is in these similarities that their significance in Labour history lies.

Both first held ministerial office in the Attlee Government; both pay affectionate and perceptive tributes to Attlee's character and achievements; both can best be understood politically as Attlee's children. The term is most obviously appropriate for Jay. 'Attlee',

152

he wrote, 'was a straightforward Victorian Christian, who believed one should do one's job and one's duty, whether as an Army Officer or Member of Parliament or Prime Minister'; his own father, he added, 'was in character a similar type, and sprang from a similar background; so that the characteristics were not unrecognisable to me'. Stewart did not make an explicit comparison of that sort, but the reader senses a similar response:

> The reliable, self-respecting working man and his wife, who have learned that if they want justice they must strive for it themselves, not wait for the gentry to give it to them – these are the rock on which the Labour Party was built, and it was these who Clem not only represented, but came to personify. . . . Starting with conventional middle-class – and working-class – beliefs in King, Country and empire, he had the vision to see how these ideas must develop in the 20th century: defence of the country required not only adequate forces but collective international action, and the Empire must become a multi-racial Commonwealth. . . . As the record of his Government shows, he was 'left-wing' on matters of public ownership and the distribution of wealth, but had no patience with those who asked for the moon or expected everything to be done at once.[4]

It is a good picture of Attlee and, for that matter, a good picture of Stewart. For those, like me, who grew up when the Attlee Revolution was in full swing, it is also an immensely attractive picture. Attlee was not the saintly figure some Labour mythologists have depicted. But the government he headed did more good to more people than any other British government of this century, and did it in a more honourable and honest way. As that formulation implies, it was, of course, a distinctly paternalist government, anxious to do good to people rather than to create the conditions in which people might do good to themselves and to each other: 'the reliable, self-respecting working man' is apt to have a short way with the unreliable and unself-respecting. But although we are now conscious of the limits of paternalism, even of the most attractive sort, it would be anachronistic to blame Attlee and his colleagues for operating as they did. In 1945, no non-paternalist option was available. The choice lay between Fabian paternalism and Tory paternalism. There can be no question that the Fabian variety was more generous, more compassionate, and closer to the attitudes and aspirations of its beneficiaries. The real trouble is that reliability – whether working man's or Wykehamist's – is no longer enough. Fabian paternalism has run its course, but the Fabian paternalists – precisely because paternalism was so successful thirty years ago – have hardly begun to recognise the fact. On the evidence presented here, Stewart and Jay were still unaware of it when their memoirs were published. They brought it home just the same.

Harold Wilson: Alibi for a Party?

For nearly thirty years, Harold Wilson personified the Industrious Apprentice. From the Wirral Grammar School he won an exhibition at Jesus College, Oxford, where grinding hard work won him the Gladstone prize, the Webb Medley junior and senior scholarships and a glittering First. At twenty-nine, he was a Member of Parliament and at thirty-one a Cabinet minister. His resignation with Aneurin Bevan three-and-a-half years later temporarily interrupted the onward march of his career, but the interruption gave him that most precious of Labour Party assets, the reputation of being a man of the left. At thirty-six he was elected, on the Bevanite slate, to the constituency section of the National Executive. At thirty-eight, he took Bevan's place in Labour's shadow Cabinet; at thirty-nine, he was shadow Chancellor of the Exchequer. Another interruption came at the height of the party's nuclear agonies in 1960, when he challenged Gaitskell for the party leadership, only to be beaten by a majority of more than two to one. But even that interruption may have done him more good than harm, consolidating his hold on the left, without doing him irreparable damage on the right. When Gaitskell died in 1963, he won the leadership with an ease that surprised only the ill-informed. When he entered 10 Downing Street at forty-eight, he seemed set fair to be one of the most successful British Prime Ministers of the century as well as the youngest.

In the event, few modern British governments have disappointed their supporters more thoroughly than his. After thirteen years in opposition, Labour returned to office in 1964 on the ticket of technical competence, purposive planning, faster growth and higher social spending. Socialism, as Wilson put it, would be harnessed to science, and science to socialism. When he and his colleagues limped back into opposition six years later, it was hard to tell which half of the promise had been more comprehensively belied. His Government had wrecked its own National Plan less than a year after announcing it, achieved a lower annual growth rate than that of the Conservatives and consumed vast quantities of energy and time in a bitter struggle with the trade unions, in which it was humiliatingly defeated. What Wilson had christened the 'social wage' did indeed absorb a larger share of the gross domestic product, but that was only because the whole economy had grown more slowly than expected. His second incarnation as Prime Minister was even less happy than his first. In 1974, Labour promised 'an irreversible shift of power and wealth to working people and their families', to be achieved through a social contract with the unions, entailing higher social spending and an end to wage controls. Two years later, Wilson resigned, having presided over record levels of inflation and unemployment, having launched an incomes policy patently designed to reduce real wages and having started the long series of expenditure cuts which were to destroy all hope of putting Labour's election pledges into effect.

How far these failures could have been avoided is a matter for argument. How far the responsibility for them can be laid at Wilson's door is still harder to determine. It is beyond dispute that they did enormous damage to Labour's self-confidence and unity. Clive Ponting may be wrong in implying that the Wilson governments of the 1960s could have followed different policies if they had tried to do so, but his verdict that they were guilty of 'breach of promise'[1] is impossible to fault. The jilted bride behaved accordingly. Within a few years after its fall, Labour men and women were looking back on the 1945 Government through a haze of nostalgic pride. Its successors of 1964 and 1974 have been objects of apology at best, and of shame at worst. More damagingly still, each side in the endemic struggle between left and right was fortified in its hostility to the other. The left concluded that its opposition to social democratic revisionism had been vindicated; that the Wilson governments had failed because they had not been truly socialist, and that they had not been truly socialist because they had been led astray by the right. Thoughtful people on the right increasingly came to suspect that the revisionist project could succeed only in an explicitly revisionist party, which had no need to truckle to the left. In this sense, if in no others, the Bennite upsurge of the late 1970s and the SDP breakaway of the early 1980s were both Wilson's children. The man whose proudest boast was that he could unite the party had divided it beyond repair.

The damage went wider and deeper than that. For most of the post-war period, the prevailing interpretation of modern British history – certainly on the left, but not only on the left – was essentially, if often unconsciously, whig. The Attlee Government was seen as part of a long continuum of progress, going back well into the nineteenth century if not before. To be on the left was to be part of this continuum; to be on history's side and to know that history was on one's side. Even Conservatives half-accepted this instinctive whiggery. Their role was to make sure that history did not go too fast; to consolidate the advances made by non-Conservatives; to graft new projects on to old traditions. But although they often resisted change when it was first mooted, they generally absorbed it into their bloodstream once it was accomplished. In the 1950s, it is true, the left lost ground in three successive general elections. A certain triumphalism appeared on the right, and a corresponding demoralisation on the left. Neither undermined the pervasive whiggery of the political nation. Conservatives were more anxious to extend the post-war settlement than to whittle it away; they were triumphalist as honorary whigs. However gloomy they might feel about their performance in the polling booths, Labour people rarely doubted that the onward march of progress would resume sooner or later, or that they would be in the van when it did. In the early and middle 1960s, their hopes seemed vindicated. By 1962, it looked as if Labour might win the next election after all. By 1963, it looked as if it would. By 1966, it had won the third largest anti-Conservative majority of the twentieth century. The 'thirteen wasted years' of Conservative rule, it seemed, had only been an interregnum. The road to Jerusalem was open again.

The Wilson governments mocked these expectations; more importantly, they called into question the assumptions which had underpinned them. Heavy deflation; a forced devaluation; a statutory wage freeze; defeat over the *In Place of Strife* white paper; temporising with the Smith regime in Rhodesia; support for the American war in Vietnam; the arbitrary removal of the immigration rights of the East African Asians; the botched and ultimately unsuccessful 'reform' of the House of Lords; above all, the atmosphere of shabby expediency which hung over the Government like a pall – these and other miseries of the long travail of 1966–70 could hardly fail to shake the whiggery of the progressive left. After the even harder travail of 1974–9 – mounting unemployment; endemic inflation; unprecedented currency depreciation; swingeing expenditure cuts; the switches of line towards Scottish and Welsh devolution; the agonised humiliation of the winter of discontent – whiggery had virtually disappeared. The road to Jerusalem, it seemed, was not open after all; perhaps it did not even exist. History had turned traitor. The left and centre–left were no longer in the van of change. They were forced to defend themselves and their achievements against an increasingly aggressive and self-confident right.

The Wilson era has, in short, a special significance – and a special poignancy – in the history of the British left. It was an era of lost innocence, of hopes betrayed. Partly because of this, it is an extraordinarily difficult era to assess, above all, perhaps, for those who were politically active during it. Were the hopes of the early 1960s really betrayed, or were they doomed from the start? Might innocence have been retained with better luck or better judgement, or is its loss a sign of maturity? Could the undoubted failures of the period have been avoided, or were they the products of structural factors or unforeseeable contingencies beyond the control of any government? The same applies, with even greater force, to Wilson's own reputation. It fell precipitately during his time as party leader, and has fallen still further since he retired; for him, at any rate, it has never been glad confident morning again. Was the fall justified? Was he responsible for the failures of his governments and the disappointments those failures have bred? Or has he become the scapegoat for his ministers and his party, much as Ramsay MacDonald became a scapegoat for the Labour Government of 1929?

On one level, the answer is straightforward. Prime Ministers get the credit when their governments do well; it is not unreasonable to blame them when their governments do badly. As Prime Minister, Wilson was responsible for the central direction of his governments; in that technical, but not trivial, sense, the lion's share of the blame for their shortcomings is inescapably his. But the real question goes deeper than that. From the perspective of this book, at any rate, it is historical responsibility that matters, not technical responsibility. Could Wilson, knowing what he knew, leading the party he led, facing the constraints that faced him, have acted differently? If he had, would things have gone better?

Here the answers are more complicated. Plainly, the key must lie in the governments of the 1960s, and above all in the 1966 Government, not in the dismal coda of 1974–6. Judged by its record, it is true, the 1974 Government ranks as one of the worst of the century. But for its first few months it had no majority at all, and even after the second 1974 election its majority was exiguous. More important still, the external environment facing it was so unpropitious, and it was so hagridden by the legacies of the outgoing Heath Government on the one hand, and of Labour's European split on the other, that it had virtually no room for manoeuvre. In any case, by the 1970s innocence was already lost, the road to Jerusalem patently closed. No one had high hopes of the 1974 Government, least of all its own members. The brave talk in the election manifesto had been a weapon in an internal faction fight, not a declaration of intent. The 1966 Government was a different matter. It had a comfortable parliamentary majority throughout. There were divisions within the party, of course, but they were the normal, inescapable divisions inherent in the structure of the Labour coalition, not an unbridgeable chasm. To be sure, Labour had inherited a large balance of payments deficit, an inheritance on which Wilson was to dwell with obsessive frequency. But, although the size of the deficit was unexpected, the fact was not. In any case, a party that made so much of its commitment to economic planning might fairly have been expected to cope with even a large deficit. And still the Government failed. It did not produce the economic growth on which it had based its claim to power. Most of the institutional reforms on which it expended so much time and energy went off at half-cock. Above all, it gradually lost its hold on that elusive, but indispensable element in the politics of the left, the liberal conscience. At a great rally at the beginning of the 1964 election, Wilson called for 'men with fire in their bellies and humanity in their hearts'.[2] Whatever might have been said in the Government's defence in 1970, no one could seriously pretend that the fires were still alight.

It would be absurd to suggest that Wilson was solely responsible for the detailed decisions that put them out. His reverence for the pieties of the British constitution was shared by virtually all his colleagues apart from Richard Crossman and Tony Benn. Callaghan, not he, deserves most of the blame for revoking the citizenship rights of the East African Asians and for postponing the changes in parliamentary boundariers agreed upon by the non-party Boundary Commission – perhaps the two most disgraceful decisions of the whole period. Michael Stewart, Foreign Secretary for most of the time, was at least as committed as he was to the American cause in Vietnam, support for which did more than anything else to disillusion the idealistic young. The East of Suez policy, which tightly constrained the Government's economic policies in its early years, was Denis Healey's as well as his. The *In Place of Strife* white paper, the repercussions of which came near to wrecking the Government and did wreck Wilson's reputation, was originally conceived by Barbara Castle. It is true that the most obviously disastrous decision of the entire six years – the decision not to devalue in the summer of 1966 – can be laid at Wilson's door. George Brown was by now in favour of devaluation, as were Crossman, Benn and Barbara Castle from the left of the party, and Tony Crosland and Roy Jenkins from the right. For a while, even Callaghan wobbled. To be sure, Wilson had no trouble in rallying the rest of the Cabinet against devaluation, but if he had wished to he would have had even less trouble in rallying it in favour.

Yet even on devaluation, the heaviest cross which his reputation has had to bear, the circle of responsibility is wider than it looks at first sight. By 1966, the best part of two years had been spent defending the \$2.80 parity. The Government in general, and Wilson in particular, had staked a great deal on its defence. Devaluation in these circumstances would have dealt a heavy blow to their political credit. That does not excuse the failure to devalue, of course; had devaluation come voluntarily in 1966 rather than involuntarily in 1967, many of the other failures of the period might have been avoided. It does, however, help to explain it. In doing so, it pushes the argument back to the real moment of truth – to the fatal morning in October 1964, the day after the Government took office, when Wilson, Callaghan and Brown agreed together to rule devaluation out. It was then, not in 1966, that the Government put its hand to the deflationary plough which it was never able to relinquish. Wilson, with all the authority of a newly installed Prime Minister behind him, was easily the most powerful member of the trio, as well as the most experienced. It would have been difficult for the others to gainsay him, even if they had wished to do so. The point, however, is that there is no evidence that they did so wish. Morally, as well as technically, the decision was theirs as well as his.

The picture of a Cabinet of brave and wise idealists, held back by a craven, foolish and unprincipled Prime Minister, does not, in short, stand up to examination. A better Prime Minister would doubtless have given a better lead; a better lead might have produced better results. But that is only to say that Wilson failed to rise above the level of his colleagues, not that he fell below it. Labour's retrospective indignation with his policy tergiversations and failures is the political equivalent of Caliban's horror at seeing his own face in the glass. He was not an American president or presidential candidate, catapulted into national leadership by the vagaries of primary elections or the contingencies of the nominating convention. He was elected as party leader by his colleagues in the Parliamentary Labour Party, with whom he had lived and worked for nearly twenty years. They knew his strengths and weaknesses; and they chose him in that knowledge.

They also sustained him thereafter. They had, after all, plenty of opportunities to get rid of him. More than once in the 1966 Parliament, young backbench critics tried to muster support for a challenge to him. Indeed, my own most abiding memories of the summers of 1968 and 1969 (summer is always the season for parliamentary plotting) are of small knots of conspirators holding excited meetings to check off the names of potential anti-Wilson putschists. These attempts never got anywhere, because there were never enough putschists; because the serried ranks of age and experience which surrounded us were unbudgeable. Having knowingly chosen Wilson, the Parliamentary Labour Party knowingly kept him. And what applies to the parliamentary party applies with much greater force to the Cabinet. A Cabinet revolt might have got rid of him; short of defeat in war, a Cabinet revolt is probably the only way to get rid of a sitting prime minister who wants to stay. But for all the talk in Fleet Street and the lobbies, and the agitated manoeuvring of Wilson's entourage, the Cabinet never came within spitting distance of a revolt. The conclusion is irresistible. Cabinet and parliamentary party alike kept Wilson because they wanted to keep him: because, as Dick Crossman once put it, he was the leader who divided Labour least: because his conservatism, his vacillation and his corrupting mixture of left-wing talk and right-wing deeds were also theirs.

To be sure, that does not dispose of the case against him. His critics were not primarily concerned with his policies. Their charges have to do with his personal style and conduct, and still more with the way he managed his colleagues – with the atmosphere of febrile and malicious intrigue that hung around his Kitchen Cabinet; with the disloyalty and distrust, the leaking and counter-leaking, 'the unease and suspicion' as Douglas Jay called them later,[3] that seemed to spread like some mysterious viral infection from the Prime Minister to his colleagues and that slowly destroyed the Government's cohesion and sense of purpose; with the self-deception, small-mindedness and short-sightedness that so often seemed to govern Wilson's actions; above all with the concentration on tactics and neglect of strategy that caused the Government to slide further and further from the high ground of politics. Since Wilson had 'neither political principle nor much government experience', Denis Healey wrote in his memoirs,

> he did not give Cabinet the degree of leadership which even a less ambitious prime minister should provide. He had no sense of direction, and rarely looked more than a few months ahead. His short-term opportunism, allied with a capacity for self-delusion which made Walter Mitty appear unimaginative, often plunged the government into chaos. Worse still, when things went wrong he imagined everyone was conspiring against him. He believed in demons and saw most of his colleagues in this role at one time or another. . . .
>
> . . . The steady deterioration of the economy following his victory in 1966 led him to see enemies in every corner; at worst he began to behave, in the words of an uncharitable journalist, like 'a demented coypu'.[4]

Healey was, of course, an old Gaitskellite, who had served his political apprenticeship as the party's international secretary when Bevin was at the Foreign Office. He and Wilson had been on opposite sides in the Bevanite blood feud of the early 1950s, and again in the battle over nuclear weapons in the early 1960s. His criticisms might perhaps be discounted as the residue of an ancient grudge. As time went on, however, many of Wilson's old supporters in the centre and the left became disaffected as well. As early as September 1966, Crossman, a close ally since the early 1950s and Wilson's campaign manager in the leadership election, was complaining of his 'methods of getting round every corner without any strategic thinking. . . . Central coherent purpose was, after all, the main thing which Harold laid down as the characteristic which distinguished our method of government from the spasmodic drooling of the Tories; now we are drooling in a not very dissimilar way.'[5] By the end of the year he was 'more doubtful than ever whether he's going to lead us anywhere, whether he has any real vision of a future for this country. . . . His main aim is to stay in office. That's the real thing and for that purpose he will use any trick or gimmick.'[6] In April 1968, when memories of the forced devaluation of 1967 were still fresh and talk of a change of leadership was mounting, Crossman noted that Wilson had become:

> a tarnished leader. Of course he still retains the qualities which

brought him to the top, above all his resilience, his power to take punishment and to come up fresh each morning fighting fit. His india-rubber resilience is linked of course with self-deception. No man can be the kind of boy scout Harold is and read aloud Kipling's 'If' as often as he reads it to me without a great deal of self-deception in his make-up. . . . I suppose that self-deception reached its zenith when he appointed himself head of the D.E.A. last autumn with Peter Shore as his henchman and from last October until devaluation day lived in a mood of continuous self-deception, week after week believing in recovery when we were running a £600 million trade deficit. . . .

. . . In his personal relations he still has a strong preference for the second-rate and the undistinguished. He's managed to collect round him in no. 10 the most undistinguished group of civil servants. . . . Apart from Tommy [Balogh] and myself, he allows no one of ability in his entourage – Gerald Kaufman, Trevor Lloyd Hughes, Peter de Cheminant, incredibly dim people. . . .

. . . [H]e will always prefer a whole series of empty meetings to one unpleasant row. He will always postpone a decision until forced to accept the inevitable and then, when he does accept it, he will congratulate himself on the brilliant execution of a well-laid plan.[7]

Tony Benn, another warm admirer in happier days, was also quick to lose his faith. 'The trouble is that Harold is very paranoid and I think he is, in a sense, creating the very thing he is afraid of, namely a plot against himself . . .', he noted in the spring of 1968. 'I think it's probably because he is afraid and isn't quite up to the job.'[8] Wilson, he complained a year later, was 'a very small-minded man'.[9] After describing a 'tense' Cabinet meeting at the height of the *In Place of Strife* battle he reflected that Wilson 'did emerge as a small man with no sense of history and as somebody without leadership qualities'.[10] Tom Swain, the grizzled old miners' MP, put it more succinctly: 'If Harold Wilson swallowed a sixpence, he'd shit a corkscrew.'[11]

The indictment is formidable, and the evidence on which it is based cannot be dismissed. Wilson was, by any reckoning, a bad Prime Minister. Beneath the bluster and conceit, which struck officials who worked with him even in the Attlee Government,[12] ran a corrosive streak of insecurity. Despite his agile mind, tactical resourcefulness and early academic brilliance, he surrounded himself with mediocrities: the dead weight of Wilson's appointments in the 1960s and 1970s was still pulling Labour down ten years later. If the memoirs of his press secretary, Joe Haines,[13] are to be trusted he allowed himself to be bullied unmercifully by his egocentric and neurotic personal secretary, Marcia Williams, whom he eventually ennobled; though her influence on policy was almost certainly negligible, there is not much doubt that she fanned his suspicions of his colleagues and followers, and exacerbated the sense of isolation which lay behind them. As Benn guessed, the plotting of which he complained was largely of his own making: real conspiracies were set on foot because endless false accusations of conspiracy drove independent-minded ministers and backbenchers to conclude that only a change at the top could save the Government from disintegration. Deeper and more destructive insecurities, partly social and partly intellectual, made themselves felt as well. As Crossman constantly complained, Wilson was, in a strange way, not merely unintellectual but positively anti-intellectual; though he had the cleverness of the good examinee, ideas, and people who cared about ideas, made him ill at ease. He felt more comfortable with the dim businessmen who figured in his honours lists or the placemen who stuffed his private entourage. At Oxford, he 'could not stomach all those Marxist public school products rambling on about the exploited workers';[14] as Prime Minister he had equally little stomach for those who believed that good government entailed thinking long. Well before he became Prime Minister, pragmatism had become a kind of religion, leading Aneurin Bevan to make the famous comment that Wilson was 'much more dangerous than Gaitskell because he isn't honest and he isn't a man of principle, but a sheer, absolute careerist, out for himself alone'.[15]

And yet, and yet, and yet. Weak, insecure, devious and lacking in vision though Wilson was, Crossman's judgement that he was the only possible leader of the Labour Party is much harder to fault in retrospect than enthusiastic young Gaitskellite backbenchers like me imagined at the time. No one could deny that weakness and insecurity are defects in a leader, but deviousness and lack of vision may have been the necessary conditions of leading a party hagridden by factionalism. Even Attlee, the only successful Labour Prime Minister there has ever been, was constantly criticised for failing to give his colleagues a lead; and in Attlee's day the party had a much more obvious mission and a much more coherent governing philosophy

164

than it had in Wilson's. Wilson may have been, in Benn's contemptuous phrase, a 'small man', but his followers were not comfortable with big men. He inherited the leadership of a party exhausted by battles over principle, and desperate for an ideologically quiet life. That, at least, he gave it. It was his party's fault as well as his that the gift it wanted from him was poisoned. When he finally retired, it is worth remembering, he was followed by another adroit and guileful politician, with no interest in ideas and no discernible vision of the future. Of course, it would have been better for the country if the Labour governments of the 1960s had been united, coherent and courageously led. We cannot know whether a different leader would have produced Labour governments of that sort. To put it at its lowest, the record does not suggest that it would have been an easy task.

Tony Crosland:
The Progressive as Loyalist

I first met Tony Crosland in the middle 1950s at a seminar at Nuffield College. I took an instant dislike to him. I was then a rather priggish Bevanite, and I was shocked by his politics. I was even more shocked by his manner. He seemed to typify what I most disliked about the Southern English mandarinate. He had a cut-glass accent. He was insufferably sure of himself. He was appallingly and gratuitously rude. Then I read *The Future of Socialism*. Slowly, reluctantly, and with many backward glances, I was converted. Capitalism, it seemed, had changed, after all. Public ownership was not essential to socialism. It was merely a means to an end, and not a very important means. What mattered was equality, and equality could be achieved in other ways. Bevan dropped out of my pantheon, and Gaitskell took his place. Crosland did not join the pantheon, exactly, but he became a sort of candidate member. The next time I met him, the qualities which had previously shocked me seemed forgivable, even endearing. I was captivated by his exhilarating mixture of affection and astringency, and captivated even more by his robust iconoclasm and refusal to follow the crowd. Very well, he had a cut-glass accent. Who can help his upbringing? Very well, he was sure of himself. If the author of *The Future of Socialism* did not have a right to self-assurance, who did? Very well, he was rude. That was a sign of a fundamental seriousness and egalitarianism.

By the mid-1960s, when I got into Parliament, I had become an admirer, as well as a disciple. Gaitskell was dead, and the revisionists needed a champion. George Brown was too unreliable, and Roy Jenkins too remote. Crosland seemed to be the man. More than any of the other Gaitskellites, he cared about ideas. He had none of the stultifying self-importance that afflicts so many successful politicians. Above all, he was the high priest of revisionism. He had charted its course in happier days. Who better to lead it through the storms that followed Gaitskell's death? For most of my first Parliament –

the strange, confused, ultimately tragic Parliament of 1966–70 – I thought of myself as a Croslandite. I used to go to clandestine meetings in his room in the House, where an ill-assorted group – Christopher Price, David Owen, John Mackintosh, Jack Ashley and myself – drank whisky and talked devaluation. When devaluation finally came, I hoped he would become Chancellor of the Exchequer. When he did not, I hoped – incredible as it seems in retrospect – that he would save the Party by helping to lead a *putsch* against Harold Wilson.

Then came the 1970 election defeat, and the Common Market split. It seemed to me then, and it seems to me now, that a Crosland-ite revisionist was logically bound to support entry into the Community: that the xenophobia and Little Englandism which seemed to me to lie at the heart of the opposition to it, and which would have been hugely reinforced had it been defeated, were irreconcilably opposed to the values for which Crosland had always stood, and to which *The Future of Socialism* was the most eloquent recent testimony. Believing that, I also believed that it was necessary to vote for entry even if it meant splitting the Labour Party and keeping the Conservatives in office. As everyone knows, Crosland did not agree. Community membership, he declared when David Owen and I tried to persuade him to sign a declaration in favour of it, was seventeenth (or perhaps seventh or seventieth, I cannot now remember) on his list of priorities. He was still in favour of it, of course. But the workers of Grimsby were not interested in it, and it was nothing like as important as housing finance. It was certainly not worth a split in the Labour Party and we should stop being so childish about it.

At the time, this felt like a betrayal. Crosland was not any old revisionist, after all. He was not a superior apparatchik, like Denis Healey, or a figure from the past, like Douglas Jay. He was the revisionists' guru – our teacher and mentor. We were what we were, in part at any rate, because of him. To watch him sulking in his tent, when the cause being fought over was, in reality, his cause, and when the troops fighting for it were his troops, was unbearably painful. In such a situation, the myth of the Lost Leader is a comforting stand-by. Many pro-Marketeers – myself, I regret to say, among them – found comfort in it. Crosland, we told ourselves, had deserted us. His motives might perhaps have been honourable. But desertion was still desertion.

We were wrong, of course – how wrong, Susan Crosland has

made clear in her sensitive and moving portrait of her late husband.[1] Not that her account of the episode is complete. She has tried to depict the Crosland she knew, and to describe the experiences which made him what he was, not to write a chapter of contemporary British history. Sensibly, she makes no pretence at objectivity; and she concentrates on the private man, not on the public figure. Her picture of his upbringing – an extraordinary mixture of upper-middle-class conventionality and ferocious nonconformity – is particularly sensitive and full of insight. Crosland's father was a scholar of Trinity College, Oxford, and a high-ranking civil servant at the War Office. His mother was an MA of Bedford College and an authority on medieval French literature. They lived first in Golders Green and then in Highgate, and sent their son to Highgate School, from where he followed his father to Trinity. But their superficial conformity to the norms of the higher salariat of their generation went hand in hand with a deep, unswerving commitment to the most extreme kind of religious dissent. Both had been born into what Mrs Crosland nicely calls 'the intense, austere, narrow Christianity' of the Exclusive Plymouth Brethren, 'whose pleasure lay in the Word of God and endless discussion of it'. Both remained utterly loyal to it all their lives, and although Crosland broke away from it in his teens, there can be no doubt that it marked him for ever. Mrs Crosland's description of what it meant in practice could hardly be bettered:

> The Exclusive Brethren had a creed, but it was difficult for an outsider to gather what it was. They didn't have rules: there were pressures, things one didn't do – these shibboleths. They didn't do that; they did do this. They didn't go to opera; they did go to concerts. They had some way of making the two consistent when they weren't. Ritual was shunned. Pleasure for its own sake was eschewed. Love for another human being must not overwhelm: total surrender to the physical and natural beauties of life could shut out the Spirit. When a beloved died, grief was curtailed: one should rejoice that the creature wrenched away was now with Jesus.[2]

Crosland, she added, 'had been inculcated with the sense of being apart from other people'.[3]

We also learn a good deal about the wartime Fusilier and paratrooper, about the swashbuckling, hard-drinking Oxford don and

Labour MP of the 1940s and early 1950s, and about the husband and stepfather of the 1960s and 1970s. But we learn very little about the author of *The Future of Socialism*, and although we learn a lot about the Cabinet Minister and would-be Labour leader, we do not learn much about the political context in which he operated. There is a lot of excellent gossip, some of which is illuminating. But, with one important exception, it illuminates character, not events. It tells us what Crosland thought was happening – or rather, what he told his wife he thought was happening – not what happened. That does not mean that it is valueless. He told her a great deal, and her memories of it have the ring of truth. The fact remains that the account she has given us is a one-sided picture of what was a one-sided picture even at the start.

Thus the 'Jenkinsites', as Mrs Crosland calls them, march through her pages like a malevolent phalanx, drilled by Bill Rodgers. When he tells them to advance, they advance. When he tells them to turn, they turn. Recognising that Crosland's balanced judgement of the European issue is a threat to them, they decide to blacken his character and question his motives. Later, they decide to punish him for his refusal to march with them, and deny him the Deputy Leadership when Jenkins resigned it. The confusions and uncertainties, the bruised feelings and angry swings of mood, the divisions and jealousies which in fact characterised that motley coalition of future Social Democrats and old-style Labour right-wingers are not recorded. They could not be recorded, of course, because Crosland did not know about them. But, because they are not recorded, the truth is simplified and distorted. And the truth is that the 'Jenkinsites' had mostly been Croslandites as well. They reacted as people who feel that they have been let down usually do react. No one told them to react in that way. No one needed to.

But what would be a weakness in a historian of the Labour Party of the 1970s is a strength in a biographer of Crosland. Mrs Crosland's pages may not contain the Truth, with a capital 'T', but Truth with a capital 'T' is a notoriously elusive commodity. They do contain her late husband's truth. This *was* how things seemed to him. Housing finance, the workers of Grimsby, above all the unity of the Labour Party really did matter more to him than the future pattern of Britain's relations with the European mainland, and he was shocked by our failure to agree with him. If we saw him as a deserter, he saw us as frivolous and irresponsible schismatics. He was not a Lost Leader after all. No handful of silver had seduced him from his allegiance. He had not shared our allegiance in the first place, or, if he had, he had ceased to do so. It was not his fault that he fell off the pedestal on which we had placed him. It was our fault for putting him there. Whatever might have been true of the Crosland of the 1950s, the Crosland of the 1970s was no longer our sort of Croslandite. The swashbuckling, iconoclastic ex-paratrooper had settled down, politically as well as in his private life. He stuck unswervingly to the content of his earlier revisionism, but he no longer pursued it with his earlier irreverence. We persisted in seeing him as our mentor, but he did not want to be the mentor of a divisive and potentially heretical sect. He wanted to be a sober, respectable departmental minister in the mainstream of the labour movement – not for base reasons, but because he genuinely believed that that was how he could make his most effective contribution. We still thought of him as the author of *The Future of Socialism*. He thought of himself as a once and future Secretary of State. And he took it for granted that the only possible vehicle for the things he believed in was the Labour Party – icons and all.

On one level, he was probably right. Croslandite revisionism did not fare well in the Labour Party of the 1970s and 1980s, but, as Crosland never ceased to complain, it might have fared better if the pro-Marketeers had not divided the Labour right against itself and, in doing so, allowed the left into the citadels of party power. In any case, no other vehicle was available and there is no reason to believe that Crosland (or, for that matter, anyone else) could have constructed one. It is true that, a few years after his death, former Croslandites seceded from the Labour Party to set up the SDP, among them his lifelong friend Philip Williams, Gaitskell's biographer. But the SDP was never a Croslandite party and Crosland would never have felt at home in it. Its purpose – never realised, of course – was to revise the revisionism of the 1950s, not to become a vehicle for it. By the 1970s, in fact, Croslandism and Labourism were symbiotically linked – a symbiosis nicely symbolised by the decision of that arch-Labourist, James Callaghan, to make Crosland his Foreign Secretary. For Croslandism could flourish, if at all, only in the Labour Party, while Labourism could acquire intellectual respectability, if at all, only by wearing Croslandite clothes.

On a deeper level, however, there was a tragic irony in the transition from revisionist *enfant terrible* to responsible Labour statesman. The symbiosis between Croslandism and Labourism was a symbiosis of exhaustion. Even in the old Labour fortresses, the old working-class culture, whose child Labourism was, had become narrower, more introverted and more brittle. Elsewhere, it was in retreat. Partly because of this, the familiar, sixty-year-old tension between movement and party – between the claims of working-class solidarity and the imperatives of winning and exercising power in an advanced industrial society, in which the organised working class is only one social interest among many – had become more acute than ever before. In the struggle over trade union reform in the late 1960s, that tension had almost destroyed the second Wilson Government. In the so-called 'winter of discontent' two years after Crosland's death, it did destroy the Callaghan Government. Labourism could still flourish in opposition, when its built-in tensions could be disguised with the rhetoric of unity. In government, it either had to evade hard choices or risk self-destruction.

If Labourism had come to the end of its tether, so, in a different way, had Croslandism. Though Crosland did not put it in this way himself, Croslandite revisionism is best understood as a historic compromise between British parliamentary socialism and a more inchoate 'progressive tradition' going back, by way of Keynes and Beveridge, to the New Liberalism of the early century. Like New Liberalism, it was quintessentially optimistic. Capitalism, Crosland argued, was no longer capitalism. Because of this, socialism could be a different kind of socialism. Thanks to the reforms of the post-war Labour Government, and still more to the Keynesian Revolution in economic thought, socialist ends could now be realised through New Liberal means. For the real end of socialism was equality; and to that the traditional socialist means of public ownership was no longer essential, or even relevant.

Instead of wasting their energies on further nationalisations, socialists should give 'exceptionally high priority' to the relief of poverty, distress and social squalor; procure a more equal distribution of wealth; and improve the nation's social capital 'such that the less well off have access to housing, health and education of a standard comparable . . . to that which the better off can buy for themselves out of their private means'. All this would entail a significant redistribution of resources from private to public expenditure and from the better- to the less-well-off. That in turn would entail a high rate of economic growth. For only if growth were rapid would it be possible to win public consent for the redistribution which lay at the heart of the whole project. 'We cannot even approach our basic objectives at the present rate of growth,' Crosland wrote in 1970.

> For those objectives . . . require a redistribution of wealth and resources: and we shall not get this unless our *total* resources are growing rapidly. I do not of course mean that rapid growth will automatically produce a transfer of resources of the kind we want; whether it does or not will depend on the social and political values of the country concerned. But I do assert dogmatically that in a democracy, low or zero growth excludes the possibility. . . . In a utopia (or a dictatorship) perhaps we might transfer x per cent of near-static GNP towards 8 million pensioners and better housing and clearing up pollution. In the rough democratic world in which we live, we cannot.[4]

In short, no growth, no redistribution – and no redistribution, no revisionism. Growth was the solvent which made the Croslandite compromise possible: the whole intellectual system rested on the twin assumptions that rapid growth could occur, and that governments knew how to make it occur. In the long boom of the 1950s, when *The Future of Socialism* was written, both assumptions seemed almost self-evident; and Crosland's tone was appropriately relaxed. Even with the current growth rate, he pointed out genially, Britain's standard of living would double in twenty-five years. A socialist government should try to do better, but there was no need 'to strain every nerve' for maximum growth at any cost.[5] By the 1970s, the tone was more anxious. After six years of Labour rule, Crosland conceded, 'unemployment was higher, inflation more rapid and economic growth slower than when the Conservatives left office' – a 'wretched showing', which exacted 'a calamitous cost in terms of welfare'. But there was no need to question the fundamental revisionist assumption that faster growth was, in principle, possible. The economic failures of the Wilson Government were self-inflicted. Ministers had had the wrong priorities. They had sacrificed growth to the balance of payments; above all, to the defence of an unrealistic exchange rate. But these priorities could and should be changed. Faced with balance of payments problems, future Labour ministers should devalue the currency rather than deflate the economy; faced with inflation, they should prefer an incomes policy to higher unemployment. If they had the intelligence to choose these priorities and the resolution to stick to them, growth would duly materialise.

Hand in hand with the assumption that it lay within the power of a British government to procure faster growth if it wanted to went the less obvious, but equally critical, assumption that the external world imposed no significant constraints on internal policy. Though much of the argument of *The Future of Socialism* was based on American and Swedish experience, Croslandite revisionism (in striking contrast to the contemporaneous revisionism of John Strachey) was an essentially insular creed. Foreign examples were often prayed in aid, and there were routine genuflections to the needs of the Third World, but there was no suggestion that, in an interdependent world, in which national economic sovereignty was an illusion, revisionism had to be international as well as national. Hence the approach to the European Community which so dismayed Labour pro-Marketeers in the early 1970s. Community membership was a good cause; opposition to it was a symptom of the vitality-sapping conservatism which blanketed British life. But it was a good cause in the way that reform of the licensing laws or the decriminalisation of homosexuality were good causes – a civilised, worthy, but in the last resort dispensable appendage to the serious business of egalitarian politics, not part and parcel of the whole social democratic project.

A third and more complex assumption – or perhaps a set of assumptions – deserves mention as well. For Crosland, the accepted 'Westminster Model' of parliamentary government was a given. Unlike Richard Crossman, the turbulent and unpredictable revisionist *manqué* of the period, he showed no interest in political reform and little in political theory. The possibility that it might not be feasible to realise social democratic values with and through a political system permeated with values hostile to social democracy, that if social democrats tried to work through such a system their means might corrupt their ends, does not seem to have occurred to him. Central to his whole analysis was the assumption that the way to change society, however slowly and gradually, was to win power in a parliamentary election and give social democratic ministers control of the existing government machine; that if sufficiently intelligent and resolute social democratic ministers were in office, social democratic policies would surely be carried out. Central also was the more particular assumption that the twin engines of progressive taxation and social expenditure would work as social democratic revisionists wanted them to work: that if the right people were in charge, the mechanisms of Westminster and Whitehall would produce the redistribution which was the object of the whole exercise. What applied to the accepted structure of politics, moreover, also applied – and with increasing emphasis as he grew older – to the accepted content. Such issues as 'alienation, communication, participation, automation, dehumanisation, decentralisation, the information network, student revolt, the generation gap or even Women's Lib', he wrote crustily, but not uncharacteristically, in 1971, were 'false trails': fashionable diversions from the 'hard, patient slog' of redistribution. There was no need for new aims. The old ones were 'as urgent as they have ever been'.

Herein lie the irony (and the tragedy) of Crosland's last years. His rise in the party hierarchy coincided with the gradual disintegration of the assumptions on which his system was based. He became Foreign Secretary just in time to see them collapse. If the economic performance of the Wilson Government of the 1960s was 'wretched', that of the Wilson–Callaghan Government of the 1970s was pitiable. It achieved no growth, record inflation and a post-war record in unemployment. Worse still, it was clear that no one – no one in the progressive tradition, at any rate – knew how to do better. It turned out that, in the circumstances of the 1970s, devaluation was not an alternative to deflation, after all. The Government allowed the currency to depreciate at an unprecedented rate, and then had to deflate as well. For a while, incomes policy did hold inflation in check, but before long it collapsed in confusion and recrimination. On a different level, it became clear that, in a weak and open market economy, national economic sovereignty was indeed an illusion: that no British government could stick to social democratic priorities if other governments refused to do the same. After two years of deepening crisis, the Cabinet had to seek credits from the International Monetary Fund and to cut its public expenditure programmes so deeply as to make nonsense of the platform on which it had been elected. On a different level still, it was no longer certain that high levels of public expenditure were necessarily redistributive in any case, while there was growing evidence to suggest that the complex changes of attitude and behaviour which the revisionist project required could not be commanded from Whitehall, no matter how resolute those who tried to command them might be.

The times cried out for a further instalment of revisionism – for a revisionism which would do for Croslandite social democracy what *The Future of Socialism* had done for Clause Four socialism. The Crosland of the 1950s, the daring and imaginative intellectual saboteur whose greatest delight was to demolish outworn pieties and explode ancient myths, might have responded to that cry. No doubt, he would have imposed new strains on Labour's increasingly fragile unity, but in the process he might have given the entire democratic left intellectual weapons with which to stem the advance of the neo-liberal new right. The Crosland of the 1970s was too distracted by the responsibilities of office and too encumbered by the claims of party loyalty to make the attempt. Sometimes he half-saw that the assumptions underpinning his earlier revisionism could no longer be taken for granted. In a 1975 pamphlet he even acknowledged that the engines of progressive taxation and public expenditure were not, after all, delivering the redistribution they were supposed to guarantee.

> We under-estimated the capacity of the middle classes to appropriate more than their fair share of public expenditure. They demand more resources for the schools in their areas; they complain vociferously if they have to wait for their operations; they demand that the state intervene to subsidise the prices of the rail tickets from their commuter homes to their work. Too often these pressures have been successful, and in consequence the distribution of public spending has been tilted away from the areas of greatest need to those which generate the loudest demands.[6]

But the insight was left hanging in mid-air, a momentary cry of anguish, not the starting point for a systematic reassessment. For the most part, Crosland stuck, with slightly tetchy doggedness, to the positions he had staked out twenty years before. Growth; redistribution; higher social expenditure – these, he insisted again and again, were the 'basic' questions: 'the issues which my working-class constituents want to see at the top of our agenda': the stuff of social democratic politics. Intellectuals who thought they could not be achieved within the existing system were guilty of 'lack of clarity, a flight into chiliasm and a loss of practical radical will-power'; middle-class leftists who gave a higher priority to other objectives displayed 'an elitist and even condescending attitude to the wants and aspirations of ordinary people'. And so, when the crisis came in 1976, he was intellectually defenceless. He could see that the expenditure cuts demanded by the IMF and favoured by the Treasury made a mockery of all that he had stood for. He saw too that the siege economy of the Labour left and the so-called Cambridge School was not a satisfactory alternative. But, when battle was joined, it became clear that his own alternative amounted to little more than an impotent and corrosive regret.

On all this, Mrs Crosland is as illuminating about politics as she always is about personality. She quotes an agonised entry in his commonplace book, written in the summer of 1976, a few weeks before the crisis broke, in which he analysed the political situation as the Government's moment of truth approached.

(a) Demoralisation of decent rank & file: Grimsby L.P. . . . (b) strain on T.U. loyalty. . . . Outstanding success of last 2 years has been implication & involvement of T.U.s. in national economic policy. If this survives, will struggle thru: if not, disaster. (c) breeding of illiterate & reactionary attitude to public expenditure – horrible. (d) collapse of strategy which I proposed last year. . . . Now no sense of direction and *no* priorities: only pragmatism, empiricism, safety first, £ supreme. (e) and: unemplyment, even if politically more wearable, = grave loss of welfare, security, choice: very high price to be paid for deflation & negative growth.[7]

When he learned the details of the IMF terms in late November, he asked her gloomily: 'Even if the Government survives, does it make such a difference if Labour measures can't be implemented? What the press cannot understand is that this is the most right-wing Labour Government we've had for years.'[8] When the Cabinet met, he led a motley group of lesser ministers, including Roy Hattersley, Shirley Williams and Harold Lever, in opposition to the Treasury line. But, when Callaghan made it clear that he intended to back the Treasury, Crosland's resistance crumbled. Though the Prime Minister was wrong, he insisted, it was necessary to support him: if he were defeated, the party might be smashed. As everyone knows, the Prime Minister and Treasury got their way. Croslandism had been sacrificed on the altar of Labourism. Six weeks later, Crosland was dead.

Even now, more than a decade later, the story seems to me unbearably painful. Even at the best of times, Secretaries of State are two-a-penny. In the Labour governments of the 1970s, they were a glut on the market. The labour movement – indeed, the whole progressive tradition in British politics – was collapsing from intellectual anaemia. It had no special need of competent *apparatchiki*; Callaghan's Cabinet was stuffed with them, and even Wilson's had a fair number. What it needed was a blood transfusion of ideas. Crosland was the author of one of the half-dozen greatest works of socialist theory written in this country in this century. For him to narrow his horizons to the Department of the Environment or even to the Foreign Office was, in a way, a betrayal – not of others, but of himself. It was as though Beethoven had decided that his real vocation was to become bursar of a musical college, and had then been forced to devote all his energies to saving it from bankruptcy, only to see it go bankrupt in the end.

Why did he do it? This is the question that matters most about Tony Crosland: the question that future biographers will wrestle with. Mrs Crosland does not ask it, much less answer it. Still, she gives an invaluable hint. It is contained in the dedication: 'for the people of Grimsby and the Labour Party'. The dedication is, of course, hers, not her husband's. But the central message of her book is that he would have approved of it. He did identify himself with the 'people of Grimsby', or at least with what he imagined the people of Grimsby to be. It was not a pose: it was part of him. By the same token, and probably for the same reasons, he identified himself with the Labour Party. It was for him what the Exclusive Brethren had been for his parents: the unquestioned structure giving meaning to his life; the embodiment of a commitment which was now beyond argument. His loyalty to it was not, as party loyalty so often is, a superficial matter of convenience, or habit, or personal ties. It sprang from the deepest recesses of his complex and elusive character. For him, breaking with the Labour Party was unthinkable. It followed that thoughts which might have led to a break with the Labour Party were unthinkable too. But a sustained, rigorous, no-holds-barred attempt to revise his earlier revisionism – an attempt to do for the fragile and exhausted labour movement of the 1970s what he had done for the enormously more confident movement of the 1950s – would have been worthless without thoughts of that kind. Whether he realised this consciously, I do not know. I cannot believe that he did not sense it. The increasingly curmudgeonly tone of his later writings; the mournful fatalism of his comments to his wife during the IMF crisis; the impression one gets of emotional and intellectual hatches battened down – all these suggest a decision, conscious or unconscious, not to ask awkward questions in case the answers turned out to be intolerable. The price of party loyalty has often been high. Few have found it higher than Tony Crosland.

David Owen:
The Progressive as Meteor

For the best part of a decade, the 'radical centre' of British politics, as Roy Jenkins once called it, was haunted by the coruscating, baffling, driven personality of David Owen. His part in creating the SDP was second only to Jenkins's own, and in some ways not even to his. Jenkins's Dimbleby Lecture lit the fuse. He had thought the unthinkable; and not only thought it, but talked it in front of the television cameras. In doing so, he had forced others to think about it too. The point of lighting a fuse, however, is to produce an explosion; and the explosion was David Owen's. He came around to the idea of a new party comparatively late, but once he was converted his conversion was characteristically total. He rallied the MPs who eventually broke away, he set the pace of the breakaway and he largely dictated the tactics. Once the new party had come into existence, his role in defining its stance and identity was second to no one's. *Face the Future*,[1] his earnest attempt to give policy substance to the co-operative, decentralist, non-statist tradition in British socialism, was the nearest thing to a philosophical credo which the new party had. Much more important than his writings, however, were his strangulated, yet gripping passion on the public platform, his relentless mastery of committee detail, his driving, sometimes almost self-lacerating, energy, his personal magnetism and his unsleeping will. He never won the party's heart. In the only leadership election it ever held, Jenkins easily defeated him. Shirley Williams always evoked more warmth than he did. For all that, he did more than any of the other leaders to shape its policies and determine its style.

Then came the 1983 election, Jenkins's fatal resignation from the leadership and Owen's effortless assumption of it. In the eyes of the media and the public, at any rate, he was now the SDP and the SDP was him. He had only five followers in the House of Commons, most of them worthy but unexciting figures of the second rank.

Once the excitement of the election was over, the political world – most notably and most damagingly the political journalists whose assumptions and prejudices determine the shape of the political information available to the public – returned to business as usual; and in Britain, political business is two-party business. With extraordinary, almost breathtaking skill, Owen managed to keep himself in the spotlight, in spite of all the pressures of the system. The first three years of his leadership, at any rate, were a virtuoso performance, to which it is hard to think of a parallel in twentieth-century British history. The nearest is Lloyd George's brilliant, but doomed campaign to breathe new life into the dying Liberal Party in the late 1920s which I discussed in Chapter 2. But the differences are more striking than the similarities. With all its weaknesses, the Liberal Party had, after all, been the governing party of the country well within the memory of a large part of the electorate. It still had deep roots and organised loyalties. Lloyd George himself was a former prime minister – and not just any old former prime minister, but the prime minister who had Won the War, a latter-day Chatham and a world statesman into the bargain.

Owen had none of these assets. His party was less than three years old. Its support was evanescent, as shallow as it was broad. He had sat in a Cabinet for only two years. He had, of course, been foreign secretary – a cow he milked with remorseless, sometimes rather tedious, assiduity – but, truth to tell, his tenure of the Foreign Office had not been an unqualified success. Yet with marvellous effrontery, he contrived to be taken at his own valuation: as a heavyweight national politician whose sayings and doings were important simply because he said and did them; as the leader of a serious party, which might, in the not too distant future, help to shape the destiny of the country. Of course, there was a price to be paid. The party itself – including, most damagingly, the other three members of the original Gang of Four – was dwarfed. It connived at, even applauded, its own eclipse. How could it not connive? Without Owen it would have disappeared from sight, and it had the sense to see that. But its applause was tempered by twinges of unease which a more sensitive leader would have detected. Owen does not seem to have detected them: or, if he did, he refused to pay them any attention. For the time being, however, all this was under the surface; and what happened under the surface had no immediate political significance. What was significant was that the leader of the smallest and most fragile party in United Kingdom politics had forced himself into the front rank, against all the odds.

Nemesis was appropriately swift and deadly. On the morrow of the 1987 election, Owen was the most forceful and glamorous figure in the Alliance ranks, as well as the most powerful influence on its policies. He had dominated its election campaign; on any rational calculation of the odds, he was also the favourite to become the leader of the united Alliance party which an overwhelming majority of the Liberals and a comfortable majority of the SDP both wanted. Yet in a few short weeks, he threw all this away. Any tyro could have seen that the question of merger between the two Alliance parties was bound to be raised once the election was over. It is inconceivable that Owen did not realise this. Yet when David Steel actually raised it, he behaved as though it were a monstrous and unpredictable bolt from the blue. Though he had opposed merger before the election, he had been careful not to rule it out thereafter. He could perfectly well have accepted it now, trumping Steel's card and capturing the substantial anti-Steel vote in the Liberal Party. Alternatively, he could have played for time and waited to gauge the true, under-the-surface feelings of the SDP rank and file. Instead of doing either of these things, he rushed into all-out opposition; pulled the SDP MPs out of joint spokesmanships with the Liberals in the House of Commons; and insisted on an immediate ballot of the SDP membership. Then, in an atmosphere of petulant menace, he refused to abide by the ballot result. The darling of social democracy had emerged as its Achitophel, resolved to ruin what he could no longer rule.

The rest is history – the bitter, bruising split in the SDP; the mean-spirited, self-destructive bickering between the new merged party and the Owenite remnant; the remorseless slide of both successor parties in the opinion polls; the slow political eclipse of Owen himself; and, worst of all perhaps, the dreadful, all-pervasive, sense of waste. Whether the Alliance project could ever have succeeded I do not know. In retrospect, it is clear that the structural obstacles, some of which I discuss in the next chapter, were always far greater than they seemed in the euphoria of 1981 and early 1982. What is certain is that the enterprise need not have ended in the acrimony and misery of 1987 and 1988. It is equally certain that the blame goes wide. No one who played any part in the merger debate and its sequel can look back on it with pride. SDP mergerists, like me, were far too cavalier about the reservations of ordinary party

181

members who did not wish to see the structure they had helped to build engulfed in something else. Opponents of merger often displayed a narrow-minded sectarianism quite at variance with their proclaimed belief in power-sharing and coalition politics.

When all the qualifications have been made, however, it still seems to me that Owen was the chief author of the catastrophe as well as its most prominent victim. His authorship started early. The merger split and the disasters that followed were only the last chapter in a saga which began at the earliest meetings of the newly formed SDP's national committee. Even before the SDP was launched, it was clear that it would have to have close relations with the Liberals. In an electoral system made for two parties there was simply no room for a fourth party, occupying broadly the same social and ideological terrain as the third, but in contest with it. The Liberals and SDP did not, of course, have to merge: Owen was quite right about that. But they did have to fight together; and if they were to carry conviction in fighting together, they had to have a common platform and to support each other's candidates. Owen did not quarrel openly with that logic, but he constantly kicked against the conclusions to which it led.

As he made clear in a series of interviews with Kenneth Harris, published, ironically, at the height of the merger battle,[2] he had been implacably opposed to an alliance of principle with the Liberals from the moment it was first mooted. On no evidence that I can see, he appears to have believed that the infant SDP could have forced the Liberal Party to give it a clear run in more than half the seats in the country, without agreeing a common programme. He told Harris that he would have liked Shirley Williams to fight the Croydon by-election in the early autumn of 1981 against a Liberal, and that he half-wished that Roy Jenkins had joined the Liberal Party when he came back from Brussels, thus allowing the SDP to develop 'without constantly looking over its shoulder as to its relationship with the Liberals'. Once the Alliance had come into existence, he became a dedicated and unswerving opponent of all attempts to being the allies closer together.

In the four years of his leadership, the energies of the SDP National Committee were consumed by an endless series of petty, but extraordinarily bitter squabbles over relations with the Liberals. Which party should fight which seat? Should local parties be allowed to select candidates jointly with the local Liberal Associations if they wished to do so? How should Alliance policy be decided? Should there be joint Alliance spokesmen in the House of Commons? The substantive issues at stake in any particular dispute were mostly trivial, but they were invested with portentous emotional and political significance. For the first time in my life I began to understand what it must have been like to dispute the finer points of Marxist theory with the exiled Lenin or the subtleties of predestinarianism with some Calvinist divine in the seventeenth century. By the summer of 1987, so much bad blood had accumulated that the option of closer co-operation short of merger – the option which might, in an ideal world, have had most to be said for it – was no longer feasible. The supporters of closer co-operation could not trust Owen to co-operate. Because they did not trust him, Owen could not trust them not to use co-operation as a stalking horse for merger. The merger split, in short, was not really over merger at all. It was over David Owen's singular vision of social democracy and of the proper relationship between the SDP and the Liberal Party.

Yet on close inspection, the vision turned out to be extraordinarily cloudy. Owen's interviews with Harris contain a good deal of muffled growling about the need for a 'hard' as opposed to a 'soft' centre, and some imprecise hints about the need for a 'competitive' as opposed to a 'privatised' economy. But these scarcely amount to a social philosophy. In a defiant article immediately after the merger vote, he implied that the real obstacle to merger was that Social Democrats wished to remain faithful to social democracy as it was practised within Western Europe. To judge by the positions he adopted on the practical questions of economic and social policy, however, the consensual, quasi-corporatist, solidaristic social democracy of Scandinavia, Federal Germany and Austria, with its emphasis on group loyalty and its distaste for individualistic liberalism on the Anglo-American model, was profoundly alien to him. Indeed, by this criterion, the pro-merger members of the Gang of Four, and perhaps even David Steel, were better social democrats than he was.

Owen and his admirers often spoke as though the essence of the matter was his notion of the Social Market. Unfortunately, it was never clear what the Social Market really meant. The term was imported into British politics by Sir Keith Joseph and the Conservative New Right. To them, it meant what we have come to know as 'Thatcherism'. Despite occasional indications to the contrary, Owen did not mean that; the charge of 'sub-Thatcherism', which some of his less-considered utterances certainly invited, was unfair. Did he, then, mean a mixed economy – an economy in which resources are largely allocated by the market, but in which public power intervenes to alter market outcomes and constrain market forces for public ends? Not according to him. The notion of the mixed economy, he insisted, was a symptom of 'mixed thinking',[3] which blurred the differences between the public and private sectors. So what did he mean? The answer, I suspect, is twofold. On one level, the level of emotional and political symbolism, the Social Market was a banner, a rallying cry, an assertion of identity. It told the world that the SDP was new and different and that David Owen was new and different; in a phrase beloved of Owen's followers, it gave the party and its leader a 'cutting edge' which was theirs and theirs alone. That was the level which really mattered to Owen, and which explained his fierce attachment to the phrase. The trouble was that, if he wished to be taken seriously, he could not operate on that level alone. And on the level of intellectual substance, the level revealed when the emotional detritus was cleared away, the Social Market meant nothing more precise than an efficient and competitive mixed economy, with a vigorous and profitable private sector, as opposed to an inefficient and uncompetitive one. But Roy Jenkins had called for an efficient and competitive mixed economy in the Dimbleby Lecture and it had been part of the stock-in-trade of the Liberal Party since the days of Lloyd George and the 'Yellow Book'. To put the point another way around, the Social Market was not the source of Owen's differences with the Liberal Party and the pro-merger camp in the SDP. It was a way of legitimising them.

What, then, *was* the source? The obvious answer is ambition; and it is beyond dispute that no one gets as far as David Owen did without being ambitious. But what one might call conventional ambition – the calculating, odds-assessing, rationally directed ambition of the ordinary front-bench politician – would have pointed towards merger, not away from it. Not long after the 1983 election, I told him I thought he could be the leader of a merged party if he wanted. I still think I was right: more importantly, I also suspect he thought I was right. And whatever may have been true in 1983, there was never any doubt that the stand he took in 1987 was more likely to lead to a Powellite isolation than to power or even influence. There was, of course, a conventional, odds-assessing, rational calculator in Owen. An important factor in the course he charted as SDP leader was his belief that the Labour vote had been squeezed down as far as it would go, and that new votes could only come from the Conservatives. But the rational calculator held sway only on the surface. In the volcanic depths beneath, which gave him his extraordinary energy and magnetism, was a gambler, a free spirit chafing against the constraints of odds-assessing rationality and prepared to risk everything on a single throw. It was the gambler who took Owen out of the Labour Party in the first place, and it was the gambler who took command during the merger row. On both occasions he was gambling for psychic space, for the freedom to be himself and to follow his instincts wherever they might take him. On both occasions he was, at least for a blessed moment, beyond calculation.

But that only pushes the question one stage further back. Why should the gambler have wanted to gamble in this way? Why could he not find psychic space in a merged Alliance party? If ideology and ambition do not explain Owen's vision of social democracy and its relationship with the Liberal Party, what does? At the time, I was inclined to find the answer in an emotional blind spot – in the absence of the elusive mixture of self-confidence and humility which makes it possible to win and hold the trust of equals, and which, for that reason, is the most important single attribute of a political leader in a parliamentary system. (Presidential systems may well be different: I have often thought that Owen would have been a marvellous candidate for the White House.) In his eyes, I thought, the SDP was a essentially an instrument – the violin to his Paganini or the Old Guard to his Napoleon. The reason he did not want merger was that he knew that a merged party would be less malleable: that even if he led it, it would not be an extension of his personality in the way he hoped SDP would be.

I still think there is something in it. Certainly, the Harris interviews reveal a remarkable inability to establish relations of trust with associates who possessed independent political weight of their own. The Mike Thomases and John Cartwrights – moons reflecting the Owen sun – receive warm tributes. The other members of the Gang of Four are a source of repeated betrayals and disappointments. Owen trusted Shirley Williams and wanted her to lead the SDP, but she let him down and he was forced to realise that 'she could, on occasion, be indecisive and that this would become a problem'. He trusted Bill Rodgers, but Bill let him down too. While they were both still in the Labour Party, Bill stood for the Shadow Cabinet. Then, at the launch of the SDP, he announced that it and the Liberals should fight an equal number of parliamentary seats – a concession from which 'we were never able to recover the concept of an electoral pact'. Worse was to follow. No sooner was the party founded than Bill and Shirley went off to the Anglo-German conference at Koenigswinter, there to engage in unauthorised discussions with David Steel – the moment when 'the development of SDP relations with the Liberals went critically wrong'. Roy Jenkins is pretty suspect throughout; even before the SDP was founded Owen could see that 'if the party was launched and the world thought Roy was predestined to be its leader, we would be finished before we had started'. But Roy too sank further as time passed. In his last appearance in the book, he sponsors the nuclear freeze movement – a peculiarly shocking deed since the retention of nuclear weapons is a necessary condition of becoming a 'can do, will do' Britain.

In the end, however, a narrowly personal explanation will not suffice. There was more to Owen than a masterful ego. For a brief moment, he represented something outside himself. Like Mrs Thatcher, he was part of the iconography of the 1980s: a focus for the hidden yearnings and insecurities which helped to shape the character of that curiously tormented decade. It is difficult to describe this aspect of his political appeal in words: iconography is a matter of style rather than of content. A good starting point is a passage from the Harris interviews describing a labouring job which he took in the summer of 1956 before going up to Cambridge:

In 1956, when the Suez crisis broke, there was Gaitskell on television and in the House of Commons criticizing Eden, and here were these men working alongside me, who should have been his natural supporters, furious with him. The *Daily Mirror* backed Gaitskell, but these men were tearing up their *Daily Mirror*s every day in the little hut where we had our tea and sandwiches during our break. . . . My working mates were solidly in favour of Eden. It was not only that they taught me how people like them think; they also opened my eyes to how I should think myself. From then on I never identified with the liberal – with a small 'l' – establishment. Through that experience I became suspicious of a kind of automatic sogginess which you come across in many aspects of British life, the kind of attitude which splits the difference on everything. The rather defeatist, even traitorous attitude reflected in the pre-war Apostles at Cambridge. I suppose it underlay the appeasement years. Its modern equivalent is a resigned attitude to Britain's continuous post-war economic decline.[4]

This was the authentic voice of the age – or, at any rate, of a crucially important part of the age. Three features stand out. The first and most obvious is populism: a mystic faith in the untutored common sense of ordinary folk, whose simple wisdom inoculates them against the sophistries of the over-educated, and whose hearts beat in time with the heart of their populist spokesman. The second is the gruff, Plymouth-Dockyard, southern English nationalism which explains Owen's lukewarm Europeanism as Foreign Secretary and his nuclear obsessions thereafter. The third is a yearning for hard, clear, simple solutions and a corresponding contempt for compromise and compromisers, for 'splitting the difference', for 'fudge and mudge', in other words for the humdrum processes of negotiation and consensus-building which muddy the clarity and glory of heroic leadership.

In all this, Owen – like Thatcher – was the symbol and product of a complex cultural and status upheaval. Like her, he spoke to and for the raw, down-to-earth, thrusting New Men who saw themselves as the harbingers of a new age of realism and enterprise: for the self-proclaimed 'achievers', whose anxious climb up the status hierarchy seemed blocked by a patronising old establishment, which they half-despised and half-envied. To be sure, most New Men were Conservative (or at least Thatcherite: the two are not the same) in politics. But even Conservative New Men had a soft spot for Owen. In any case, some New Men – perhaps because of their social origins or early political loyalties; perhaps because they worked in the public rather than in the private sector – were not Conservatives. Owen was not himself a New Man; he came from a comfortable professional background, and went from public school to Cambridge. But he increasingly looked and sounded like one. For 'every 60–year-old establishment figure', he insisted in the SDP's early days, it must have 'a late thirties/early forties radical thinker'.[5] 'What this party needs', he told one of the SDP's leading feminists, 'is balls'.[6] In his manifesto for the leadership election he promised 'a spirit of adventure, "guts" and drive',[7] implying, none too subtly, that Roy Jenkins, his opponent, lacked these attributes. Increasingly, the non-Conservative New Men became his real constituency. For him, as for them, small 'l' liberalism, with its emphasis on compromise and civility, and its willingness to see the other side's point of view, was inherently suspect. Like them, he saw it as the badge of the enervate old elites, with their clubs and their claret and their mocking irony, which the Costains building workers had taught him to disdain. To him, as to them, it reeked of defeatism and weakness. Small 'l' liberals were the people whose nerve always cracks: the appeasers who refused to glory in the Falklands war; the squeamish who did not want to see the miners crushed; the sentimentalists who saw shortcomings in the ethic of private-sector business; the wimps who questioned the virtues of 'macho' management in industry and 'macho' leadership in politics. Since big 'L' Liberals were mostly small 'l' liberals as well, conflict was inevitable.

The irony was that the Liberals were mostly new as well, but in a quite different way from Owen. Most of them were much further from anything that could reasonably be called an establishment than he was. The battle between Owen on the one hand and the Liberals and their SDP sympathisers on the other was not a battle between old and new, or between friends and enemies of the establishment: beneath the veneer of tolerance, the British establishment has always been deeply illiberal, as its treatment of heretics and dissenters demonstrates. It was a battle between rival challenges to the establishment, and rival responses to the crisis with which the old ways had failed to cope. One response was essentially managerial – heroic leadership; no-nonsense populism; hierarchical structures; in a word, the reassertion of authority. The other was participatory – a politics of negotiation and compromise; the extension of democracy. The combatants fought all the more fiercely because, in certain respects, they were on the same side: theirs was a civil war, and civil wars are notoriously more bloody than ordinary wars. Though Owen seems to have fallen on his own sword, the battle continues. It is the central battle of our times.

Labourism Resurgent

Mrs Thatcher's first Government presided over a post-war record in unemployment, a sharp fall in manufacturing output and a swathe of bankruptcies in exporting industries. Yet in the general election of June 1983, the Conservatives increased their majority over all parties from 43 to 144 – the second-largest majority in post-war history. The Labour Party suffered a net loss of 60 seats and came back with 209 – its smallest contingent since 1935. The recently formed SDP–Liberal Alliance won twenty-three, outshining any Liberal performance since 1931.

The result in votes was, in some ways, even more remarkable. The Conservative share of the popular vote fell from nearly 44 per cent to a little more than 42 per cent. Labour's share fell from 37 per cent to a little less than 28 per cent. The Alliance won a little more than 25 per cent – an increase of almost 12 per cent on the Liberals' performance in 1979. It was Labour's worst performance since 1918. The Alliance did better than the Liberal Party had done since 1931. The Conservatives fared worse than in 1950 or 1964, when they had gone down to defeat. To be sure, the 'mould' of British politics still held: Labour was still the chief opposition party and, once memories of polling night faded, public discussion of politics was still dominated by the familiar two-party jousting of the House of Commons. But the party system of which these jousts were the epiphenomena looked more vulnerable than at any time since it had taken shape in the 1920s, while the Labour Party, whose emergence as a potential party of government had been the chief catalyst of that system, seemed to many (including many Labour supporters) to be in terminal decline.[1]

Three years later, it was clear that rumours of its death had been exaggerated. In late August 1986, the *Guardian*'s running average of the last five opinion polls taken before the end of the month showed Labour at 38 per cent, the Conservatives at 34 per cent and the Alliance at 26 per cent. When the general election finally came in 1987, however, Labour's hopes were dashed. By common consent, it fought a brilliant campaign, but its performance in the polling booths remained mediocre. It only managed to push its share of the vote up to 30.8 per cent – the same percentage that it had won in the catastrophic election of 1931. It won only 229 seats – a worse result than in any post-war election, apart from 1983. Alliance hopes were dashed even more cruelly. Its share of the vote fell to 22.6 per cent, and it suffered a net loss of one seat. Only the Conservatives had any cause for self-congratulation. Still with only a little more than 42 per cent of the vote, they nevertheless won 376 seats and a majority over all parties of more than 100. The historically minded among them could note that no British political party had won three general elections in a row since 1959, and that no British Prime Minister had done so since the Great Reform Act.

Three years later, all was changed. The old two-party system had been restored to health. The SDP had split; the Alliance was in ruins; its successor parties bumped along in the opinion polls with ratings well below 10 per cent; and the sudden emergence of the Green Party as a serious, if minor, player in national politics still further divided what was misleadingly called the 'centre' vote. Partly as cause and partly as consequence, the Labour Party had recovered as well. It broke through the famous 40 per cent barrier which it had consistently failed to surmount in the previous Parliament, enjoyed opinion poll leads over the Conservatives of 20 per cent and more and scored ratings of more than 50 per cent. It still faced great difficulties, of course. To win an overall majority in the House of Commons, it would have to achieve a bigger swing than any party had achieved since the war. It would have to make substantial gains in the south-east of the country, where it had fallen back even in 1987, when it was recovering elsewhere. It would also have to win a number of seats where it had come third in two successive general elections. Formidable though these feats might be, however, its chances of performing them were better than anyone would have thought possible in 1987.

In broad outline, that is the essence of the electoral history of Britain in the 1980s. It has three outstanding features; if we are to make sense of the present position and likely future prospects of the British centre–left, their implications must be pondered with some care. The first and most obvious is that the supposed Thatcher Revolution has been procured from an extraordinarily narrow electoral base. Mrs

Thatcher's election victories were real enough, but they were won with a much smaller share of the total vote than Eden's or Macmillan's in the 1950s, or even than Heath's in 1970. The Conservative Party of the middle and late 1950s was the party of nearly half the country. Mrs Thatcher's was the party of only a handful more than two-fifths of it. It is true, of course, that the anti-Labour and, for that matter, anti-Alliance majorities were even larger than the anti-Conservative one. But that is hardly to the point: Labour and the Alliance were not using the machinery of the state to reshape a reluctant civil society in the image of a minority ideology. The revolutionaries' base, moreover, actually shrank a little as the revolution continued. They may or may not have succeeded in creating an 'enterprise culture', in destroying 'socialism' or in laying the foundations for a new and thrusting 'people's capitalism'; such claims are virtually untestable. What is certain is that their third election victory was won with slightly fewer votes than their first.

The second outstanding feature is the failure of the biggest centre–left party – at any rate until the closing months of the decade – to keep abreast of the economic and cultural transformation of the times. Though Thatcherites liked to pretend otherwise, that transformation was neither the product of Thatcherism nor, in itself, specially friendly to Thatcherism. It was a worldwide phenomenon, which took different forms in different societies, depending on the constellation of social and political forces in the society concerned; as Mitterrand and Gonzales showed in continental Europe, and Hawke showed in Australia, parties of the left could turn it to their advantage as well as parties of the right. In Britain, however, the Labour Party remained trapped, culturally and psephologically, in the past – a product of the age of steam, hobbling arthritically into the age of the computer. It spoke to the casualties of change, rather than to the pacemakers; to declining areas, rather than to advancing ones; to those who looked back in resignation rather than to those who looked forward in hope. In 1987, it won more of the inner-city seats north and west of the Severn–Trent line than it had ever won before. Among manual workers in the south of England, it came a bad second to the Conservatives.

That leads on to the third obvious feature of the electoral history of the 1980s – the Alliance's failure either to overtake the Labour Party in popular votes or to make significant inroads on its core constituency. There is nothing new about these failures, of course; in one form or another, similar failures have dogged the Liberals since the 1920s. But in the heady days immediately after the creation of the SDP, it looked as though the factors responsible for them might be about to disappear. Traditional loyalties to the two big parties had been fading for some time, and a large, volatile constituency of the 'de-aligned' seemed to be available for mobilisation. Alongside it was a smaller, but burgeoning, constituency – mostly middle-class; relatively well educated; anti-Conservative, but non-Labour – which seemed positively attracted by the promise of a new politics of institutional reform, social justice and market economics.[2]

These two groups had, of course, provided the social base for the Liberal revival of the middle 1970s, and that revival had nevertheless fizzled out. One reason why it had done so, however, was that the Liberals had suffered from two great weaknesses. No Liberal had held ministerial office since the war, and the Liberal Party had never come near to breaking Labour's hold on traditional Labour loyalties. When the SDP was formed, many believed that it would plug these holes. Its 'gang of four' were all recent members of the Cabinet and included both a former Chancellor of the Exchequer and a former Foreign Secretary. Nearly all its founders had joined it from the Labour Party. Some saw it as a potential successor to Labour as the main left-of-centre party in a still class-based party system; most assumed that it would be more successful in winning over working-class Labour voters than the Liberals had been on their own. The same view shaped early conceptions of the Alliance. The Liberals, the assumption went, would peg away at their existing constituency; the SDP would bring, as its dowry, a new, ex-Labour, working-class constituency, which the Liberals could not reach. These hopes perished in the 1983 election. There was no discernible difference between the two parties' capacities to appeal to working-class voters; after the election, they were equally unable to halt Labour's partial recovery. That central fact of electoral sociology holds the key both to the Alliance's gradual decline between 1983 and 1987 and to the savage internal conflicts which tore it apart thereafter.

The implications go wide, but one crucial implication stands out above all the others. This is that Britain's electoral history in this period is a Labour history rather than a Conservative or a Liberal one. Whatever may be true of the Cabinet table, the story that matters in the polling booths is not a story of triumphant Thatcherism; it is a story of enfeebled Labourism. The Conservatives did not gain ground in the 1980s; they lost it. The reason they stayed in power was simply that Labour's losses were far greater. The British people were not converted to Thatcherite values. Survey after survey makes it clear that, if anything, they were less Thatcherite in outlook at the end of the 1980s than they had been at the beginning.[3] The trouble was that Labour could not translate diffuse and unsystematic sympathy for broadly social democratic values into Labour votes on polling day. By a strange paradox, however, the story was not only one of enfeebled Labourism; it was also one of enduring Labourism. For most of the decade, Labour was too weak to provide an alternative to Thatcherism, but it remained strong enough to smother the Alliance alternative. It was no longer an effective partner in the old two-party system, but it could – and did – abort the birth of a new system.

Two obvious questions follow. Whence came this strange mixture of weakness and strength, enfeeblement and endurance? What does it portend for the future of the centre–left?

On one level, the answer to the first question is reasonably straightforward. After the 1979 defeat, the gathering boil of resentment, bitterness and sectarianism which had been building up under the inept and visionless Wilson–Callaghan Government came to a head, and burst. As after 1931 and 1951, only more so, the result was a prolonged swing to the left, marked most conspicuously by Michael Foot's election as leader when Callaghan retired, and culminating in the 'longest suicide note in history' on which the party fought the 1983 election. Humiliating defeat in that election, however, brought the party to its senses. Simply as a machine, as an instrument dedicated to the business of getting votes and anxious to stay in that business, the Labour Party turned out to be much tougher and more resilient than its propensity for self-mutilation in the 1979 Parliament suggested it would be. The younger generation of telegenic professional politicians which rose to leadership positions after the 1983 catastrophe – the generation of Neil Kinnock himself, John Smith, John Cunningham, Bryan Gould and Robin Cook – may have been a little short on ideas, but it was impressively long on that most crucial of political attributes, the will to win. More remarkably still, it became clear that a strong will to win was also to be found lower down in the party, both in Parliament and in the constituencies. To put it at its crudest and simplest, a lot of people in the Labour Party very much wanted to be in power – not by any means a self-evident proposition in a party of the left – and most of them had the sense to see that if they were to get into power the party would have to say the sorts of things voters want to hear.

Because of all this, the Kinnock–Hattersley leadership which took over a few months after the 1983 defeat found it surprisingly easy to isolate the ideological left and to present a smooth, competent and moderate face to the media and the voters. Kinnock's vaguely left-wing past was, moreover, an enormous asset from this point of view. Like Ramsay MacDonald in the 1920s and Harold Wilson in the 1960s, he came to the leadership with a substantial ideological credit balance at his command. He drew on it heavily after his election, but he never quite exhausted it. Like MacDonald in 1922 and 1923 and Wilson in 1963 and 1964, he could speak to the wider, national audience which he would have to persuade in order to reach 10 Downing Street, without arousing reflex suspicions of treachery or faintheartedness in the narrower party audience which he also had to satisfy. A second, and more paradoxical, asset was the conduct and demeanour of the Thatcherite enemy. One of the strongest impulses behind the advance of the left in the late 1970s and early 1980s was the sense, hard to put into words, but almost palpable among ordinary members of the Labour Party at the time, that it was better to be in opposition than to make the kind of compromises which the Wilson–Callaghan Government had made. If the most a Labour government could do was to carry out the dictates of the IMF slightly less enthusiastically than a Conservative government would have done, why snatch at every passing floating vote in order to return a Labour government? If no advances to socialism could be made in office, why water down principle in order to get into it? Under a Macmillan- or Heath-style Conservative government such questions would have been hard to answer. Mrs Thatcher made the answers self-evident. Even a feeble, pusillanimous and non-socialist Labour Government was better than Thatcherism. It *was* worth watering down principle in order to get into office: only in office could Labour halt the Thatcherite juggernaut.

That, or something like it, is the story told on the television screens and by the political commentators in the press. It is a convincing and illuminating story as far as it goes, but it provides only a partial answer to the questions that matter. If we are to tease out the full significance of Labour's fall and rise, we must dig deeper. In particular, we must look more closely at the internal dynamics, not just of the Labour Party, but of the wider labour movement. Tension between the political and industrial wings of that movement is built

194

in to its very structure. The Labour Party exists to win and hold power in a complex society, less than half of the working population of which belongs to a trade union, and in which the unions are frequently unpopular. The unions exist to promote the interests of their own members – interests which they have notoriously seen in a much narrower and less 'encompassing' way than have their counterparts in Scandinavia and Central Europe.[4] This tension has manifested itself in recurrent waves of trade union exasperation with the inhibitions and constraints of parliamentary politics. At repeated intervals, the unions have come to feel that the politicians have let them down: that they can achieve their purposes only through direct industrial action: and that any damage this does to the party is supportable since they can, at a pinch, do without it. Two obvious examples are the periods of labour unrest immediately before the First World War, when the parliamentary party was helping to prop up a minority Liberal Government, and immediately after it, when a handful of Labour MPs ineffectually confronted the massed battalions of the Lloyd George coalition. A third is the swing towards 'Direct Action' which followed the fall of the first Labour Government in 1924, and culminated in the general strike of 1926. A fourth is the upsurge of militancy which followed the collapse of the National Plan in 1966 and the abortive *In Place of Strife* white paper of 1969 and a fifth, the 'winter of discontent' of 1978–9, which followed the expenditure cuts of 1976 and the stringent incomes policy of 1976–8.

Just as disappointment with parliamentary politics has repeatedly driven the pendulum of trade union opinion to 'Direct Action', however, so industrial defeat has repeatedly driven it back to politics. The defeat of the general strike and the anti-trade union legislation which followed it convinced the unions that they needed the party as much as it needed them. At last, the political wing of the movement had unquestioned primacy over the industrial wing – not the least of the reasons for its victory in the 1929 election. And what Baldwin did for Ramsay MacDonald in the mid-1920s Mrs Thatcher did for Kinnock sixty years later.

From the defeat of *In Place of Strife* in 1969 until the defeat of Arthur Scargill in 1985, Labour politics were conducted in the shadow of 'Direct Action'. In the battle over *In Place of Strife*, the unions discovered that they could, after all, defeat the government of the day – at any rate, if it was a Labour Government. In the 1970s, they discovered that they could defeat a Conservative government as well. The Parliamentary Labour Party fought the Heath Govern ment's industrial relations legislation line by line and clause b clause, and succeeded only in making itself look ridiculous. Th unions, however, made the resulting Act inoperative by the simpl expedient of refusing to operate it. The result of the snap electior of February 1974 was still more illuminating. It was, after all, sort of 1926 in reverse. Once again, the miners had challenged th authority of a Conservative Government. But, whereas they ha been humiliatingly defeated in 1926, in 1974 they were triumphantl victorious – and not only on the industrial ground where they knew they were strong, but on the Government's chosen electoral groun as well. Not surprisingly, primacy in the movement now lay unmis takably with the industrial wing. The Wilson–Callaghan Govern ment was in office only because the National Union of Mineworker had made up its mind to smash the previous Government's statutory incomes policy, and everyone knew it. Though ministers took vigor ous, if belated, action to cut real wages,[5] they did so only when Jacl Jones decided that it was necessary, and by methods that h approved. Yet, in spite of their assiduous servility to the unior leaders, opposition from the rank and file of the trade unions eventu ally made their policies inoperative too; and when they left office ir 1979, the industrial wing of the movement seemed more firmly ir the saddle than ever before.

Even Mrs Thatcher's victory in 1979 did not produce a decisive change in the position. High unemployment weakened the unions bargaining power, and continuing unpopularity put them on the defensive politically. But it was not until Arthur Scargill, the herc of the industrial militants, had led his troops into battle and los that everyone could see that 'Direct Action' was now a blind alley and that Thatcherism could be defeated only through the ballo box. Thereafter, 'Scargillism' ceased to be a bogey. Much more importantly, primacy in the movement returned to the politicians. The union leaders, harassed by Thatcherite legislation and haunted by declining membership, now needed Kinnock more than he needed them. In a sense which had not been true since the mid-1950s, thei block votes were once again the heavy artillery of the party leader. With this queen of the battlefield at his command, Kinnock was able to scatter his enemies on the far left, to jettison the last vestiges o the neo-socialism of the late 1970s and early 1980s and to dominate the conference as no leader had dominated it since Ramsay MacDon ald in the days of his glory. It was a remarkable achievement, which proved him to be a far more resourceful, determined and courageous man than he had seemed at the time of his election. But he could not have done it if Mrs Thatcher had not given him the chance.

There was, however, a paradox in his triumph. As Henry Drucker has pointed out, the ideology of the British labour movement has, in practice, always had two dimensions, not one. The first is the obvious, familiar dimension of 'doctrine', learned analyses of which fill multitudinous library shelves. The second is the nebulous, impalpable dimension of 'ethos' – of mood, symbol and tradition – the subtleties of which are extraordinarily hard to catch on paper, but which nevertheless provides the better guide to the party's behaviour.[6] Kinnock fought his battles with the left in the realm of doctrine. He had to, for the party had no hope of winning an election until the doctrinal victories which the left had won in the early 1980s were undone. In striking contrast to Hugh Gaitskell twenty years before, he made no attempt to challenge the party's ethos. Indeed, one of the reasons why he prevailed in the battles over doctrine was that the stubborn survival of that ethos through all the vicissitudes of the recent past played into his hands. Yet, for most of its history, it has been the party's ethos, far more than its doctrine, which has alienated those anti-Conservative but non-Labour voters whose unwillingness to identify themselves with it holds the key to its electoral failures. Ethos helped to make the party's recovery possible. The trouble is that it is also the chief obstacle to a more decisive recovery in future.

As everyone knows, the party's doctrine is 'socialism', however defined. It has always been a fuzzy doctrine, stronger on long-term aspiration than on short-term strategy. But for the first fifty of the seventy-odd years since the party committed itself to the socialist project, it was, at least, a plausible doctrine for a would-be party of government. The failures of the minority Labour ministries between the wars were, no doubt, disconcerting, but they could be explained away. In any case, they were overshadowed by the achievements of the great reforming Government of 1945–50. By the 1950s, it is true, the kind of socialism which the party had preached between the wars was beginning to look threadbare, but the 'revisionists' around Hugh Gaitskell produced an equally plausible successor. Socialism was redefined to mean what is now thought of as social democracy. It was no longer about ownership. Instead, it was about equality, to be achieved by redistributing the fiscal dividend of economic growth. There were mutterings from traditional socialists, whose attitudes still prevailed in the constituency parties,[7] but for all practical purposes, revisionist social democracy became the working doctrine of the leadership.

In the 1960s and 1970s, however, doctrine disintegrated. Between 1964 and 1970, Gaitskellite revisionism was tried and found wanting. A government elected on the ticket of faster growth, and stuffed with the flower of the Oxford PPE School, steered the nation into a forced devaluation, wrecked its own, highly promising, incomes policy, fatally discredited the notion of consensual economic planning and contrived a somewhat lower rate of growth than that of the 1950s. More ominously still, these experiences called into question two of the central premises on which the whole revisionist project was based: the assumption that the existing machinery of the British state could be used as the revisionists wanted to use it; and the related assumption that revisionist policies could be carried out within the frontiers of a single, medium-sized West European nation-state, with an open market economy. This time, however, no successor was in sight. The old, Bevanite left of the party had never had a doctrine, only a series of intuitions. It had been against the rather bloodless and two-dimensional revisionism of the right, but it had never decided what it was for – still less, how it proposed to get it. In practice, the former Bevanites who held office in the Labour Cabinets of the 1960s and 1970s generally followed the revisionist line; its collapse left them as naked as their revisionist colleagues. The backbench right of the period (to which I belonged) occasionally sensed that something was lacking in the revisionism of the 1950s, but failed to propose an alternative. The backbench left increasingly stood, not for socialism in any recognisable sense, but for what might be called 'workerism':[8] for the twin propositions that any demand, made by any section of the organised working class, was *ipso facto* deserving of support, no matter what effect it might have on other sections of the working class or on society at large; and that the party should base its policies on the visceral intimations of its working-class constituents rather than on the theories of middle-class intellectuals.

When Labour returned to office after Heath's fall in 1974 it had become, in practice, a party without a doctrine – a fate neatly symbolised by its choice of James Callaghan, the 'Keeper of the Cloth Cap',[9] as its leader when Wilson retired. The radical intelligentsia, whose adhesion to the Labour Party during the inter-war period had turned it from a trade union pressure group into a potential party of government, and given it cultural and intellectual hegemony over the rest of the centre–left, became increasingly alienated from it – the most important single reason for the emergence of the SDP a few years later. For, although the Wilson–Callaghan Government contained some highly intelligent people, it displayed a kind of blank indifference to ideas and to the producers of ideas. Its motto was the First World War refrain: 'We're here because we're here because we're here.' It existed only to exist. At best, it stood for a kind of mitigated monetarism; for a slow, reluctant and humane retreat from post-war Keynesianism as opposed to a fast, enthusiastic and callous one. At worst it stood only for keeping Labour bottoms on the Treasury bench rather than Conservative ones.

Into this void swept the confused and passionate neo-socialism of the late 1970s and early 1980s, the legacies of which Kinnock has spent his leadership uprooting. It was a mood at least as much as a doctrine, this neo-socialism, and like many such moods it was articulated in a bewildering variety of accents. Some of its manifestations were generous and outward-looking, reflecting the 'post-materialist' idealism[10] and commitment to participative democracy which were also reflected in the community-politics wing of the Liberal Party, the feminist movement and the Green movement. Others were hard, dogmatic and intolerant, products of a peculiarly crude and rigid class-war Marxism. Insofar as it *was* a doctrine, however, the logic behind it pointed either to a kind of despairing negativism or to a quasi-Leninist political strategy for which the Labour Party was hopelessly unsuited and for which there was no mass support.

The doctrine contained two main elements, one primarily political and the other primarily economic. Central to the first was a theory of institutional seduction, oddly reminiscent of the arguments put forward fifty years earlier to explain Ramsay MacDonald's backsliding in 1931. Labour ministers, the argument went, had been captured by the civil service establishment and the institutions of global capitalism. They had then used the powers and patronage available to any British government to impose their policies on a supine parliamentary party. To ensure that this never happened again, Labour MPs should be made accountable to, and removable by, the activists in their constituency parties. Only then could the rank and file be sure that future Labour governments would remain firm in their socialist faith. Hand in hand with the theory of institutional seduction went a theory of what might be called the 'escape of the meso-economy', the chief British proponent of which was Stuart Holland.[11] Holland held that the growth of a 'meso-economy' of giant, often multi-national, firms had invalidated both classical and Keynesian economics. These giants were too powerful to be controlled by the sovereign consumer of classical theory. Nor could they be controlled by the sovereign nation-state. They could frustrate its monetary policies, through their access to credit beyond its boundaries, and its fiscal policies, through transfer prices which lowered their profits in high-tax countries and raised them in countries where taxes were lower. They could also frustrate its attempts to manage the exchange rate; and, since their investment horizons were longer than those Keynes presupposed, their investment intentions did not respond to Keynesian pump-priming. Meso-economic power, in short, had made Keynesian demand management unworkable; revisionist social democracy, which depended upon Keynesian demand management, was therefore obsolete. Salvation lay in a combination of central planning, public ownership, import controls and industrial democracy.

Particularly when coupled, as they were, with a commitment to unilateral nuclear disarmament and to withdrawal from the European Community, these conclusions implied a radical reconstruction of the political economy and an even more radical reorientation of the country's position in the world. More significant than the conclusions, however, was the logic behind them. Bennite neo-socialism was intended to challenge the revisionist social democracy of the 1960s and 1970s. By implication, it posed at least as fundamental a challenge to the gradualist democratic socialism which the revisionists had hoped to supersede. If the neo-socialist analysis was right – if Labour ministers could so easily be captured by the civil service establishment; if the giant firms of the meso-economy were strong enough to frustrate the Keynesian state; if, in other words, the prevailing balance of social power was such that revisionist social democracy could not be put into practice – there was no reason why gradualist democratic socialism should enjoy a happier fate. On neo-socialist assumptions, in other words, it would not be enough to elect a Labour government, even one committed to neo-socialist policies. It would also be necessary to overturn the prevailing balance of social power and crush the opposition which such policies would be bound to engender. The neo-socialists did not explain how they proposed to do this, but it did not take much perspicacity to see that they would almost certainly have to break with the norms of pluralist democracy.

The neo-socialists did not win an outright victory in the battle for party power which erupted after the 1979 defeat. But they enjoyed a long period of ascendancy, provided the occasion, if not the cause, for the creation of the SDP and left a profound impress on Labour's policies and stance. Kinnock's central objectives were to destroy their influence and to undo their work: to divide them against themselves, to isolate the dogmatic, class-war core from the generous, potentially outward-looking fringe, to drive the former to the margins of party decision-making and to weed out all the legacies of their ascendancy from the party's programme. By the summer of 1989 it was clear that he had succeeded. Bennite neo-socialism was as though it had never been. Unilateral nuclear disarmament, import controls and withdrawal from the European Community were no more. Public ownership had been replaced by a pale, if protean, creature called 'common ownership', which turned out to mean either employee ownership or a variety of forms of public regulation. The Labour Party was unmistakably another European social democratic party, committed, like its continental sister parties, to further European integration, continued membership of the Atlantic alliance and a market-oriented mixed economy, combining private enterprise with public power. Judged by results, Kinnock was now a better – or, at any rate, a more successful – revisionist than Gaitskell had ever been.

Unfortunately, there were at least three flies in the ointment. Gaitskell's revisionism was doctrine-driven. It sprang from an analysis of society and a vision of the future. To be sure, the analysis was flawed; that was one of the reasons why the vision remained unrealised. But Gaitskellite revisionists at least had a compass to steer by. Kinnock's do not. Their revisionism has been opinion-survey-driven. The object of the 1989 Policy Review was not to mobilise a constituency behind a set of principles; it was to tailor a programme for a set of constituencies. Opinion research told the party managers what themes would 'play' with the voters. The review groups then did their best to weave the themes concerned into a plausible whole.[12] At a time when a tired and unpopular government is running out of ideas, this may well be a good way to win an election, but it cannot be a way to produce a governing philosophy, capable of guiding decision-makers through the unforeseeable contingencies of power. Too much doctrine may produce a blinkered dogmatism that hardens into self-righteousness and intolerance. Too little is apt to lead to the kind of beleaguered opportunism that tore the soul out of the Labour Party in the late 1960s and 1970s. To be sure, the party is less beleaguered today than it has been for nearly thirty years. The fact remains that it has been better at following opinion than at shaping it. And, whatever may be true of oppositions, reforming governments cannot be content to follow.

The second fly is closely related to the first. Though Labour's new revisionism is not doctrine-driven, it belongs to a familiar doctrinal family. It is the younger brother of the revisionism of the 1950s and 1960s. Because it is not rooted in any social analysis, however, it is a curiously unquestioning and unhistorical younger brother. Like the Gaitskellites of thirty years ago, its proponents wish to use the machinery of the British state to make British society more productive and more just. There is no suggestion that that machinery may not be fitted for such purposes, still less any hint that past attempts to use it in this way have failed, or any enquiry into the reasons why. Though it makes occasional nods in the direction of the new, post-materialist, non-economist politics whose growth has been one of the central features of the age, these are half-hearted and unconvincing. Despite its air of novelty, the Policy Review is, in reality, a distinctly Bourbon document – the product of an intellectual restoration, not the herald of a revolution.

Partly because of all this (and this is where the third fly makes its appearance), Labour has not yet recaptured its lost cultural and intellectual hegemony over the rest of anti-Conservative Britain. It is overwhelmingly the dominant anti-Conservative party in votes, but hardly in ideas. More new thinking has come from the minuscule Communist Party than from all Labour's review groups. *Marxism Today* has a better claim to be the organ of the radical intelligentsia than the *New Socialist*, and the cross-party Charter 88 has evoked more enthusiasm from it than has any initiative of the Labour front bench. For all the ability and decency of its leaders, the Labour Party cannot yet claim to embody the progressive conscience, to speak to and for a broad swathe of centre–left opinion extending far beyond its own ranks, in the way that it could claim to do in the early 1960s or in 1945. As a result, its dominance in votes is not as complete as it looks at first sight. Even after the implosion of the Alliance, around 15 per cent of the electorate remained unwilling to support either of the major parties. Labour's hold on its core constituency is virtually unshakeable. Outside the core, it still has significant, if weakened, left-of-centre competitors.

At this point in the argument, re-enter ethos. Whatever may be true of Labour's doctrine, one of the central themes of the last ten years of British political history is the extraordinary toughness and durability of its ethos through all the buffetings which it has had to suffer. That ethos is, of course, almost indefinable. It is an amalgam of inherited habits, values, assumptions and expectations, derived, not from theory, but from experience and memory: the sediment left by nearly 200 years of working-class history. Any attempt to put it into words is bound to be arbitrary, and at the same time misleading. It is, above all, the ethos of the underdog: of life's losers: of the objects of history, on whom the subjects act. Perhaps Richard Hoggart caught it best in his famous evocation of the world of 'them' as seen from the vantage point of 'us':

> 'They' are 'the people at the top', 'the higher-ups', the people who give you your dole, call you up, tell you to go to war, fine you, made you split your family in the 'thirties to avoid a reduction in the Means Test allowance, 'get yer in the end', 'aren't really to be trusted', 'talk posh', 'are all twisters really', 'never tell yer owt' (e.g. of a relative in hospital), 'clap yer in clink', 'will do y' down if they can', 'summons yer', 'are all in a click (clique) together', 'treat y' like muck'.[13]

When Hoggart published that passage thirty years ago, it was beginning to sound out of date. Hoggart's world, we revisionists assured ourselves, was dead or, at any rate, dying. It was a product of the poverty and hardship which a combination of Keynesian economics and revisionist politics would gradually eradicate. Another decade or two of rising living standards, progressive taxation and growing social expenditure, and the whole notion of a powerless 'us', facing an alien and impervious 'them', would lose its resonance. And so, for a time, it seemed. But only for a time. The sunlit uplands of ever-increasing material prosperity, on which the revisionists pinned their hopes, suddenly receded beyond the horizon. The end of 'growthmanship', the collapse of the Keynesian system, the disappearance of large sectors of manufacturing industry, the rise in unemployment and the fall in expectations which all this brought with it[14] – in the forlorn council estates and bedraggled

203

terraces of Labour's heartlands, these gave Hoggart's world a new lease of life. In 1983, it was overwhelmed by the residue of late-1970s neo-socialism. The ebbing of the neo-socialist tide made it possible for Labour to take advantage of its resurgence.

That, of course, was the real meaning of the 1987 election. As Anthony Heath, Roger Jowell and John Curtice have shown, the well-worn notion that class voting has been on the wane, and that the secular decline in the Labour vote since the early 1950s is the product of a breakdown in the old association between class and voting, is dangerously over-simplified.[15] If classes are divided, not by income, as in most studies of voting behaviour, but by conditions of employment, a much more complex picture emerges. The association between class and voting has not declined. Rather, it has fluctuated. Labour is still the party of the working class, defined as 'rank-and-file manual employees'. Its problem is not that the working class is less likely to vote for it than it used to be, but that there are fewer workers: not the *embourgeoisement* of the proletariat, but its erosion. In the long run, of course, that is cold comfort for Labour's leaders. They do not want to be the undisputed chieftains of a shrinking proletarian enclave. They want to govern the country. All the same, they would have had no hope of winning over the rest of the country if they had not first won back the parts of the enclave which their predecessors lost between 1979 and 1983. That was what they did (or to put it more precisely, that was what they nearly did) in 1987. And it was the resilience of the Labour ethos that enabled them to do it.

In a more complicated way, ethos also helps to account for the collapse of the Alliance. For the Alliance's strategic problem was the mirror image of the Labour Party's. Where Labour found it hard to break out of its enclave, the Alliance found it almost impossible to break in. Without at least part of that enclave, however, it had no hope of replacing Labour as the main anti-Conservative player in a restructured two-party system: though it had won over most of the radical intellectuals who had been alienated by the bleak defensiveness of the Wilson–Callaghan Government, they were too few to turn it into a major party. There were three possible solutions. The first was to tackle the problem head-on: to accept that class was still a major factor in voting behaviour and to try, by one means or another, to detach Labour's working-class base from its old allegiance. The second was to circumvent it: to try to transcend the class divisions which had held the Liberals back in the past by putting forward a view of society and politics to which class was irrelevant, and to persuade the electorate that that view was correct. The third was to accept that, for the time being at any rate, the problem was insoluble and that Labour would continue to be the party of the working class in a system which was, at least, partly class-based; and to seek new Alliance voters not from the old Labour heartlands, but from the Conservatives. The vacillations and ambiguities which dogged the Alliance's 1987 election campaign sprang from a fatal unwillingness to choose between these solutions. The split which tore it apart thereafter reflected an earlier, suppressed, but bitter split over which solution to choose.

Broadly speaking, the first solution was that of the community-politics wing of the Liberal Party. Realising that many of the old Labour heartlands were ill served by sclerotic Labour machines, which took their working-class constituents for granted, the community politicians concluded that if they campaigned unremittingly on the bread-and-butter local issues which concerned Labour voters, they could gradually capture what had originally been safe Labour seats. Whatever its possible advantages in the distant future, however, this strategy offered only scanty and uncertain gains in the short, or even the medium, term; and although it had some support among the Liberal rank and file, the Alliance's leaders barely toyed with it. For the most part, the leadership oscillated between the second and third solutions. Sometimes, it campaigned for a 'new politics' of electoral and constitutional reform, cutting across the lines of class, party and economic interest. Sometimes, it offered a brisk, purportedly tough-minded mixture of neo-liberal economics and social concern, best described as 'Thatcherism with a human face' and designed to appeal to potential defectors from the Conservative Party. Unfortunately, its flirtations with the second solution were too cautious to attain the object of the exercise, while its flirtations with the third outraged many of its own members. When the election came in 1987 it was clear that, although the Alliance stood, in principle, for constitutional reform, it did not have sufficient faith in it to trust its future to it. More damagingly still, it was equally clear that it was hopelessly divided between a sub-Thatcherite faction led by David Owen and a larger, if more confused and less united, faction led by David Steel, for which Thatcherism was the main enemy. In the circumstances, the surprising thing is not that it lost some ground, but that it held on to so much.

Last, but by no means least, the resilience of Labour's ethos

205

provides a large part of the explanation for Kinnock's victories over the left. One reason is that, in a sense true of surprisingly few of his predecessors, Labour's ethos is also his ethos. He is unmistakably and unaffectedly a product of the working-class culture of the South Wales valleys, with all the strengths and weaknesses that that implies. The language of 'our people', which can so easily sound false or patronising, comes naturally to him because they really are his people. The myths and symbols of Labourism, which he manipulates with such artistry, are his myths and symbols: that is why the artistry is so successful. In many Labour front-benchers, his evocative 1987 phrase – that he was 'the first Kinnock in a thousand years' to go to university – might have sounded strained or mawkish. In him, it sounded authentic and moving. Another reason is that, in the circumstances of the 1980s, Kinnock's unyielding determination to make his party electable again fitted the essential defensiveness of the Labour ethos like a glove. Under a different Conservative Prime Minister, it might have pulled in a different direction: in normal circumstances, it is an ethos of opposition rather than of government. But, in the 1980s, the circumstances were not normal. As never before in this century, the labour movement, the labour culture, the values and practices which made up the labour ethos and the institutions which embodied those values and practices were all under attack. The Thatcher Revolution was inspired by a fierce hatred of what Mrs Thatcher called 'socialism', but what was in reality Labourism, and an equally fierce determination to destroy it. Labour people could see this; and, like Kinnock himself, they drew the conclusion that the adventurism of the neo-socialist left was a luxury which the movement could not afford.

But if the resilience of the party's ethos was an asset, it was also a liability. It enabled Labour to fight off the Alliance challenge; to reassert its hold on its core constituency; to break the neo-socialist spell which had done it so much damage in the early 1980s; to embrace a new version of the revisionism of the 1960s; and to become, once again, the only serious alternative to the Conservatives. Unfortunately, it also hampered the party's efforts to run with the grain of the technological and cultural changes which were steadily widening the gap between its core constituency and the society beyond, and made it difficult for it to respond emotionally to the new moods and new demands which those changes had brought with them. It stood in the way of an open, responsive and pluralistic political style appropriate to an increasingly diverse and hetero-geneous culture, and shored up the inward-looking defensiveness which cut the Labour movement off from non-Labour strands of opinion. And in doing all this, it fortified the doubts of the uncertain millions who yearned for an end to Thatcherism, but for whom the myths and symbols of Labourism were meaningless or threatening. The Labour Party had faced essentially the same problem since the 1920s: how to transcend Labourism without betraying the labour interest; how to bridge the gulf between the old Labour fortresses and the potentially anti-Conservative, but non-Labour hinterland; how to construct a broad-based and enduring social coalition cap-able, not just of giving it a temporary majority in the House of Commons, but of sustaining a reforming government thereafter. It was nearer to solving that problem in 1990 than it had been for a quarter of a century. As seventy years of Labour history bore witness, a near-solution was not enough.

Revisionism Revisited

A spectre is haunting Whitehall, the spectre of social democracy. One reason is that, on the mainland of Europe, it is much more than a spectre. In France and Spain, nominally socialist, but in reality social democratic, governments are in power. In Italy, a similar party is a significant partner in a coalition government. Social democratic parties also share power in the Benelux countries. In Federal Germany, the Social Democrats are in a stronger position than for nearly a decade. The socialist group, again largely social democratic in practice, is the largest group in the directly elected European Parliament; and, as Mrs Thatcher has spotted, the policies of the European Commission are essentially social democratic in orientation. Though it is too soon to tell what the political complexions of the former Soviet satellites in Eastern and Central Europe will be, it seems fairly clear that disillusion with neo-liberal dogma will eventually lead them to the mix of social welfare, market forces, political democracy and public intervention which is social democracy's hallmark.

Britain, as so often, lags behind the rest of Europe. But even in Britain, there is growing evidence that the Thatcher Revolution is beginning to approach the Thermidorean Reaction which lies in wait for all revolutions. Conservative ministers now talk of 'citizenship', 'stewardship' and 'responsibility'; Burke is returning to favour and Adam Smith is beginning to pall. Outside formal politics, the pendulum of concern is swinging away from private interest and back to public concern. Market failure once again looms larger in the public mind than government failure; and the erosion of community seems more alarming than the excesses of collectivism. Partly as cause and partly as consequence, it is becoming increasingly clear that the neo-liberal experiment of the last ten years has not ended the century-long relative decline of the British economy. Meanwhile, its social costs are becoming more visible and less tolerable. The problems which cry out most loudly for solution – poorly developed human capital; accelerating environmental degradation; decaying public services; fraying social ties – have all become more serious in the decade since the post-war settlement collapsed. Above all, there is growing evidence that the threat of ecological disaster can be averted only by a huge, unprecedented shift of attitude and behaviour which cannot conceivably be accomplished through the free competitive market. And, as I tried to show in the last chapter, the main opposition party is now essentially social democratic in approach.

All this suggests that Britain may be about to return to the social democratic middle way foreshadowed by the New Liberal theorists before the First World War and embodied in the reforms of the Attlee Government after the Second. Yet there is an irony here, which the reviving left and centre–left are understandably reluctant to confront. The strange amalgam of Tory politics and neo-liberal economics which has come to be known as 'Thatcherism' was, after all, a response to the crises of the 1970s and to the despairing negativism of the Wilson–Callaghan Government in the face of those crises. That negativism had many causes, some of which were discussed in the last chapter. One cause, however, stands out. Revisionist social democracy – the tacit governing philosophy which had guided the Labour leadership since the closing years of the post-war Labour Government – had fallen into disarray. Revisionist social democrats were adrift in seas which their philosophy had not charted, and through which it could not guide them. They lost the battle with the neo-liberal new right, and almost lost the battle with the neo-socialist new left, because they no longer knew what they were fighting for: because, on the deepest level, they were no longer fighting *for* anything, but only *against* something. The Thatcher Revolution (or, more properly, counter-revolution) was the legatee of their intellectual and moral exhaustion.

The values embodied in the social-liberal, social democratic middle way – a combination of personal freedom and social justice; of individual fulfilment and public purpose – are as compelling as they always were. But, as earlier chapters of this book have shown, the instruments through which the revisionist social democrats of the 1960s and 1970s tried to realise their values broke in the hands of the governments which relied upon them. To return to the middle way of Anthony Crosland and Hugh Gaitskell, or for that matter to the middle way of David Lloyd George and the authors of the Liberal 'Yellow Book', would be to return to a cul-de-sac. If revisionist social democracy is to recover intellectually as well as politically, if it is to serve as a governing philosophy after an election as well

209

as providing a basis for a platform from which to fight one, it must itself be revised.

If it is to be revised, it must first be revisited. One of the reasons for the neo-liberal ascendancy of the last ten years is that the neo-liberals had a ready-made explanation for the failures of the 1960s and 1970s; one of the reasons why the neo-liberal experiment has failed to solve the problems which baffled the 1960s and 1970s is that the explanation was over-simplified and misleading. The social democratic middle way, said the neo-liberals, was doomed from the start. It led inexorably to a vicious circle of excessive public expectations and excessive government commitments. Politicians were driven by the appetites of their electorates to promise more than they could perform; in trying to honour their commitments, they forced the state's reach beyond its grasp. The inevitable consequence was inflation in the economy and overload in the polity. The solution was to prune the state back and to damp down popular expectations.

The trouble with this explanation was that it ignored the experience of other Western industrial societies. By any measurable criterion – the share of GDP going to public expenditure, the rate of increase in that share, the level of welfare spending, the extent of government intervention in the economy – the British state was not exceptionally overloaded. On the contrary, it was close to the middle of the Western industrial range. On one point, however, the neo-liberals were right. No other European country saw a crisis of middle-way social democracy on the scale of Britain's. Partly because of this, no other European country saw as violent a swing to a radical new right. The neo-liberals gave the wrong answer, but they asked the right question. They saw that something went badly wrong with the middle-way social democracy of the post-war period, and they saw that that something had to be explained. So what is the explanation? Why *did* the revisionist social democracy of the post-war period fall into disarray in the 1970s? Why *were* the revisionists adrift?

Part of the answer, of course, is that the social democratic revisionists had the misfortune to be in power when the long-drawn-out British crisis of economic maladaptation entered its acute phase. Revisionist policies were associated with economic failure and the symptoms of economic failure: record inflation; rising unemployment; stagnant output; borrowings from the IMF; quarrels with the unions. But that provides only part of the explanation for the disarray of their authors. Economic failure did not come suddenly from a clear sky. It was the product of deep-seated structural flaws which had been discussed for years. If any school of thought could claim expertise in the economic sphere, it was the revisionists; they, above all, should have been able to foresee the crises which assailed them and to tackle the underlying causes. In any case, the crisis of economic maladaptation was only one facet of a much deeper political and institutional crisis; and the revisionists were as baffled by its non-economic manifestations as by its economic ones. Their periods in office were marked by repeated institutional tinkering – an abortive 'reform' of the House of Lords, half-hearted 'reform' of the civil service, abortive devolution for Scotland and Wales, half-hearted 'reform' of the system of parliamentary committees – but most of their changes were *ad hoc*, designed to buy off trouble in the short term rather than to reconstruct the system as a whole. As so often, in such circumstances, the trouble continued. There were growing signs of public disaffection from the political system,[1] and the governments of the period found it increasingly difficult to mobilise consent for the measures which they believed to be necessary to overcome the economic crisis.

It would be absurd to suggest that these failures, confusions and hesitations sprang from a single source. All the same, a common thread runs through most of them. One way to identify it is to look at the things the social democratic governments of the 1960s and 1970s did not do – at their failures, for example, to give the House of Commons investigative committees teeth, to reform the Official Secrets Act, to liberate council-house tenants from the tyranny of petty officials, to give parents more say in the education of their children, to devise schemes of devolution for Wales and Scotland with a fair chance of working or to promote labour co-operatives in the profitable sectors of the economy. At the heart of these failures of omission – as well as of the more obvious failures of commission which characterised the period – lay a certain attitude of mind. It was a venerable attitude, the roots of which can be traced back to Peter Clarke's distinction between 'moral' and 'mechanical' reform, discussed in Chapter 3.[2] The New Liberals, Clarke suggested, were essentially 'moral' reformers. They believed that reform came, in the last resort, from inner changes of value and belief and therefore put their faith in argument and persuasion. The early Fabians, by contrast, put theirs in 'mechanical' reform, pushed through by the coercive power of the state. Revisionist social democracy was the child of New Liberalism as well as of Fabianism, of course, but the Fabian element in its inheritance had gradually swamped the New Liberal element.

Despite the humanity and generosity of its founders, it degenerated, in practice, into a system of social engineering, perilously dependent on the positivist social sciences of the day. Social scientists, it was assumed, knew or could easily find out what levers the engineers would have to pull in order to put their values into practice. The engineers could then pull the levers in the knowledge that the machine would respond as they wished. There was no doubt that society could be changed by social engineering from the top: there was also no doubt that it was right to change it from the top. Social democrats wanted to do good, but they were more anxious to do good to others than to help others do good to themselves. As they saw it, the role of public intervention was to provide, to manipulate, or to instruct, rather than to empower. They reorganised the school system instead of trying to foster an appetite for learning. They tried to maintain full employment by macro-economic manipulation from the centre, instead of giving local communities the instruments with which to develop their economies. They sought to dispense medical care, instead of trying to help people to become less dependent on medicine. In spite of its commitment to personal freedom, social democracy in practice gave a lower priority to spontaneity, creativity and autonomy than to efficiency, tidiness and uniformity; perhaps because of this, or perhaps because the social scientists on whom it relied often thought in this way themselves, it also gave more weight to the quantitative and the measurable than to the qualitative and the intangible.

Hand in hand with all this went a curiously simplistic attitude to the state and to the relationship between the state and the web of intermediate institutions and voluntary associations which make up a civil society. The state was seen as an instrument (or set of instruments) which social democratic ministers could use as they wished. Civil society was seen, all too often, not as an agent but as a patient: as an inert body, lying on an operating table, undergoing social democratic surgery. The surgeons acted for the best, of course, but they acted on the patient from without; the patient merely received their ministrations. But in reality, of course, civil society is not in the least like a patient. Even in Stalin's Russia and Hitler's Germany, it turned out to have a mind (or minds) of its own, which could not be bent to the dictator's will. In Britain, it was far more recalcitrant.

Instead of lying passively on the operating table, it insisted on arguing with the surgeon, or at least on trying to do so. Employers, trade unionists, parents, doctors, teachers, civil servants, investors – none of these were content to abide by the decisions which social democratic ministers took on their behalf. And because revisionist social democracy had no place for the notion of civil society, the surgeons were hopelessly disorientated by this behaviour. In the simplest sense, they no longer knew what to do.

An obvious question follows. Why did revisionist social democracy come to rely on 'mechanical' rather than on 'moral' reform? Why did its exponents put so much faith in top–down social engineering? Why did they view the relationship between civil society and the state in such an over-simplified fashion? Why, above all, did they assume so readily that the institutions of the central state were the appropriate instruments for the ends they wished to pursue?

A complete answer would have to range wide. Like all doctrines, revisionist social democracy was the child of its time. Hubristic scientism, grandiose projects, institutional giantism, technocratic arrogance – these were the stigmata of the age, marking political leaders of the right as well as of the left, and private sector hierarchies as well as public sector ones. Underlying all of these was a common mentality; and a complete account of the revisionists' assumptions would have to explore their relationship with that mentality. My scope will be narrower. I shall start by looking at the revisionists' historiography: at their assumptions, tacit rather than explicit, about the logic underlying the growth of the modern state and the development of its functions.

These assumptions can be traced back to the debates which took place before the First World War and which I discussed in Chapter 1. One revealing source for them is that masterpiece of compression, *Liberalism*,[3] written by the New Liberal theorist, L. T. Hobhouse, and published in 1911. Liberalism, says Hobhouse, is about freedom. But the struggle for freedom has changed direction. In the old days, Liberals fought for equality before the law, for representative government, for freedom of speech, belief and association. But these battles have now been won, or largely won. The goal now is more complex. Liberalism is now about positive freedom, or freedom to, rather than about negative freedom, or freedom from. Its task is to enable men and women to realise themselves to the full; to do that it must use state intervention to guarantee to all individuals a share in the common stock large enough to ensure that their personalities can flourish. What Hobhouse advocated, later thinkers postulated. In his seminal essay, 'Citizenship and Social Class',[4] published in 1949, T. H. Marshall put forward an essentially Hobhousian view of the way in which the concept of citizenship and of the rights of the citizen had evolved. Citizenship, said Marshall, had three elements – civil, political and social – and over the preceding three centuries the struggle for citizenship rights had shifted from the first to the second, and then from the second to the third. Civil citizenship, manifested in equal civil rights, had been established in the eighteenth century. Political citizenship, equality of political rights, was largely the work of the nineteenth century. In the twentieth century, the focus had shifted to social citizenship, to the struggle for equal social rights.

A similar view was implicit in the writings of Anthony Crosland, the high priest of social democratic revisionism. His central message was, of course, that socialism was about equality, not about ownership; and that the path to greater equality lay through a combination of economic growth, high welfare spending and progressive taxation, not through further nationalisation. If only by implication, however, the whole Croslandian edifice rested on the premise that the primordial social democratic ends of greater social and economic equality – in effect, the full realisation of Marshall's vision of social citizenship – could perfectly well be achieved by and through the existing political system, since that system was already egalitarian. In this country, Crosland and his followers assumed, political citizenship and political rights were secure. Because they were secure, democratic socialists could and should concentrate on social reform and leave the polity to take care of itself.

Against that background, the crisis which overtook revisionist social democracy in the 1970s takes on a new significance. In a now famous study, Albert Hirschman suggested that there are two mechanisms with which consumers may control producers.[5] One is Exit: taking one's custom elsewhere: ceasing to buy the product: the quintessential mechanism of the market. The other is Voice: nagging, argument, persuasion, complaint. That is quintessentially the mechanism of politics. And, says Hirschman, Voice goes with and depends upon Loyalty: upon ties of mutuality which endure through time. That insight, I believe, throws a vivid shaft of light on the whole story.

The growth of social citizenship – indeed, the very notion of social citizenship – implies a smaller role for the market and a greater role for politics. Exit does less and Voice does more. The pioneers of social citizenship were well aware of this, but they saw no problems in it. Indeed, they rejoiced in it. They assumed that the new social citizenship would supplement the old political citizenship: that the struggle for political rights and political equality had been won: that democracy, having triumphed in the political sphere, should expand into the social sphere, where the battle was still going on. Taking this for granted, they also took it for granted that the institutions and practices of the social-citizenship state would be subject to popular control: that Voice would not only have a larger role to play, but would in practice be able to play it. To use my earlier metaphor, the surgeon was entitled to operate on the patient because, in the last analysis, the patient controlled the surgeon. As the 1970s wore on, that assumption was increasingly called into question. Voice, it began to seem, was not playing the enhanced role assigned to it after all. The institutions of social citizenship were not effectively subject to popular control, or not, at any rate, in a fashion which the supposed citizens themselves – the patients in the doctor's waiting room, the parents outside the school playground, the crowd waiting to approach the DHSS counter – considered satisfactory. At the point where the shoe pinched, at the point where ordinary members of the public brushed up against the institutions which were supposed to be acting in their names, the social citizenship state did not feel like a citizenship state at all. All too often, it felt more like a rather ramshackle, on the whole benevolent, but often remote and high-handed despotism. And, as anyone who played any part in electoral politics in the 1970s can testify, there arose, from the ranks of the supposed social citizens, a swelling chorus of complaint.

All this was grist to the new right's mill. The new right held that, in this field at any rate, Voice could not possibly work and that the only sensible course was to rely on Exit. To them, it seemed self-evident that the whole project of social citizenship had always been an absurdity; the troubles of the 1970s proved, what was in any event obvious, that the time had come to abandon it. That was not, of course, the only possible conclusion. Another was that Hobhouse, Marshall, Crosland and the rest had been dangerously over-optimistic: that they had tried to build the top floor of citizenship before the first floor was in place. For the pioneers of social citizenship were wrong in supposing that political citizenship had already been achieved. In the most profound sense, Britain's (or, at least,

England's) was not really a civic culture. The British were not, and never had been, citizens of a state, with the rights and duties that go with citizenship; they were subjects of a monarch. By a strange irony, however, the culture of subjecthood gave extra resonance to the arguments of the new right. When they were told that Voice was bound to fail, that they would never be able effectively to control the institutions of social citizenship, that the social citizenship state was bound to be bureaucratic, top-heavy and remote and that dignity, autonomy and choice could be enhanced only by giving greater scope to the market, large numbers of people – including large numbers of working-class people who had formerly voted Labour – nodded in bemused agreement.

They did not do so because they shared the new right's hostility to the values of social citizenship; as I pointed out in the last chapter, survey data suggest that those values remain popular. They nodded for two reasons. Experience had convinced them that there was something in the new right's critique of the way in which the values were put into practice. And because their assumptions had been shaped by a non-civic culture, by a subject culture with little or no place for active and participatory citizenship, they could see no grounds on which to quarrel with the new right's inference. Because of this cultural inheritance, the top–down statism of the left and the neo-liberalism of the right appeared to be the only feasible alternatives. The case for non-statist, decentralist, participatory forms of public intervention was rarely made, and still more rarely heard. Exit won the argument, in short, because the culture provided too little space for Voice. Social citizenship faltered because political citizenship was lacking.

That leads on to a more complex point. The notion of citizenship implies a notion of the City: of the *polis*; of a community which endures beyond the lifetimes of its present members and to which they have loyalties that transcend their own immediate interests. Hirschman recognised this when he suggested that Voice went with Loyalty. That part of his insight also throws much-needed light on the fate of social democratic revisionism. Not only did the revisionists fail to see that Voice was too weak to play the role they allotted to it. They also failed to see that their whole project depended upon Loyalty as well; that social citizenship, like political citizenship, could be made a reality only in a community held together by ties of mutual obligation. In more familiar language, they sought equality

216

and made ritual genuflections towards liberty, but forgot about fraternity.

The reasons go deep. Occasional dissenters apart, the British left has never managed to emancipate itself from a set of attitudes to man and society – to the relationship between individual purposes and social purposes – which has permeated the political philosophy and dominated the most influential social sciences of the English-speaking world for around two centuries, and which I shall call reductionist individualism. Reductionist individualism can make sense of Exit and Voice. Loyalty, however, is alien to it. Central to it is the assumption that society is made up of separate, sovereign, atomistic individuals. The obligations which these individuals owe to their society derive ultimately from the fact that it can be shown that it is to their advantage to belong to it. They follow their own purposes, which they choose for themselves. These purposes may be altruistic as well as egoistic, but in either case they are individual, not social; and even altruistic purposes are pursued in the same manner as egoistic ones. Firms, colleges or research institutes may have common purposes, but whole societies do not. The notion that politics is, or should be, a process through which a political community agrees its common purpose is therefore nonsensical. Politics is about reconciling conflicts between individually chosen purposes; it has no business with the choice of purposes. Indeed, in some versions of the intellectual tradition which has inspired this way of looking at society, the notion that politics might have something to do with the choice of purposes is at least incipiently tyrannical. Freedom means *my* freedom to choose *my* purposes for myself, and to pursue them in my own way, provided only that I leave others free to choose and pursue their purposes in their ways. To allow others to take part in the process through which I choose my purposes would be to allow them to trespass on psychic space which belongs to me – space which it is my right to keep inviolate.

The reductionist picture of society has been underpinned by an extraordinarily tenacious, though frequently only half-acknowledged, set of psychological assumptions. In it, as Brian Crowley brilliantly demonstrates, the three-dimensional self of the real world – the self which has been fashioned by constant interaction with other selves, in a structure of common traditions, interlocking histories and shared meanings; the self which is, so to speak, 'permeable' by other selves – is replaced by an impermeable self. This impermeable self is, as he puts it, 'radically individuated and unencum-

217

bered': isolated, atomistic, in an important sense a-social and therefore historyless.[6] Such a self can command, or obey, or exploit, or trade with other selves, but it cannot engage with them. It is the self which Mrs Thatcher posited when she said there was no such thing as society, but only individuals and their families. It is incapable of the relationships which enable members of a society to learn from each other and which lead them to define themselves as social creatures: of the relationships which teach us who we are and which enable us to become something different from what we once were. Such a self can be a subject, but scarcely a citizen – a fit recipient for the ministrations of 'mechanical' reformers, but not the learning creature presupposed by those who put their faith in 'moral' reform.

Reductionist individualism has great achievements to its credit. It helped to liberate our ancestors from superstition and oppression. Unfortunately, however, its legacy has constricted the imagination as well as enriching it. For it can picture only two ways of living together in society, and make sense of only two ways of co-ordinating the actions of men and women in society. One way is through command and the other is through exchange. Co-ordination may be imposed from the top down or it may emerge spontaneously from free exchanges of one kind or another. Society is either a kind of hierarchy, held together because those at the bottom obey those at the top, or it is a kind of market, held together by the calculating self-interest of its members.[7] The objection to this picture is not that it is false. Hierarchies and markets both exist; and both are easily recognised and understood. The objection is that it is incomplete; that the exchange relations characteristic of markets and the authority relations characteristic of hierarchies do not exhaust the repertoire available to real men and women in real societies. The familiar dichotomies of exchange versus command, market versus state, around which so much political argument has revolved in the last two centuries, contain only part of the truth. Alongside the command and exchange modes of co-ordinating the actions of people in society, there is a third, more elusive mode, which is in some sense fraternal or communitarian. We collaborate with our fellows, not only because we have been ordered to or because we calculate that it is in our interests to, but because we have learned to, because we believe that it is our duty to, because the ties of mutual obligation which derive from membership of a community impel us to. For, in the real world, the self *is* permeable; real people in real societies are social creatures, genetically programmed for sociability. People do not only command, obey and exchange one good for another. They also teach and learn, and become different people in doing so. Because of this, the mirror which the tradition of reductionist individualism holds up to us reflects only part of our true natures.

On the level of everyday life this is scarcely an epoch-making discovery. It is common sense. But everyday life is one thing; social theory is another. In the English-speaking world, at any rate, reductionist individualism has had enormous influence. Indeed, Britain's political culture has been saturated with it. Many have knowingly adhered to it. Many more – including, not least, many of the pioneers of the social democratic middle way – have been unconsciously shaped by it and still more, perhaps, by the psychological assumptions underlying it. And so the image in the mirror has been taken for reality, not just by the political right, but even by the left and centre–left.

The consequences are multifarious, but one stands out ahead of all the others. It is that there was a vacuum – perhaps a contradiction – at the heart of the revisionist project. Croslandian social democrats had broken with the conclusions which the classical and neo-classical economists of a previous generation had drawn from their reductionist-individualist premises, but they had not constructed an alternative set of premises. In the political class and, for that matter, among the academic and quasi-academic technocracy on which the political class relied for advice, the individualist paradigm continued to hold the field – not on the level of everyday practice, of course, but on the level of principle and theory. While the practices worked, no problems ensued. When they started to run into trouble, however, the gap between practice and theory became increasingly obvious, and the practitioners found it increasingly difficult to justify their practices to themselves. They also found it increasingly difficult to justify them to others. New-right liberalism is much closer to the individualist paradigm than was revisionist social democracy, and the neo-liberals could therefore appeal much more convincingly to it than could the revisionist social democrats whom they were trying to displace.

All this applies to the plane of ideas and argument; to revisionist social democracy as a system of belief competing with other systems of belief. Even more damagingly, much the same was true of the practical plane: of social democracy as a guide to policy and action. The revisionist middle way depended on negotiation, power-sharing

219

and mutual education among and between the state and the myriad intermediate institutions on the health of which the health of civil society depends – in other words, on the kinds of relationships which depend upon the ties of common citizenship and community. But because they were trapped in the individualist paradigm, its intellectual defenders did not (perhaps could not) realise this; and because they did not realise it, their system was fatally flawed. Central to it was the notion of a mixed economy, in which resources are largely allocated by the market, but in which public power intervenes on a significant scale to supplement, constrain, manipulate or direct market forces for public ends. Public intervention, however, implies a public purpose. But if reductionist individualism is true how can there be a public to have a purpose?

That is a rather abstract way of putting it, but the consequences were all too concrete. Almost by definition, public intervention is designed to change behaviour; otherwise there would be no need for it. In order to change behaviour, the interventionists had to influence choices and purposes. In principle, there were two ways of doing this. They could influence them through a mixture of punishments and rewards – perhaps indirectly, by manipulating the punishments and rewards of the market, perhaps directly, by regulation and prohibition. Or they could influence them by argument and persuasion. But in order to argue they would have had to listen to the arguments of others, and create a structure within which argument could take place. In order to persuade they would have had to appeal to a communitarian ethic of some kind, capable of generating a sense of mutual obligation and civic duty. But, because they had never broken out of the reductionist-individualist framework and the command–exchange dichotomy associated with it, they could do neither of these things. The notion that social change might come through arguing and listening rather than through commanding and obeying was alien to them; and they had no communitarian ethic to appeal to. Only rewards and punishments were left.

The result was a paradox. Revisionist social democracy depended on communitarian ties, but it could not speak the language of community. That was why it became a technocratic philosophy rather than a political one: why its view of government and of the relationship between government and governed was 'mechanical', rather than 'moral'. In the halcyon days of the long post-war boom, that view provided an adequate basis for policy-making. When the economic climate began to turn cold, however, mechanistic social engineering became more and more difficult; and governments had to turn to argument and persuasion after all. Since the changes they sought were often painful, moreover, they had to argue on non-hedonistic grounds: on grounds of fraternal solidarity or community loyalty. But their philosophy gave them no basis on which to develop arguments of that sort, and no language in which to phrase them. Resurgent economic liberalism easily drowned the resulting silence.

I have argued that the revisionist social democracy of the 1960s and 1970s failed for two reasons. In Hirschman's terminology, Voice was too weak to provide a satisfactory substitute for Exit; Voice was too weak because Loyalty was lacking. In ordinary language, social citizenship was not achieved because the institutions – and still more the practices and assumptions – of political citizenship were feeble or absent. Revisionist policies failed because they were not sustained by the communitarian ties upon which a social demo-cratic political economy depends. Behind all this lay a deep-rooted failure of political imagination. Revisionist social democracy focused on policy and neglected process. It had to do with outcomes rather than with procedures; with results rather than with the methods by which they were pursued. It forgot that, in the real world, process and policy are inextricably entangled; that good policies are likely to be twisted out of shape by bad processes. At its heart lay the old, social liberal notion of positive freedom; of freedom to; of self-fulfilment. But because it concentrated on policy and underestimated process, it failed to see that positive freedom could not be handed out from on high to a grateful society, like chocolate bars at a children's party; that its vision of a fairer society, in which autonomy and dignity would be enhanced and the human personality would flower, could be realised only in action and by the members of the society themselves; that, in this crucial sense, process *is* policy. Hence its increasing reliance on social engineering; hence too its disarray when the social engineers found that their instruments had broken in their hands.

A revised revisionism would have to put process first. To use a phrase of Zygmunt Bauman's, it would be a philosophy of interpreters rather than of legislators:[8] of facilitators rather than of blueprint-makers: of listeners and persuaders rather than of com-manders or manipulators. Like the revisionism of twenty-five years ago, it would be a philosophy of social citizenship and the mixed economy. Unlike the older revisionism, however, it would recognise that, without political citizenship, social citizenship cannot be achieved. Also unlike the older revisionism it would not be trapped in the conventional dichotomy of state versus market, command versus exchange, and it would therefore see the mixed economy, not as a mere 'middle way' between undesirable extremes, but as a distinctive entity, desirable in its own right. For the same reason, it would try to call on the third, communitarian mode of social coordination to redress the balance of the other two. It would, in other words, lay more emphasis on what Charles Lindblom calls 'preceptoral' relations, and less on the more familiar relations of authority and exchange. Its conception of citizenship would be civic-republican rather than liberal-individualist, implying that citizens have duties to the city as well as rights against it. It would seek to restore the fraying bonds of community, to offset the pressures which atomise the individual and fragment the ties that bind individuals to each other, to create spaces in which the language of community can be spoken. Above all, it would try to find an idiom in which an ethic of fraternity and mutual obligation can resonate in a diverse, medium-sized, multi-cultural late-twentieth-century society in an increasingly interdependent world.

Almost by definition, no one can be certain how to do this. The revisionist social democracy of the 1960s and 1970s ended in an impasse because it lacked the intellectual and moral resources to transcend the authority–exchange dichotomy, because its approach to man and society was saturated with assumptions which made communitarian relations incomprehensible, if not inconceivable. All the same, one or two points seem plain.

'We do not learn to read or write, to ride or swim, by being merely told how to do it,' wrote John Stuart Mill, that strange amalgam of civic republican and liberal individualist, 'but by doing it.'[9] We restore the ties of community by practising its habits: we acquire citizenship by acting as citizens. Where High Tory communitarians see the community as the unwilled, supra-rational child of blood and soil and instinct, a social democratic communitarian would see it as a construct, endlessly made and remade by the decisions of its members. But these values – the values of active citizenship as opposed to passive subjecthood – cannot be taught. They can only be learned; and they have to be learned in use. Social democratic communitarians will therefore seek the widest possible diffusion of responsibility and power – not only in what is conventionally thought of as the political sphere, but in what Mill called 'the business of life', at work, in the school system, in the health service, indeed wherever discussion and debate can help to determine collective purposes. Unlike their predecessors of the 1960s and 1970s, the revisionists of the 1990s would not deploy public power only, or even mainly, through the central state. But, where the neo-liberals tried to resolve the crisis of central-state social democracy by narrowing the scope of public power, the new revisionists would do so by widening access to it; and where neo-liberals draw in the frontiers of politics and citizenship, new revisionists would extend them.

It hardly needs saying that such a politics would run against the grain of the 'deferential' elements which have helped to give Britain's political culture its characteristic flavour, and which political commentators since Bagehot have taken to be the predominant ones. But it would be wrong to despair of it on that account. It is not clear that the British were ever as 'deferential' as their rulers would have liked them to be; even if they were, it is not clear that they are so still. Cultural determinism is as dangerous as any other sort of determinism. One of the reasons why the Thatcher Revolution went as far as it did is that its supporters defied orthodox assumptions about the culturally imposed limits to change. In that respect, if in no others, a revised social democracy would do well to take a leaf out of the Thatcherites' book.

Towards a New Progressive Coalition?

In a thought-provoking essay, the American economist Albert Hirschman once suggested that one of the features of present-day society is a continuing cycle whereby periods of 'intense preoccupation with public issues' oscillate with periods of 'almost total concentration on individual improvement'.[1] Each phase in the cycle, he thought, breeds its own excesses; sooner or later, these lead to disappointment and disillusionment; these, in turn, cause the pendulum of opinion and involvement to swing back again. So the privatism of the 1950s gave way to public activism in the 1960s, and the activism of the 1960s and early 1970s to a new kind of privatism in the 1980s. As a new decade begins, there are signs that Hirschman's cycle is on the move again. 'Markets', 'enterprise', 'choice' – the bugle calls of the neo-liberal counter-revolution which seemed destined to carry all before it in the early 1980s – are beginning to sound as empty as the cries of 'planning', 'strategy' and 'intervention' sounded ten years ago. As in early 1960s, when Jack Kennedy was elected to the presidency of the United States on the ticket of active government and the Conservative Government of Harold Macmillan began the switch from arm's-length Keynesianism to indicative economic planning, privatism seems to be losing its charms, while a tentative and uncertain collectivism is beginning to return to favour.

The opposition parties can hardly fail to rejoice at this. Albeit in different ways, all of them – even the nationalists – stand for public involvement of some kind. Just as Kenneth Galbraith's famous paradox of private affluence and public squalor provided fertile soil for their predecessors in the early 1960s, the emerging, if still undefined, neo-collectivism of the 1990s may provide fertile soil for them now. But they would be unwise to rejoice too much: 'may' should not be mistaken for 'will'. Hirschman's cycle seems to be shifting back from the private sphere to the public and therefore from neo-liberalism to interventionism. It does not follow that the political right is bound to suffer and the political left to benefit. However odd it may seem at first sight, there are signs that the Conservative Party has sensed the change in the public mood and that it is preparing to fight on the new terrain which that change is likely to bring into being. Douglas Hurd's thoughtful call for 'active citizenship', Christopher Patten's promotion and Mrs Thatcher's partial, but unmistakable, greening all suggest that their party is bracing itself for a change of emphasis and direction.

It is true, of course, that such changes often damage those who make them. The Attlee Government's bonfire of controls in the late 1940s, Macmillan's switch to planning in the early 1960s and Denis Healey's enforced conversion to monetarism in the middle 1970s all made the opposition case seem more plausible than it had been before and paved the way for a government defeat at the subsequent general election. But it does not follow that governments can never carry conviction if they change policy wardrobes in this way. Everything depends on the skill and panache with which the switch is made, and that in turn depends on the extent to which those who make it feel comfortable with their own conduct. New-right rhetoric notwithstanding, it would be a mistake to assume that Conservative ministers could not possibly feel comfortable with a switch away from individualistic neo-liberalism.

Individualistic neo-liberalism is by no means the only strand in the Conservative inheritance, and not necessarily the most important. In its long history, the Conservative Party has been on different sides of more than one argument at different times. It has been for protection and for free trade; for imperialism and for Little England; for the free market and for planning. That, of course, is why it is the oldest right-of-centre party in the world. Where its rivals have gone through agonies of introspective revisionism when circumstances changed, it has simply drawn on a different strand in its constantly evolving tradition. As the sacred names of Burke, Disraeli and Joseph Chamberlain bear witness, that tradition can easily support a kind of Tory collectivism.

Even Thatcherism is not to be equated with new-right market liberalism. There is a coincidence between the two, of course, but the first is both wider and narrower than the second. Like Gaullism, Thatcherism was born of the sense of despair, almost of panic, which a generation of apparent national decline had provoked in a certain section of the political class. Its central purpose was to make Britain great again; since the heyday of market liberalism had coincided with the heyday of the British Empire, it assumed that market liberalism was the key to greatness. In Andrew Gamble's phrase, it is has always been about the 'strong state' as well as the 'free economy';[2] about British (or rather English) nationhood as well as the profit motive; about history, identity and, above all, authority as well as economics. For most Thatcherites, the strong state, English nationhood and authority come first. They objected to the soft, liberal and, as they saw it, over-extended state of the 1970s and wanted to prune it back. But they wanted to prune it because they wanted to strengthen it, because they believed that softness and liberality were the products of over-extension, not because they objected to the state as such. They wanted to put authority back on its throne, to restore social discipline. They were for the market, not just because they saw it as the realm of individual freedom, but because they believed that market discipline and social discipline went together. They were, and are, individualists, but in a strange way they are collectivists as well. They are willing, in some cases even eager, to use collectivist instruments to procure the right kinds of individuals; and they want the right kind of individuals because they want the right kind of collectivity.

The end of new-right neo-liberalism, in short, would not necessarily spell the end of Thatcherism. Still less would the end of Thatcherism necessarily spell the end of Conservative rule. The Conservative Party, having experienced an individualistic mutation in the 1970s, could perfectly well experience a collectivist mutation in the 1990s. Collectivism, after all, comes in different flavours. It can be authoritarian as well as participative: repressive as well as tolerant: High Tory as well as social democratic. Between the wars, Conservative or Conservative-dominated governments were in office for nearly twenty years. In the 1920s they tried (not very enthusiastically, it must be admitted) to return to the market-liberal order of the past. In the 1930s, their stance was at least as collectivist as the outgoing Labour Government's had been. Partly because of this, their long hegemony was still unshaken at the end of the decade, and would probably have continued into the 1940s if the war had not intervened. The fact is that, since the coming of manhood suffrage in 1918, Conservative rule has been the norm, not the exception. That does not mean that it is bound to continue into the 1990s. History is indeterminate, and there is no iron law to say that the future will resemble the past. It is, however, a corrective to the instinctive whiggery – to the comforting assumption that History was a capital 'H' is naturally progressive in direction, and that only temporary accidents occasionally wrench it off the rails of progress – which lurks in the subconscious of the British left and centre–left. In modern Britain, left-of-centre governments are rare. There is nothing in the present political conjuncture to suggest that they are about to become commonplace.

Analysis of the complex and paradoxical condition of the anti-Conservative oppositions should begin at this point. Labour, the Greens and the Liberal Democrats together overwhelmingly outnumber the Conservatives. If the votes which went to the Alliance in the last election could be added to the votes which went to Labour, the Conservatives would certainly lose. The smaller opposition parties plainly have no hope of assembling such an electoral coalition. In spite of a strong local government base, the Liberal Democrats' showing in the national polls is no better than the Liberals' showing used to be before the Alliance came into existence and considerably worse than it used to be in good Liberal years. In spite of their sudden upsurge in the 1989 European elections, the Greens' showing is now even poorer than the Liberal Democrats'. Labour's chances of doing so are, of course, far better. By the early months of 1990, opinion polls were putting it ahead in all social classes except the professional and managerial. But in spite of its sedulous moderation, its social democratic posture and the upsurge in its poll performance which followed its Policy Review, it has captured only part of the Alliance's old constituency and not the whole of it; its hold on the part it has captured, moreover, is less secure than it seems. The elements of a winning anti-Conservative coalition undoubtedly exist on the ground. So far, no one has managed to put them securely together.

The question is, why not? One of the chief reasons, I believe, is that part of what is normally thought of as the centre is no longer conventionally centrist in assumption or aspiration, while part of the left is not, in most of the familiar senses of the phrase, genuinely on the left. Because of this, the familiar language of right, left and centre now confuses at least as much as it illuminates. More importantly, the mental universe which that language reflects, and in which most people who use it are imprisoned, prevents its inhabitants from coming to terms with the complex and baffling social and cultural transformation of the age. Because they cannot come to terms with that transformation, they are equally unable to come to terms with the divisions between the opposition parties which are its product. And because they cannot come to terms with these divisions, they cannot overcome them.

The language of the right, left and centre dates, of course, from the French Revolution. It is also saturated, however, with assumptions born during the Industrial Revolution. One of the legacies of the first is that the left is supposed to be the party of the Revolution and the right of Reaction; that the left stands for Movement and the future, and the right for Order and the past. Thanks to the second, the left is also supposed to be the party of the exploited – by definition, the proletariat – and the right of the exploiters, by definition the bourgeoisie. Implicit in the whole terminology of right centre and left, in other words, are three crucial assumptions. The first is that the 'left' is in favour of change and the 'right' against it. The second is that change – radical and far-reaching change, at any rate – is inherently 'progressive', emancipatory and anti-exploitative, to be welcomed by the dispossessed, and feared by their dispossessors. Though this is less obvious, a further implication is that, in the epic contest between progress and reaction, the 'centre' stands on the margins – uncertain, pusillanimous or even hypocritical, in favour of trivial changes, perhaps, but not of fundamental ones: sympathetic towards the exploited, but unwilling to make war on the exploiters.

These assumptions have been shaky for quite a long time. More than twenty years ago, Samuel Brittan argued with some force that the choice between left and right was a 'bogus dilemma' and showed that the language of right and left distracted attention from important divisions of political opinion.[3] With all its weaknesses, however, the terminology did at least have some purchase on political reality. (If only for the sake of simplicity, I have frequently used it in this book.) Everyone knew that the divisions between the parties were blurred, and that some significant divisions of opinion and attitude cut across them. But, for the purposes of everyday discussion, it made a kind of sense to talk as if the spread of political allegiance could be pictured in linear terms, with a left at one end and a right at the other. In the last few years, however, the assumptions underpinning that familiar view of politics and political belief have broken down. New issues have arisen and new identities have taken shape around them. These can be assimilated to the categories of left and right only by doing violence to their true meaning. Because of that, the very notion of a mass party of the left, whose mission is to lead the forces of progress towards their historical destiny –

228

the notion which has been central to the mythology and culture of the entire labour movement since the late nineteenth century – has now collapsed in ruins. So, of course, has the corresponding notion that the onward march of the left is barred by an anti-progressive right.

Some concrete examples may help to pin down the argument. The most obvious is perhaps the Greens, both in their narrower manifestation as a political party and in their wider manifestation as a movement of opinion. Are they right or left or centre? More importantly, what does it add to our understanding – either of them or of the political scene – to describe them as right or left or centre? The programme put forward by the Green Party is more radical – indeed, in some respects, more socialist – than anything proposed by the Labour Party. The assumptions on which it based, however, challenge most of the assumptions which have been central to the socialist tradition (and, of course, to all other political traditions) for most of the last century. The same applies, even more obviously, to the Green movement and to what might be called the Green perspective. As Christopher Patten has pointed out, elements in that perspective are uncannily reminiscent of Edmund Burke; other elements remind one of William Morris and the early Independent Labour Party. But a laborious attempt to trace the ideological ancestry of the Greens – however intriguing as an exercise in the history of social thought – would contribute very little to understanding their role in the politics of today. The important thing about them is that they are new, the product of an issue and a set of identities which simply did not exist when the language of right, left and centre was invented and which that language cannot encompass.

The Greens are not alone in this respect. Much the same applies to nationalism and feminism – perhaps the two most potent reshapers of identity in the recent past. One of the most striking features of present-day Europe is the revival of ancient and, until recently, dormant ethnicities – Basques, Catalans, Welsh, Bretons, Flemings, Scots, Corsicans – in the face of the homogenising pressures of the twentieth century. In the eyes of progressive-minded intellectuals from the 'classical', metropolitan nations, the nations whose nationhood is embodied in and guaranteed by statehood, that revival often looks bizarre, irrational, even reactionary, just as the comparable revival of the Slav peoples of Central Europe looked irrational and reactionary to Marx and Engels more than 100 years ago. But the metropolitan nations are metropolitan only because they (or, to put it more precisely, the dynasties at whose courts their languages were spoken) happened to be the winners in struggles for power which might have gone the other way. No immutable law of progress decreed that Paris should be a metropolis rather than Avignon, Madrid rather than Barcelona, London rather than Edinburgh. It is hard to see why the loser nations should be thought of as unreasonable or backward-looking because they now wish to unpick the seams stitched long ago by the accidents of battle, dynastic marriage and inheritance. In any case, they do not think of themselves as backward-looking. On the contrary, they believe, with some justification, that theirs is the wave of the future. But they stand athwart the conventional left–right spectrum; and their view of themselves, of their futures and of the political projects on which they are engaged cannot be articulated in left–right language.

Feminism is in some ways the most striking example of all. No social change in my adult lifetime has been more dramatic or more far-reaching in its human consequences than the changes which have taken place in the status of women and, still more, in the claims made by women. The forces responsible for these changes are still in full spate and are likely to produce further, perhaps even more dramatic, changes in future. In every corner of experience, from the most intimate to the most public, gender roles are being redefined and gender identities reconstructed. That redefinition and reconstruction, moreover, is the result of public debate, persuasion and agitation – in short, of politics – as well as of the private transactions of individual men and women. But although some feminists sometimes speak the language of right and left, and try to assimilate their claims to its categories, that is best seen as an unconscious tribute to the weight of the past from which they are trying to escape.

In reality, feminism is neither left nor right. To phrase its claims and express the experiences which lie behind them in the language of right and left is, in an odd way, to diminish them. Women are not an exploited class, denied their fair share of society's resources: they are not a *class* at all. Nor are they an ethnic or religious minority suffering unfair discrimination. They are half the human race. There are obvious analogies between their experiences and the experiences of exploited classes or of minority groups which have been discriminated against, and these analogies can help to illuminate the predicament against which feminism is a protest. But analogies are not equations. The central, fundamental proposition which give point to the feminist perspective is that, in certain crucial respects, women

230

qua women have common interests which cut across their class interests and that society should be transformed to take account of these common interests. That proposition cannot be put in a language which presupposes that the interests of women can be assimilated to the interests of their menfolk: that, as a matter of fact, women *qua* women have no place in the public sphere at all.

That is only the beginning of the story. These profound shifts of identity and aspiration are not the only ones which the old right–left language cannot capture. Since the middle 1970s, Britain has been caught in the backwash of two overlapping crises. The first is a worldwide crisis of rapid technological change, intensifying international competition and lagging societal adaptation. This crisis is the product of three interconnected developments. The first might be termed 'globalisation'. Markets, capital, companies have all become global, in a sense which was not true in the past; partly, but only partly, because of this, no national government can manage its economy in isolation from other national governments. The second might be termed 'miniaturisation'. Its origins lie in the information revolution which has made possible the growth of 'flexible specialisation' and small-batch production in industry; because of it, traditional mass-production manufacturing and the nexus of values and institutions associated with traditional mass-production manufacturing – what has come to be called 'Fordism'[4] – have sharply declined in importance. The third is best understood as the child of the first two. It is the emergence of what is sometimes called 'disorganised capitalism' in place of the organised capitalism of the post-war period.[5] These developments have imposed extraordinary strains on the adaptability of the societies which have experienced them and on the managerial capacity of their institutions, national and international. Huge, disruptive changes have taken place in the balance of wealth and power, both within societies and between them; and although the pluralist democracies of the West have weathered these storms far more successfully than have the one-party regimes of the East, it is clear that, even in the West, the social and political stability associated with the long, 'Fordist' post-war boom is a thing of the past.

The second crisis is connected with the first, but analytically distinct from it. It is a peculiarly British crisis of legitimacy, authority and civic solidarity. In part it is the product of relative economic decline and of the social tensions associated with relative economic decline. In part in reflects a complex set of cultural and social changes – increasing social heterogeneity, the decline of deference, the growth of a 'post-materialist' ethic of autonomy, authenticity and diversity – which, between them, began to undermine the moral basis of the institutions of the British state and to call into question the central assumptions of Britain's unwritten constitution. For the moment, however, the causes matter less than the consequences. And the chief consequence was that it became progressively more difficult for British governments, buffeted by the worldwide storms described in the last paragraph, to operate a mixed economy, dependent on public intervention and therefore on public support for the institutions of intervention.

Like the shifts of attitude and identity I described a moment ago, only in some ways even more decisively, this double crisis has shattered the categories of the old, left–right language and made nonsense of the assumptions embedded in it. It no longer makes sense to assume that the left is for change, the right against it and the centre undecided. By a terrible irony, Thatcherism has, until recently at any rate, been the most radical, change-welcoming and change-promoting tendency in British politics. It is a moot point whether the most conservative, change-fearing and change-opposing has been the Militant hard left, what remains of the old-fashioned, traditional, blue-collar Labour right or the equally demoralised remnants of traditional, *noblesse-oblige* Tory paternalism.

What is true of ideas is equally true of interests. In the short term, at any rate, the unionised, heavy-industry, manual working class, locked into the old technologies and the mind-set they engendered, can only lose from the disappearance of the 'Fordist' order of the past. Alongside it on the change-fearing side of the barricades is the growing under-class of the handicapped, the unskilled and the desperate – the late-twentieth-century equivalent of the undeserving poor who haunted the imaginations of respectable Victorians. Equally, if less blatantly, conservative in interest is the old-established, upper-middle-class, public-sector professional salariat, which used to manage the now diminished institutions of the post-war settlement. Ranged against all of these, on the change-welcoming side of the divide, is a motley army of, among others, small builders, acupuncturists, millionaire stockbrokers, health-insurance salesmen, garage mechanics, whole-food restaurateurs, software designers, desk-top publishers, property dealers, corporate managers, travel agents, gutter-press magnates, council-house purchasers, electricians, makers of garden furniture and members of workers' co-operatives.

If we are to pick our way through the confusion, and make sense of the way in which the double crisis of the 1970s and 1980s has impacted on our politics, we must, as a first step, supplement the categories of 'right', 'centre' and 'left' with the categories 'conservative' and 'radical'. Thatcherism then emerges as a radical-right response to the crisis. Its most obvious feature is the rather provincial, defiantly insular, mildly xenophobic and occasionally strident British (or at any rate, English) Gaullism I mentioned earlier. Linked with that have been a most un-Gaullist neo-liberal economic ideology, an almost Jacobin determination to thrust aside the intermediate institutions which embody alternative values and assumptions and a much trumpeted, if slightly bogus, populist contempt for the old elites which can be made the scapegoats for national decline. To be sure, there are limits to its radicalism. As Harold Perkin has pointed out, one of the central themes of the social history of the last twenty years is a struggle between the public-sector professionals, whose interests lie in more public intervention, and their private-sector counterparts who compete with the public sector for scarce resources.[6] Looked at in that light, Thatcherism is the ideological stalking horse for corporate big business; and big private-sector corporations are at least as conservative in instinct and behaviour as big public-sector ones. When all the necessary qualifications have been made, however, there is no doubt that the thrust of the whole ensemble has been radical. There is no doubt either that its radicalism has given it an *élan*, a sense of mission and an internal cohesion which go far to account for its political success.

The opposition to Thatcherism has, however, been divided against itself – obviously by party and ideology, but much more importantly by mood, assumption, instinct and approach. Parts of what is conventionally classified as the centre have offered radical-left responses – notably, though not exclusively, the community-politics wing of the pre-merger Liberal Party, in many ways the closest British equivalent to the West German Greens. Sections of the Labour 'soft left', most of the Greens themselves, parts of the feminist movement, sections of the Scottish and Welsh nationalist parties and some of the socialist groupings outside the Labour Party also belong in the radical column. David Owen's social market was a sort of sub-Thatcherite sub-radicalism. On the other hand, 'wet', *noblesse-oblige* Toryism, 1950s-style Croslandite revisionism, middle-of-the-road pre-Grimond Liberalism, Morrisonian state socialism and, most obviously of all, traditional, mainstream Labourism are quintessentially conservative.

Against that background, the confusions and uncertainties of the anti-Thatcher oppositions begin to fall into place. There is no truth in the notion that Thatcherism is, for some mysterious reason, unstoppable – the wave of the future, which we must all ride or drown. It is, at most, a wave of one possible future. It is riven by contradictions, and if I am right in thinking that Hirschman's cycle of involvement is now moving back towards the public phase, some of these contradictions will be more difficult to resolve in the next ten years then they have been in the last. But, although it can, in principle, be beaten, it will not be beaten either by a miraculously renascent 'centre' or by an indomitable and triumphant 'left'. It can be beaten only by a new, late-twentieth-century version of the progressive coalitions over which the Liberal Government uneasily presided before 1914 and which, for a brilliant but fleeting moment, the Labour Party managed to mobilise in 1945. Such a coalition would have to embrace both what is conventionally thought of as the centre and what is conventionally thought of as the left. But thinking of it in that way only makes it more difficult to bring it into existence. Successful social coalitions of this sort cannot be cobbled together by procuring some quick fix through which all the constituencies of all its putative members can be delivered to the same camp on election day. They need a mission, an idea, a project. For the reasons discussed above, the kind of project which is needed – the kind of project which will speak to the new identities and new aspirations of the age – cannot be described in the language of right and left. To put the point another way around, a successful anti-Thatcher coalition would have to include conservative interests and tendencies as well as radical ones. But it would have to be radical-led, or at any rate radical-inspired. And focusing on the old, left–right dichotomy makes it more difficult to think in radical ways.

One of the most striking features of British politics in the 1980s was the stubborn persistence of an amorphous, fluctuating, but nevertheless unmistakable anti-system constituency. For a while, the SDP–Liberal Alliance captured a good deal of it, perhaps even most of it. But, as anyone who played any part in Alliance politics can testify, both the Alliance parties always faced in two directions. They tried to appeal, at one and the same time, to radicals and to conservatives: to the adventurous and dissatisfied who wanted change and to the timorous or established who feared it: to those alienated by the ancient pieties of the British state and to those who respected them: to those who looked forward to a turbulent and unpredictable citizen democracy, and to those who wanted to erect a barrier against 'extremism'.

Because of this, and because their leaders were children of the existing system and shaped by its imperatives, the Alliance parties did not speak unambiguously to or for the anti-system constituency on which they partially depended. Because their message was ambiguous, conventional commentators – also children of the system – failed to decipher the anti-system subtext it contained. Yet the anti-system Alliance constituency existed, and helped to give the Alliance its early successes. The traditional left–right language belittled (and still belittles) it, just as it belittles the nationalist and feminist constituencies. For anti-system voters do not fit on the left–right spectrum: the assumptions embedded in the left–right spectrum are part of the system against which they are in revolt. In left–right language, theirs is a mere 'protest vote' – negative, unpredictable and, in an odd way, faintly underhand. It would be much more convenient for those who think in left–right categories if they disappeared. Then the protagonists in the left–right struggle could get on with the economic and social issues which really matter. But although the collapse of the Alliance has rendered the anti-system constituency even more amorphous and uncertain of its allegiance than it was before, it still exists. It is an indispensable element in any progressive coalition worthy of the name.

The question that really matters, in short, is not how to assemble an anti-Thatcher coalition. It is how to assemble an anti-Thatcher coalition capable of offering a convincing radical alternative to the radicalism of the right, while at the same time appealing to non-radical interests and opinions. Almost by definition, none of the anti-Conservative parties can do this by itself. For different reasons, the nationalists and the Greens do not even aspire to do so. The Liberal Democrats, the miscalled centre, present a more complicated problem. In some respects, they are better placed than Labour to spring the trap in which anti-Thatcherite Britain is caught. Their structures are suppler and more open to new currents of thought and feeling. They have no institutional or sentimental ties to the old 'Fordist' order – no sacred rites of proletarian solidarity or solemn memories of the martyred dead – and most of them also have a much smaller ideological stake in it. Indeed, by a strange irony of cultural mutation, their largely pre-'Fordist' ideological inheritance – an amalgam of nineteenth-century popular radicalism and early-twentieth-century social liberalism – speaks more easily to the post-'Fordist' late twentieth century than does the top–down Fabianism which has always been so strongly represented in the Labour Party. Much the same is true of their approach to the crisis of ebbing political legitimacy. Though Liberal Democrat parliamentarians succumb as easily as Labour ones to the narcissistic *mores* of the Palace of Westminster, the party as a whole is instinctively suspicious of the central state and, as such, willing to be convinced that its institutions need drastic reform.

The trouble, of course, is that these advantages are more than outweighed by corresponding disadvantages. The most obvious is the precipitous fall in the former Alliance parties' opinion-poll standing which followed the split of 1987 and 1988. The most serious is the imperviousness of the core Labour constituency to non-Labour appeals. Had the Alliance come ahead of Labour in 1987, it might have been able to squeeze the Labour vote in subsequent elections, as the French socialists have squeezed the communist vote. But it didn't; and, for the foreseeable future, it won't. Except in a handful of inner-city constituencies where Liberal community politicians had managed to build a local base, the Alliance's themes struck no chords with traditional Labour voters. It is a fantasy to imagine that the Liberal Democrats will make more inroads on Labour's core constituency in the 1990s then the Alliance did in the 1980s. And, without that constituency, no progressive coalition is possible.

Can the Labour Party do better? Can Kinnock succeed where MacDonald, Attlee, Gaitskell and Wilson all failed? He and his party have made huge strides in the last few years. To judge by the policy review, a Labour government would approach the conventional economic and social issues which can still be described in conventional left–right language with competence and flair. If a new progressive coalition could be mobilised around a broadly social democratic approach to those issues, Labour would be well set to mobilise it. The trouble, of course, is that it cannot be. Competence and flair in handling the conventional issues of the left–right spectrum are not enough. Something else is needed as well – an ability to speak *and* *listen* to the amorphous anti-system constituency I mentioned earlier; a respect for the new identities and new aspirations born of the cultural and technological paradigm shift through which we are now living; a recognition that politics have escaped from the categories of left and right which most Labour politicians learned at the political equivalents of their mothers' knees. And that something else runs against the grain of the labour movement.

The reasons are more complicated than they may seem at first sight. *Pace* most media comment, Labour's problem is not that it is a socialist party in a post-socialist era. The socialist tradition is enormously variegated, and some of the strands in it are remarkably well adapted to the needs of a post-industrial society in the late twentieth century. The real problem is threefold. Ever since Labour became a potential governing party, most Labour socialists – like most Labour social democrats – have taken it for granted that they could achieve their purposes by taking control of the central British state, and using it to engineer change from the top down. Ever since the foundation of the Labour Representation Committee, moreover, mainstream Labour socialists – again like Labour social democrats – have taken it for granted that their ideologies would have to be mediated through the institutions, values and collective memory of British Labourism. Thirdly, Labour has never been able to shake off the assumption that the battering ram of historical change is and must be a hegemonic mass party of the 'left', with its own unique vision of the future and its own unique mandate to translate that vision into reality.

The last assumption is the most damaging. It dates from the emergence of the mass political party in the late nineteenth century. The first socialist party to embody it was the German SPD of the late nineteenth and early twentieth centuries. Ironically, British Labour did not adopt it until comparatively late in the day. By a familiar paradox of cultural backwardness, however, it now clings to it more fiercely than does any of its counterparts on the European mainland. That, of course, is why Labour politicians found it so hard to come to terms with the emergence of the Alliance in the early 1980s and why they find it equally hard to come to terms with the emergence of the Greens today. For, in their eyes, history can have no place for third or fourth parties – or not, at any rate, for emerging third or fourth parties. If such parties appear on the scene, the blame must lie with the media, or with fashion or with 'protest'. The correct response is to sit tight and wait for these ephemera to burn themselves out. Then history will get back on to the rails, and the cowards and traitors whose flinching and sneering so beguiled the short-sighted will vanish from sight. That, broadly speaking, has been the working assumption of the Labour Party for the best part of seventy years. It is even more obviously out of joint with the multi-cultural, multi-valued, multi-fissured society of today than is the language of right and left with which it is so closely associated. The hallmarks of the technological and cultural changes which have shaped that society are diversity, experiment and tolerance. These must imply a different kind of politics – a politics of pluralism, negotiation and mutual education. With such a politics the fantasy of hegemony is incompatible. So long as that fantasy lurks in the mentality of the Labour Party, it can never be more than a transitory shelter for the new constituencies which a new progressive coalition would have to embrace.

So what is to be done? Of the United Kingdom anti-Conservative parties, the Greens are not – or not yet – in the business of constructing a winning electoral coalition. The Liberal Democrats dream fitfully of entering the business, but are far too weak to do so. The Labour Party is in it, but is too heavily encumbered by the legacy of its past to be sure of prospering at it. If the psephological cards all fall its way – if it fends off the nationalist threat to its indispensable majority in Scotland; if it benefits disproportionately both from the fall of the former Alliance parties and from the rise of the Greens – it may find itself in government with an overall majority, conceivably a substantial one. But such a government would be as much the prisoner of circumstances as those of the 1960s and 1970s, and as likely to see its support fade away as the constraints of economic vulnerability close in. The conventional routines of majoritarian British party politics may well produce an uncertain anti-Conservative government, speaking for only part of the broad spectrum of anti-Conservative opinion in the country. They are most unlikely to produce an anti-Conservative government backed by the kind of progressive coalition I have been advocating in this chapter. Yet electoral politicians are trapped in these routines and seem unable to break out of them. The Labour leadership still talks the language of single-party hegemony, more appropriate to the 1940s than to the 1990s. The Liberal Democrats still cannot bring themselves to admit unequivocally that the pluralistic new politics they seek can be brought into being only by a broad-based alliance, in which they would have to take second place to Labour.

Yet the prospect is not altogether bleak. On most of the conventional, 'left–right' issues of the day, and on many of the newer issues that cut across the conventional 'left–right' divide, Labour and the Liberal Democrats now have a virtually common agenda. Both are broadly social democratic in their approach to economic and welfare questions; both are at least pale green; both are in favour of closer European integration. There are differences between them, of course, but except to the eye of love the differences are much less striking than the similarities. Though passionate partisans on both sides may fail to recognise it, they also have a common interest. The seats which the Liberal Democrats might win in more favourable circumstances are seats which Labour cannot hope to win in any conceivable circumstances. It would be to Labour's advantage if they went to the Liberal Democrats rather than to the Conservatives. By the same token, the seats which Labour would have to win to prevent the Conservatives from forming a government are seats where the Liberal Democrats have no chance. On any rational calculation, it would be to the advantage of the latter if Labour won them. Sadly, that does not mean that the two parties are about to make common cause. Everyone outside electoral politics can see that there is an overwhelming case – of principle and also of self-interest – for an electoral agreement between them, but electoral politicians, conditioned by the rituals of our majoritarian system, find it extraordinarily difficult to talk publicly about co-operation with another party, whatever they may think privately. It does, however, mean that there is no insuperable obstacle to their reaching a tacit agreement not to 'strive officiously' to keep their hopes alive in seats which the other party has a better chance of winning. More important still, it means that the next election, like the elections of 1945 and 1964, will be a struggle between the Conservative Party and the rest, not between Labour and the rest.

The crux, however, lies elsewhere. It has become a cliché to say that 1989 was a year of revolutions reminiscent of 1848. All over Eastern and Central Europe, popular movements, inspired by the principles of the great French Revolution of 1789, drove out corrupt and creaking regimes which derived such legitimacy as they possessed from the memory of the October Revolution of 1917. The Declaration of the Rights of Man and the Citizen turned out to have more to say to the late twentieth century than anything in Marx or Lenin. But, as the Thatcherites are the first to point out, the principles of 1789 are alien to the parliamentary absolutism around which Britain's political culture has taken shape. Britain's *ancien régime* withstood the great French Revolution just as its only partially

239

modified successor withstood the revolutions of 1848. The result is that Britain now has a more centralised state, a less representative electoral system and fewer protections against the abuse of power than any other member of the European Community, including once-totalitarian Germany and Italy. On present form, it will not be long before we are as far behind the Poles, the Czechs and the Hungarians.

The project of a new progressive coalition should be to take a leaf out of Eastern Europe's book and carry Britain into the mainstream of European history. Official Labour may or may not be willing to take up this project. It would involve a Damascene conversion, but this is a time for Damascene conversions. There are some signs that old-style, hegemony-seeking Labourism is on the defensive within the Labour Party as well as outside it; if this is so, Labour may yet be persuaded to embrace the cause of a democratic renewal. Since hegemony-seeking Labourism is the biggest single obstacle to a convincing Labour victory, it has a strong incentive to do so. If it does, it will have an unassailable right to speak for the whole of anti-Conservative Britain; and the other anti-Conservative parties should be happy to accept its leadership. But it would be a mistake to focus on official Labour, or for that matter on the official Liberal Democrats or the official Greens and nationalists. The new progressive coalition which the times demand cannot be contrived from the top. If it is to come into being at all, it will have to grow from the bottom. The peoples of Eastern Europe, it is worth remembering, did not wait for citizenship to be handed down by a party establishment. They took it for themselves. What is needed for anti-Conservative Britain to emulate them is a marriage between the communitarian, decentralist, participatory radicalism to which the Liberal Democrats are heirs, and the communitarian, decentralist, participatory strands in the socialist inheritance: a marriage, if you like, between Thomas Paine and William Morris. Such a marriage hardly needs official blessing.

Notes

Chapter 1: The Paradox of British Democracy

1 H. G. Wells, *The New Machiavelli* (London, John Lane, The Bodley Head, 1911), pp. 325–6.
2 H. G. Wells, *A Modern Utopia* (London, Chapman & Hall, 1905).
3 George Dangerfield, *The Strange Death of Liberal England* (New York, Capricorn Books, 1961).
4 Quoted in David Marquand, *Ramsay MacDonald* (London, Jonathan Cape, 1976), p. 162.
5 *Hansard*, 3rd series, vol. LXIII, p. 46.
6 Quoted in Robert McKenzie and Allan Silver, *Angels in Marble: Working-Class Conservatives in Urban England* (London, Heinemann, 1968), pp. 4–5.
7 *Ibid.*, p. 4.
8 *Ibid.*, p. 14.
9 Anthony Heath, Roger Jowell and John Curtice, *How Britain Votes* (Oxford, Pergamon Press, 1985), especially pp. 174–5.
10 Michael Bentley, *The Climax of Liberal Politics: British Liberalism in Theory and Practice 1868–1918* (London, Edward Arnold, 1987).
11 For the notion of 'moral reform' see Peter Clarke, *Liberals and Social Democrats* (Cambridge, Cambridge University Press, 1978), pp. 1–8. For the New Liberals see also Michael Freeden, *The New Liberalism: An Ideology of Social Reform* (Oxford, Clarendon Press, 1978).
12 For this point see Harold Perkin, *The Rise of Professional Society: England Since 1880* (London, Routledge, 1989).
13 P. F. Clarke, *Lancashire and the New Liberalism* (Cambridge, Cambridge University Press, 1971).
14 David Butler and Donald Stokes, *Political Change in Britain: The Evolution of Electoral Choice* (London, Macmillan, 2nd edn, 1974), pp. 166–71.
15 Roy Jenkins, *Mr Balfour's Poodle: An Account of the Struggle Between the House of Lords and the Government of Mr. Asquith* (London, Heinemann, 1954), pp. 196–201.

16 Quoted in Perkin, *op. cit.*, p. 268.
17 Quoted in Bernard Crick, *George Orwell: A Life* (London, Secker & Warburg, 1980), p. 276.
18 Janet Morgan (ed.), *The Backbench Diaries of R. H. S. Crossman* (London, Hamish Hamilton and Jonathan Cape, 1981), pp. 769–70.
19 C. V. Wedgwood, *The Last of the Radicals: Josiah Wedgwood M.P.* (London, Jonathan Cape, 1951), p. 152.
20 Quoted in Robert Skidelsky, 'Keynes's Political Legacy', in Alastair Kilmarnock (ed.), *The Radical Challenge: The Response of Social Democracy* (London, André Deutsch, 1987), p. 87.

Chapter 2: Asquith's Ghost

1 Roy Jenkins, *Asquith* (London, Collins, 1964).
2 A. J. P. Taylor, *English History 1914–1945* (Harmondsworth, Penguin, 1982), p. 103.
3 Michael Howard, *War and the Liberal Conscience* (London, Temple Smith, 1978).
4 John Campbell, *Lloyd George: The Goat in the Wilderness 1922–31* (London, Jonathan Cape, 1977).

Chapter 3: Revolution Averted

1 Walter Kendall, *The Revolutionary Movement in Britain* (London, Weidenfeld & Nicolson, 1969).

Chapter 4: Varieties of Reform

1 Peter Clarke, *Liberals and Social Democrats, op. cit.*
2 *Ibid.*, pp. 1–8.

Chapter 5: The Politics of Deprivation

1 Margaret Cole (ed.), *Beatrice Webb's Diaries 1924–32* (London, Longmans, 1956), pp. 153–4.
2 Quoted in Marquand, *Ramsay MacDonald, op. cit.*, p. 548.
3 The speech is in *Hansard*, Fifth Series, vol. 256, cols. 72–82.
4 Michael Foot, *Aneurin Bevan, 1897–1945* (London, MacGibbon and Kee, 1962), and *Aneurin Bevan, 1945–1960* (London, Davis Poynter, 1973).
5 Ralph Miliband, *Parliamentary Socialism: A Study in the Politics of Labour* (London, George Allen & Unwin, 1961).

6   David Coates, *The Labour Party and the Struggle for Socialism* (Cambridge, Cambridge University Press, 1975).

7   Allan Bullock, *The Life and Times of Ernest Bevin*, volume 1, *Trade Union Leader 1881–1940* and volume 2, *Minister of Labour 1940–1945; Ernest Bevin Foreign Secretary 1945–1951* (London, Heinemann, 1960, 1967 and 1983). Ben Pimlott, *Hugh Dalton* (London, Jonathan Cape, 1985).

8   R. J. Skidelsky, *Politicians and the Slump: The Labour Government of 1929–1931* (London, Macmillan, 1967).

9   *Ibid.*, p. xii.

10 W. G. Runciman, *Relative Deprivation and Social Justice: A Study of Attitudes to Social Inequality in Twentieth-Century England* (London, Routledge & Kegan Paul, 1966).

11 Ibid., pp. 59–60.

12 McKenzie and Silver, *op. cit.*

13 *Ibid.*, pp. 245–6.

Chapter 6: Ernest Bevin and the Apotheosis of Labourism

1   Bullock, *The Life and Times of Ernest Bevin, op. cit.*, vol. 2, p. 103; full details of the Bullock biography are given in footnote 7 to Chapter 5.

2   Ibid., p. 44.

Chapter 7: Hugh Dalton: The Progressive as Bounder

1   Pimlott, *op. cit.*, p. 284.

2   *Ibid.*, pp. 445–6.

3   *Ibid.*, p. 445.

Chapter 8: Sir Stafford Cripps: The Progressive as Moralist

1   Ben Pimlott (ed.), *The Political Diary of Hugh Dalton 1918–40, 1945–60* (London, Jonathan Cape, 1986), pp. 181–2.

2   *Ibid.*, p. 256.

3   Ben Pimlott, *Labour and the Left in the 1930s* (Cambridge, Cambridge University Press, 1977), p. 35.

4   *Ibid.*

5   Kenneth Harris, *Attlee* (London, Weidenfeld & Nicolson, 1982), p. 104; Pimlott, *Labour and the Left*, p. 103.

6   Pimlott, *Labour and the Left*, p. 177.

7   *Ibid.*, p. 52.

8   *Labour Party Conference Report* 1935, p. 156.

9   Alec Cairncross, *Years of Recovery: British Economic Policy 1945–51* (London, Methuen, 1985), p. 509.

10 *Ibid.*, p. 308
11 *Ibid.*, p. 332.
12 Alec Cairncross (ed.), *The Robert Hall Diaries* (London, Unwin Hyman, 1989), p. 222.
13 Cairncross, *Years of Recovery, op. cit.*, pp. 307–8.
14 Philip Williams (ed.), *The Diary of Hugh Gaitskell 1945–1956* (London, Jonathan Cape, 1983), p. 56.

Chapter 9: Herbert Morrison: The Socialist as Consolidator

1 Bernard Donoughue and G. W. Jones, *Herbert Morrison: Portrait of a Politician* (London, Weidenfeld & Nicolson, 1973).
2 *Ibid.*, p. 442.

Chapter 10: Aneurin Bevan: The Progressive as Socialist

1 Donoughue and Jones, *op. cit.*, p. 518.
2 Bullock, *Ernest Bevin Foreign Secretary, op. cit.*, p. 77.
3 Pimlott, *Political Diary of Hugh Dalton, op. cit.*, pp. 539 and 650.
4 *Ibid.*, p. 529.
5 Morgan, *op. cit.*, p. 410.
6 Philip M. Williams, *Hugh Gaitskell* (London, Jonathan Cape, 1979), p. 206.
7 Pimlott, *Political Diary of Hugh Dalton, op. cit.*, p. 602.
8 Details in Chapter 5, note 4.
9 Aneurin Bevan, *In Place of Fear* (Ilkley, E.P. Publishing, 1977; first published in 1952), pp. 201–2.
10 John Campbell, *Nye Bevan and the Mirage of British Socialism* (London, Weidenfeld & Nicolson, 1987).
11 *Ibid.*, p. 245.

Chapter 11: Hugh Gaitskell: The Social Democrat as Hero

1 Williams, *Hugh Gaitskell, op. cit.*, p. 779.
2 Douglas Jay, 'Civil Servant and Minister', in W. T. Rodgers (ed.), *Hugh Gaitskell 1906–1963* (London, Thames & Hudson, 1964), p. 98.
3 Michael Postan, 'Political and Intellectual Progress', in Rodgers, *op. cit.*, p. 62.
4 Williams, *Hugh Gaitskell*, p. 582.
5 Henry Drucker, *Doctrine and Ethos in the Labour Party* (London, George Allen & Unwin, 1979).
6 Pimlott, *Political Diary of Hugh Dalton, op. cit.*, p. 518.
7 Hugh Gaitskell, 'Foreword', in Evan Durbin, *The Politics of*

Democratic Socialism: An Essay on Social Policy (London, Routledge & Kegan Paul, 5th impression, 1957), p. 9.
8   Bevan may have meant Attlee rather than Gaitskell.

Chapter 12: Richard Crossman: The Progressive as Gadfly

1   R. H. S. Crossman, *Planning for Freedom* (London, Hamish Hamilton, 1965), pp. 30–1.
2   R. H. S. Crossman, 'My Father', *Sunday Telegraph*, 16 December 1962.
3   Tam Dalyell, *Dick Crossman: A Portrait* (London, Weidenfeld & Nicolson, 1989).
4   Richard Crossman, *The Diaries of a Cabinet Minister*, vol. 1: *Minister of Housing 1964–66* (London, Hamish Hamilton and Jonathan Cape, 1975), p. 21.
5   R. H. S. Crossman, *Plato Today* (London, George Allen & Unwin, 1937).
6   *Ibid.*, p. 93.
7   R. H. S. Crossman, *Government and the Governed* (London, Christophers, 1939).
8   R. H. S. Crossman, 'Towards A Philosophy of Socialism', in R. H. S. Crossman (ed.), *New Fabian Essays* (London, Turnstile Press, 1953), pp. 14–15.
9   Crossman, *Planning for Freedom, op. cit.*, p. 110.
10   *Ibid.*, p. 71.

Chapter 13: The Tortoise and the Hare

1   Michael Stewart, *Life and Labour* (London, Sidgwick & Jackson, 1981), and Douglas Jay, *Change and Fortune* (London, Hutchinson, 1980).
2   Jay, *Change and Fortune*, p. 284.
3   *Ibid.*, p. 505.
4   Stewart, *op. cit.*, pp. 98–9.

Chapter 14: Harold Wilson: Alibi for a Party?

1   Clive Ponting, *Breach of Promise: Labour in Power 1964–1970* (London, Hamish Hamilton, 1989).
2   D. E. Butler and Anthony King, *The British General Election of 1964* (London, Macmillan, 1965), p. 110.
3   Jay, *Change and Fortune*, p. 411.
4   Denis Healey, *The Time of My Life* (London, Michael Joseph, 1989), pp. 331–6.
5   Crossman, *The Diaries of a Cabinet Minister*, vol. 2: *Lord*

President of the Council and Leader of the House of Commons, 1966–68 (London, Hamish Hamilton and Jonathan Cape, 1976), pp. 50–1.

6   *Ibid.*, p. 160.

7   *Ibid.*, pp. 782–3.

8   Tony Benn, *Office Without Power: Diaries 1968–72* (London, Arrow Books, 1989), p. 63.

9   *Ibid.*, p. 166.

10 *Ibid.*, p. 187.

11 In conversation with the author.

12 Cairncross, *Robert Hall Diaries, op. cit.*, p. 69.

13 Joe Haines, *The Politics of Power* (London: Jonathan Cape, 1977).

14 (Sir James) Harold Wilson, *Memoirs: The Making of a Prime Minister* (London, Weidenfeld & Nicolson and Michael Joseph, 1986), p. 35.

15 Quoted by Campbell, *Aneurin Bevan, op. cit*, p. 350.

Chapter 15: Tony Crosland: The Progressive as Loyalist

1   Susan Crosland, *Tony Crosland* (London, Coronet Books, paperback edn, 1983).

2   *Ibid.*, p. 4.

3   *Ibid.*, p. 10.

4   Anthony Crosland, *Socialism Now* (London, Jonathan Cape, paperback edn, 1975), p. 74. Unless otherwise stated, the quotations from Crosland in this chapter are all from this collection of essays.

5   C. A. R. Crosland, *The Future of Socialism* (London, Jonathan Cape, 1956), p. 380.

6   Anthony Crosland, *Social Democracy in Europe* (Fabian Tract 438, London, Fabian Society, 1975).

7   Susan Crosland, *op. cit.*, pp. 355–6.

8   *Ibid.*, p. 376.

Chapter 16: David Owen: The Progressive as Meteor

1   David Owen, *Face the Future* (London, Jonathan Cape, 1981).

2   Kenneth Harris, *David Owen Personally Speaking to Kenneth Harris* (London, Weidenfeld & Nicolson, 1987).

3   David Owen, 'Ownership', *Gaitskell Memorial Lecture*, University of Nottingham, 1985.

4   Harris, *op. cit.*, p. 17.

5   Ian Bradley, *Breaking the Mould: The Birth and Prospects of the Social Democratic Party* (Oxford, Martin Robertson, 1981), p. 103.

6   Peter Jenkins, *Mrs Thatcher's Revolution: The Ending of the Socialist Era* (London, Jonathan Cape, 1987), p. 353.
7   John Campbell, *Roy Jenkins: A Biography* (London, Weidenfeld & Nicolson, 1983), p. 222.

Chapter 17: Labourism Resurgent

1   For a good example of Labour forebodings, see Austin Mitchell, *Four Years in the Death of the Labour Party* (London, Methuen, 1983).
2   Heath, Jowell and Curtice, *op. cit.*.
3   John Rentoul, *Me and Mine: The Triumph of the New Individualism?* (London, Unwin Hyman, 1989).
4   For 'encompassingness' and the relative 'non-encompassingness' of British unions see Mancur Olson, *The Rise and Decline of Nations* (New Haven, Yale University Press, 1982).
5   R. J. Flanagan, David Soskice and Lloyd Ulman, *Unionism, Economic Stablisation and Incomes Policies: European Experience* (Washington DC, The Brookings Institution, 1983).
6   Drucker, *op. cit.*
7   Lewis Minkin, *The Labour Party Conference* (London, Allen Lane, 1978).
8   John P. Mackintosh, 'Socialism or Social Democracy?', in David Marquand (ed.), *John P. Mackintosh on Parliament and Social Democracy* (London, Longmans, 1982), pp. 156–68.
9   Peter Jenkins, *The Battle of Downing Street*, (London, Charles Knight, 1970).
10 For 'post-materialism' see Ronald Inglehart, *The Silent Revolution: Changing Values and Political Styles among Western Publics* (Princeton, New Jersey, Princeton University Press, 1977).
11 Stuart Holland, *The Socialist Challenge* (London, Quartet, 1975).
12 Colin Hughes and Patrick Wintour, *Labour Rebuilt: The New Model Party* (London, Fourth Estate, 1990).
13 Richard Hoggart, *The Uses of Literacy* (London, Chatto & Windus, 1957), p. 62.
14 For the fall in expectations see James Alt, *The Politics of Economic Decline: Economic Management and Political Behaviour in Britain since 1964* (Cambridge, Cambridge University Press, 1979).
15 Heath, Jowell and Curtice, *op. cit.*

Chapter 18: Revisionism Revisited

1 For a full discussion of this point and the evidence on which it is based see my *The Unprincipled Society* (London, Jonathan Cape, 1988), pp. 189–92.
2 Peter Clarke, *Liberals and Social Democrats, op. cit.*
3 L. T. Hobhouse, *Liberalism* (London, Williams & Norgate, 1911).
4 T. H. Marshall, *Citizenship and Social Class and Other Essays* (Cambridge, Cambridge University Pres, 1950).
5 Albert O. Hirschman, *Exit, Voice and Loyalty: Responses to Decline in Firms, Organisations and States* (Cambridge, Mass., Harvard University Press, 1970).
6 Brian Lee Crowley, *The Self, the Individual and the Community: Liberalism in the Political Thought of F. A. Hayek and Sidney and Beatrice Webb* (Oxford, Clarendon Press, 1987), pp. 174–220.
7 For a fuller discussion see Marquand *The Unprincipled Society, op. cit.*, pp. 228–34.
8 Zygmunt Bauman, *Legislators and Interpreters: On Modernity, Post-Modernity and Intellectuals* (Cambridge, Polity Press, 1987).
9 Quoted in Carole Pateman, *Participation and Democratic Theory* (Cambridge, Cambridge University Press, 1986), p. 31.

Chapter 19: Towards a New Progressive Coalition?

1 Albert O. Hirschman, *Shifting Involvements, Private Interest and Public Action* (Oxford, Martin Robertson, 1982).
2 Andrew Gamble, *The Free Economy and the Strong State: The Politics of Thatcherism* (Basingstoke, Macmillan Education, 1988).
3 Samuel Brittan, *Left or Right: The Bogus Dilemma* (London, Secker & Warburg, 1968).
4 For 'Fordism' see in particular Michael J. Piore and Charles Sabel, *The Second Industrial Divide: Possibilities for Prosperity* (New York, Basic Books, 1984).
5 Scott Lash and John Urry, *The End of Organised Capitalism* (Cambridge, Polity Press, 1987).
6 Harold Perkin, *op. cit.*